◆**ALTERNATIVES** *is a series under the general editorship of Eric S. Rabkin, Martin H. Greenberg, and Joseph D. Olander which has been established to serve the growing critical audience of science fiction, fantastic fiction, and speculative fiction.*

Library of Congress Cataloging in Publication Data
Main entry under title:

Hard science fiction.

(Alternatives)
Proceedings of the fifth Eaton Conference on
Fantasy and Science Fiction, held April 9–10, 1983, at
the University of California, Riverside.
Includes index.
1. Science fiction—Congresses. I. Slusser, George
Edgar. II. Rabkin, Eric S. III. Eaton Conference on
Science Fiction and Fantasy Literature (5th: 1983:
University of California, Riverside) IV. Series.
PN3433.2.H37 1986   809.3'876   84–27644
ISBN 0–8093–1234–4

HARD SCIENCE FICTION

Edited by George E. Slusser
and Eric S. Rabkin

Southern Illinois University Press
Carbondale and Edwardsville

Contents

Introduction

Insofar as one can bestow geographical centers on literary genres, science fiction may be unique in having a hard core. When science fiction writers speak of "hard SF," they seem to be designating, more than a form, a place, solid literary ground on which to resist the shocks of literary fashion. Indeed, it may be a place which resists the temptation of fiction itself. For to create this sense of substantiality at the core, science must ultimately seem to outweigh the fiction. And to do so, that science must be the "hardest" possible. In a basic sense this means that both setting and dramatic situation must derive strictly from the rigorous postulation and working out of a concrete physical problem. The method then of the hard SF story is logical, the means technological, and the result—the feel and texture of the fiction itself—objective and cold. What hard SF purports to affirm, therefore, is not the universality of human aspirations, for these are more often than not the "soft" products of our desires. Instead it asserts the truth of natural law, an absolute, seemingly ahuman vision of things. Such a vision may seem to run counter to the humanist tradition, to the basically man-centered structures of Western literature itself. Hardness here becomes hardheartedness, and risks repelling even the most open-minded literary scholar who traditionally has drawn justification for his activity from that humanism. Yet, to the degree that it remains fiction, hard SF is still part of the larger system of narrative. And by asking storytelling to adopt the procedures and conclusions of modern scientific investigation, hard SF may not reject fictional narrative so much as reshape it. To get some sense of this shape of stories to come we must, at the very least, come to grips with science fiction's hard core.

Coming to grips is exactly what the sixteen essays in this volume strive to do. Written both by scholars with scientific backgrounds or interests and by prominent scientist-writers who practice hard SF, these essays approach their subject from a broad variety of stances. Concealed beneath these diverse approaches, however, is a persistent polarity. To the question: what is hard SF, for example, we see two responses constantly emerging. For either hard SF is a new literary form, born of our modern sense of change and the future and capable of giving narrative form to the increasingly complex speculations of science. Or, on the contrary, it is merely an old form masquerading as something new, a literature quite derivable from the humanist tradition, hence reducible to its past. And concealed beneath this question is another stubborn duality, this time on the level of how we view science fiction itself. For is science fiction fundamentally defined by its "hardness" of vision? Or should not this vision, ideally, be tempered or "softened" by some sense of man's aspirations and limits? At this point we are no longer analyzing but prescribing, and our field of investigation falls into two opposing camps. To the proponents of hard SF any soft form is untenable, for human wishes and desires have no place in a universe marked by struggle between only two forces—those of determination and determinism, the iron laws of nature and the steely resolve of the scientific intelligence to master those laws. Conversely, to apologists for soft SF, the hard form, despite its claim to objectivity, itself operates on false premises. For when examined as fiction hard SF may not succeed in shaping brave new worlds of the scientific imagination. What it does instead is merely refurbish the age-old myths and fantasies of that humanity it claims to supercede. Hard SF, then, more than anything else, is a core of controversy, and this struggle for hard or soft options effectively inscribes the "two cultures" rift at the heart of science fiction as a genre.

The first group of essays provides a revealing contrapuntal exchange between practitioners of hard SF and literary theorists. In the opening paper Dr. Robert L. Forward, pioneer in gravitational astronomy and author of *Dragon's Egg* and *Rocheworld,* explains how science writes his fiction. Forward is considered by many to be today's purest hard SF writer, and his statement—that the essence of the fictional process per se is the scientifically accurate working out of a problem posed by the physical universe—has the force of a manifesto. The next essay, by astronomer-writer David Brin (author of *Sundiver* and *Startide Rising*), seeks to know why, within the broad field of science fiction today, less and less of the hard form is being written. He offers two possible explanations. For either the writers of science fiction, reversing the Campbellian tradition, have become increasingly unwilling to abdicate to science that role in the storytelling process conventionally reserved for the creative imagination, or (and Brin stresses this possibility) the science that writes the fiction may itself be running out of speculative niches. Brin offers a view of fictional originality that may seem radical, if not heretical, to the mainstream critic. For, he states, as a given hard SF writer posits and solves his particular scientific problem, he both fills a distinct speculative gap and in doing so lays claim to its fictional landscape, forcing other writers to push on to new problems and scenarios until ultimately the literary field is exhausted. As the physical and biological sciences then (as those which most inspire the hard SF writer) may be closing the gaps in our knowledge of the universe, so that mode of literature which uses its methods must do likewise in its own realm of activity.

The next four papers, written by scholar-critics, argue explicitly or implicitly against the elevation of hard SF, as a method of creating fictional worlds and as a form or genre, to new or revolutionary status in the literary system. Frank McConnell, in his paper "Sturgeon's Law: First Corollary," would deconstruct our idea of generic norms, return us to "a primal chaos of fictive forms" where all are equally privileged. McConnell argues that if science fiction is said to be primarily fiction, then can we not, turning things around, claim that all fiction may in a very real sense be science fiction. Or more accurately, technological fiction. For fiction in the Western world, he claims, is essentially the story of technology, and technology is the dynamics of our exile from the garden, the story of our subsequent struggle with the intransigence of matter. McConnell contends that hard SF, unlike the "soft" form which is technological fiction tempered or contaminated by romance, is not a newly evolved genre but instead the primal genre, that form toward which Western storytelling has been tending all along, and on which it could only dream because such a form was not till now possible to realize. Thus if science writes the fiction, it is on this unconscious level of our mythical desire to control matter.

Eric S. Rabkin's essay, "The Unconscious City," moves in this same direction. Wondering why the city, as one of hard SF's most fertile domains for extrapolative construction, seems to be a niche that never fills, Rabkin postulates that beneath what has become an icon of "hardness" lies the soft core of an "unconscious city," indeed beneath the seemingly progressivist urban experiments of hard SF we discover, shaping them, unchanging and perhaps universal preoccupations of the human mind. Analyzing a wide variety of fictional cities in works like *We* and *Metropolis,* Rabkin traces these most futuristic urban visions back to deep sources in our language and our psyche, to the fertility matrix of "mother," "womb," and "cradle."

John Huntington and David Clayton consider this same hard-soft dichotomy, respectively, as a rhetorical and ideological problem, and as a mind-set determined by even more general psychological and cultural forces. In his essay "Hard-core Science Fiction and the Illusion of Science," Huntington locates the appeal of a hard classic like Tom Godwin's "The Cold Equations" less in its form, where the exercise of scientific rationality is normally seen to control and shape the structural elements of plot and character, than in its rhetoric, where the hard language of science is made to cover a soft core of illusion. Is this rhetoric of cold objectivity, Huntington asks, any less sentimental than the rhetoric of humanist pity it professes to displace? And if not, then what are the cultural taboos that this hard rhetoric seeks to conceal or suppress?

And finally David Clayton, examining works by John W. Campbell and Robert A. Heinlein, passes from a semantic analysis of the term *hardness* to a psychocultural assessment of its meaning in terms of the ideology of modern science as we see it refracted in hard science fiction. Evoking Bachelard and Freud, Clayton digs at the sadomasochistic undercurrents of hard SF, what he sees as the struggle of our hard-edged technology against what has become, in reaction to this aggression, an even more hostile and unyielding material world. Detecting beneath hard SF's worship of "scientific law" an irrational, even Calvinist sense of predestination, and beneath its seemingly enlightened vision a deep fear of the material world, Clayton offers a new model for explaining this subgenre: a series of circles, ideologically and culturally constituted, whose innermost core is the "aggressive libidinal investments that characterize our primary relation to the world."

Each of the four preceding papers seeks to expose an underside of hard SF, some concealed subjective determinant that uses its apparently objective landscape and values as a metaphor, as a figure that strives to displace in vertical fashion, and perhaps even suppress, some fundamental "human" truth. Responding to this vision of hard SF, which seems reductionist because it ignores the very real power for change the form possesses, writer James Gunn (*The Listeners*) and writer-physicist Gregory Benford (*Timescape, Against Infinity*) discuss hard SF as an open-ended process both of reading and of writing fiction. In his essay "The Readers of Hard Science Fiction," Gunn asserts that, for these same readers, it is not so much the nature of the science depicted or its "feel" of difficulty that makes a given story "hard," but rather the way in which that science, however fanciful or improbable in itself, is treated in the fiction. Its treatment, Gunn contends, must be rigorous and objective. Thus a work like Van Vogt's *Slan* appeared hard to its *Astounding* readers because its otherwise soft concepts are presented in a way that satisfies "its readers' intellectual desire to know how we got from here to there."

Gregory Benford, in his paper "Is There a Technological Fix for the Human Condition?," identifies the two poles of this hard/soft controversy—technology and the human condition—as ideological shibboleths. Stating that people do not read hard SF to learn science, Benford would agree with McConnell that this form is primarily fiction. And yet, because he has written it and known its practitioners for many years, he realizes in an empirical sense that it is a fiction with unique, and uniquely science-connected, characteristics. These he proceeds to map on a system of coordinates. As method of literary creation, Benford asserts, hard science fiction does follow the physical sciences in demanding "constraint" and in subjecting its product, like any scientific experiment, to the test of falsifiability. In holding to the possible and the plausible in its speculations, hard SF provides verisimilitude for events in a story. And as guarantee for this verisimilitude it offers science as symbol of a new way of looking at the world. The nature of this symbol, Benford states, is determined by the climate of opinion that surrounds it. And to today's literary critic, science tends to symbolize two radically opposed views, for by means of science either we assert our mastery over nature, or we discover our limits, our thralldom to its deterministic structures. To Benford, this either/or situation stifles true critical inquiry into the idea of science and its role in literature. For if, as one side claims, there is no technological fix for the human condition, we cannot simply assume that that condition is unfixable, either. Indeed the very existence of hard SF, in Benford's eyes, raises the need for a mode of criticism capable of dealing with it—an open, dynamic model capable, like modern science itself, of being truly self-corrective.

The second group of essays continues to examine this tension between humanistic and scientific visions by focusing on individual works and on precisely defined areas of interest (or contest) across a historical span from the 17th century to the present. Paul Alkon, discussing Thomas Burnet's *Sacred Theory of the Earth*, a work of the 1680s that attempts to explain Biblical history in geological terms, asks to what extent this early narrative had already established a method and an aesthetics of extrapolation. Because its narrative sequence reverses cause and effect, giving us first the baffling phenomenon and then the theory that would explain its causes, Burnet's work, Alkon argues, may be among the first to cultivate the expository structure common both to the modern mystery story and to hard SF.

In an extended discussion of William Morris's *News from Nowhere,* Herbert Sussman examines ways in which utopian speculation, as the Victorian period's characteristic form of future history, might be considered hard extrapolation. The emphasis in modern hard SF on a continuity between the present and the future leads Sussman to draw parallels between its linguistic procedures and the fundamentally metonymic style that dominated 19th-century realism. Sussman argues that Morris, in *News from Nowhere,* created a language of the future that combines in dialectical fashion these "hard" extensions of the present and the "soft" element of the visionary leap or dream, and that this same language (along with the problems of writing about the future that it seeks to solve) is still operative in the mixture of realism and fantasy that informs today's hard science fiction.

C. S. Lewis, the subject of Michael Collings's essay, is usually thought to write the exact opposite of hard SF—a soft mode of visionary fantasy structured on the metaphorical relationship between its "speculative" future and a preordained Christian pattern. Collings argues, however, that in a novel like *That Hideous Strength,* Lewis may actually be using, within this very different mode of fiction, the Campbellian device of making soft material "hard"—in this case the angels and demons of Christian lore themselves. He does so, Collings demonstrates, by assuming for these theological presences an objective, knowable existence, and then subjecting them to the rigors of scientific investigation. If Lewis's trilogy as a whole is rightly seen as a romance, *That Hideous Strength* taken individually, with its emphasis on science and scientific method as unifying element, is nevertheless closely related in technique and function to what has come to be called hard science fiction.

For Collings the large amount of scientific discourse in *That Hideous Strength* is not merely a cosmetic factor but serves a functional purpose. Paul A. Carter, however, addressing the fiction of that bastion of hard SF, the Golden Age pulp magazine, contends not only that the scientific shop talk that fills its pages is fundamentally cosmetic, but that its use became a strategic necessity for the non-scientist writer in the face of a technologically oriented audience. Through a careful examination of testimony by both readers and writers in the pulps on the problems of writing scientific SF, Carter reveals just how little this Golden Age relied on rigorous scientific extrapolation for its characteristic effects.

The next three essays focus on works by two writers considered, for different reasons and by very different audiences, to be in the vanguard of hard SF today: James P. Hogan and Stanislaw Lem. Patricia Warrick, in her paper "Artificial Intelligence: Wild Imaginary Worlds, Wilder Realities," sees today's information technologies, with their ability to create machines that may someday outthink men, as racing far ahead of the literary imagination. She finds in Hogan's *The Two Faces of Tomorrow* a work that offers mankind the possibility of forming a partnership with intelligent computers, one of the few recent SF novels that actually meets the modern challenge of cybernetics instead of avoiding it.

The two essays that follow, those by George R. Guffey and Robert M. Philmus both see cybernetics and information theory governing the structure and direction of Stanislaw Lem's fictions. For each of these critics, however, the role this science plays is a very different one. Guffey, examining a single text, *The Investigation*, in light of the Sherlock Holmesian rationalism that forms its fictional background, finds Lem's procedural paradigm open-ended. For Guffey, Lem in this novel does not move from physics to metaphysics (thus displacing the meaning of the tale from the mere solving of a mystery to the assertion that this mystery is itself unsolvable by rational means) so much as suggest the relative inadequacy of classical physics itself. Lem's maneuver implies, therefore, the inadequacy of all fictions, detective or scientific, based on the notions of that physics.

Philmus on the other hand, ranging across Lem's entire canon from *Solaris* to the recently translated *Master's Voice*, argues that the author designs his fictions to pose the question of human identity, a question which he examines by confronting the human with the alien, and deploying cybernetic paradigms to mediate their encounter. Philmus sees the use of these paradigms as guided in each case by Lem's skeptical heritage. Yet even so, the thrust of Lem's cybernetic vision is to give us investigations that—beyond that barrier to positivist science which is mankind's ignorance of its own perceptual limits—explore a landscape of interfacing, self-organizing systems. To Lem, then, Philmus contends, the ultimate form of this cybernetic self-alteration is found in the human system of language itself. As vehicle of order, both in the phenomenal world and in the literary text, the linguistic system is looped and thus a medium of discovery which is simultaneously one of self-discovery as well.

It is interesting that, though both Guffey and Philmus consider Lem's highly methodical use of the very "hard" science of cybernetics, neither mentions hard SF once in his essay. This silence is pregnant with meaning for the volume as a whole. For each of these critics hard SF remains (as it has for many of the other essayists writing here) a concept more assumed than defined. On this level of assumption hard SF is everywhere, or it is nowhere, and "hardness" is the quality that informs all or none of science fiction. "Hard" and "soft" then may not be formal properties so much as ideological valences, vectors set on the work of fiction by those who choose to speak for it. The field of operation for these terms is perhaps only in a secondary sense the work. They may instead refer primarily to the public image of a given science fiction text, the way it is positioned and made to function in that broad ideological battlefield our century has baptised the "two cultures" clash.

Guffey and Philmus, for example, insofar as they serve as guides for Lem's texts, move increasingly, behind the silence which masks their critical assumptions, in divergent directions. On the level of form both discover, at the core of Lem's fictions, structures that, if different, are not fundamentally unrelated—the looped and open-ended patterns of cybernetics. Their interpretation of cybernetic structure, however, is, in each case, directed by radically opposed ideas as to the purpose of scientific investigation. Guffey's valence is "hard." We see this implied in his choice of analytical stategies: The single text, it is assumed, can in an evolutionary sense be seen as pivotal, a link in a developmental chain. And the vindication of statistics as investigative method in that single text is seen as offering a "scientifically sounder alternative" to the Newtonian rationality of that Holmesian backdrop from which it emerges. Philmus's approach on the other hand—careful to surround *The Investigation* and any other single text with the self-reflexive and self-corrective context which is Lem's entire *oeuvre*—is ultimately "soft." For Philmus, tellingly, the final avatar of cybernetics in Lem is not statistical logic but language, and finally something we might call metalanguage—language seen not as mankind's tool or instrument but as the system that encompasses and preserves his humanity. In Philmus's eyes Lem's main concern, relocating the alien encounter within this most human of systems, is to reveal in the self-alterations of language the process by which man becomes aware of himself, invests himself with meaning.

In the preceding essays "hard" and "soft" delineate positions that are often less adversarial than mutually exclusive. Asking why this is so, George Slusser in his essay "The Ideal Worlds of Science Fiction," considers these terms in a particular context—that of the work of art a writer makes of himself when he acts as "parent" to his production. Examining the assumptions behind a series of prominent hard/soft encounters in science fiction—such as that between Butor and Blish, that between Asimov and Pournelle, and finally that between Le Guin and Gregory Benford—Slusser argues that these terms ultimately tend to designate states of being as fixed and absolute as Platonic ideals. Alike then in their function as strategies of permanence, both soft and hard SF do not generate dynamic interchange so much as point to some fundamental inability of science fiction to be truly scientific or dialectical: to function as an open system of forms and values that embraces the tentative and hypothetical as its mode of operation. Both terms, Slusser argues, are categorical imperatives, less descriptions of some state of nature than prescriptions born of our desire to recover absolute, a priori forms from the material flux. But is not this, as we see it in the light of this hard/soft controversy, the condition of all literature today? Considering both hard SF and its soft "antagonist" as equally ideal impulses, Slusser suggests that the true countermode to science fiction may not be humanist realism but rather horror—the mode that in answer to our deep fears consigns all forms and values to the uncertain realm of material change.

All the essays in this volume are original, and all were written for the fifth Eaton Conference on Fantasy and Science Fiction, held April 9–10, 1983, at the University of California, Riverside, and sponsored by the University Library and the College of Humanities and Social Sciences of that institution. The editors wish to thank University Librarian Joan Chambers, Dean David Warren, and Jean-Pierre Barricelli of the Department of Literature and Languages for their encouragement and generous support.

Riverside, California   George Slusser
                                                         Eric S. Rabkin

HARD SCIENCE FICTION

When Science Writes the Fiction

Dr. Robert L. Forward

I don't know anything about science fiction—I just write the stuff. I don't even write science fiction. I just write a scientific paper about some strange place—and by the time I have the science correct—the science has written the fiction.

When writing hardcore science fiction, the purpose is to have the science as accurate as possible and matched to the fiction (while all the time telling a good story). There are lots of ways to make errors in science fiction stories. The goal is not to make any errors. Let me give you one example of an error in a nonscience fiction story.

"His book had sold!!! . . . leaving the office of his agent in a glow, Richard exited through the revolving doors onto a street in midtown Manhattan. Shielding his eyes from the glare of the light from the sun, he looked up Fifth Avenue, and hailed one of the rickshaws coming down the street. . . ."

Did you catch that one? If you think that the hero looked the wrong way on Fifth Avenue to see the traffic, you're wrong. I checked with the American Automobile Club maps of midtown Manhattan. Fifth Avenue is one way downtown, so you have to look up Fifth Avenue for transportation. However, rickshaws don't exist in such numbers as to clog the streets of midtown Manhattan, that was the error. Did you catch it? Good for you. You are now ready to write science fiction, for you make sure that the habits of the natives match the scientific level of the environment you have placed them in.

There are other kinds of errors if you don't do your science correctly. Here is the same scene, only now it is hard-core science fiction.

"His book had sold!!! . . . leaving the office of his agent in a

I

glow, Richard exited the revolving doors onto a street in midtown New-Manhattan. Shielding his eyes from the glare of the light from Barnard's Star, he looked up and down Fifth Avenue, and hailed one of the rickshaws coming down the street. . . ."

The story has now been transposed to a new world around Barnard's Star. You might think that by moving the scene off the earth you could get away with anything. Our hero can now look both up and down Fifth Avenue because the traffic on this Fifth Avenue is no longer limited by New York traffic regulations. It is also possible that rickshaws make a great deal more sense in New-Manhattan than they do in old Manhattan. But if you are going to use science to free you from the conventions of earth you had not only better play by the rules of science, but use its rules to help you write better stories.

Barnard's Star is a red dwarf star. It has a temperature of only 3,330 K. Living in the Barnard Star system would be like living next to a charcoal fire. If you have ever tried to read by firelight, you can appreciate what good eyesight Abraham Lincoln must have had to get his education using that light source. Yet, if you are aware of the science, you can use it to create an aura of alienness that puts the reader on the surface of that strange planet in your mind, six light-years away.

Instead of saying "shielding his eyes from the glare of the light from Barnard's star" you could say "peering through the reddish gloom of the light from Barnard's star," and you have used science to set the tone of the scene, an alien scene of rickshaws toiling up and down a Fifth Avenue under the red glow of a warm rock in the sky.

If you are going to write hard-core science fiction, good hard-core science fiction, you had better prepare yourself for a lot of work, for you are going to have to make your intellect (and personal computer) do what "common sense" does for the writer of ordinary, earth-bound, human-bound stories.

But if you do pick this genre, then literally whole new worlds open up for you. No longer are your characters limited to one sex partner (zero, four, and unlimited are only a few choices). No longer are your skies limited to one sun, one moon, a few planets, and lots of stars. One of the best science fiction short stories ever written was "Nightfall" by Isaac Asimov. It featured a world that had *NO* stars until the "day" (you couldn't really call it a day, but then there was no name on this world for "not day") turned into "night." And piled on that change for us human readers was the transposition of the world of the story from the lightly star-sprinkled sky that we see here in the outskirts of this sparse galaxy to the center of a globular cluster. I don't know how other science fiction writers write science fiction, but I know how *I* write it. First I steal a world (or worlds). If I am really desperate, I will invent a world, but there are so many around for the taking that you might as well steal them. Some you may have to ask for. After all, it *was* Frank Drake that first proposed that there might be life on a neutron star, although he didn't invent the neutron star, that had been configured long ago in the *Astrophysics Journal.* Yet when I asked Frank, I had no problem getting his permission to use his idea. Like most scientists, he was quite cooperative and even suggested a name for one of the lead characters in *Dragon's Egg,* "Amalita Shakashiri Drake." (Fortunately for the baby her mommy decided on a different name, so she doesn't have to go through life trying to match the exploits of her namesake.)

Frank Drake is like many scientists. They like to have science fiction match the reality and "magic" of real science. Before I was a science fiction writer, I was a scientist. I didn't read much science fiction, but I was starved for good stories that didn't abuse my intellect like rickshaws on Fifth Avenue. They didn't come very often, and when they did, I appreciated it. Science is full of many wonders. Worlds of ice, hot gas, water, neutrons, or dust. Each has the potential to hold that wonder we call life. We only know of one life form, but there are many others that are possible. We aren't *sure* of the science, but science can lead us into the fiction.

One can use science to create a world, an accurate, unusual world, that is completely correct as far as known science is concerned. The writer can then people that world with ordinary aliens, that have the same drives, the same fears, the same taboos, the same habits as the human creatures around us. But it really doesn't matter if you have done better than to just give them blue skin to set off their pointy ears above their purple-lipped mouths, for aliens that are humans in costume are trite. You should use the science to make the aliens alien.

When you write science fiction, you should work out the science without prejudice, then let the science write the fiction. YES, you should have an idea of the plot before you write the story, but you should not let the plot get in the way of a good fact. (Just as you should not, at least in fiction, allow the facts to get in the way of a good story. If you have a good story, and the facts [as you know them] say that the story cannot happen, then don't feel bad about rearranging the facts to make the story happen. What the people buy is the story, not a science-fact article.) Yet if the scientific facts are leading you away from your preconceived story line, don't hesitate to follow the lead. After all, the science that backs up your story has more knowledge and background than you do. (To give a simple example. I knew before I started this article that many streets in New York City were one-way streets, and that if I needed to mention looking up or down for taxicabs, I needed to consult a map on Fifth Street to find out if it were one-way, and which way.) The same care should be taken with the facts of science as the facts of New York City traffic. It is easy to do, just look up scientific facts like you look up any other facts. If you are not sure, ask your nearest scientific expert.

As examples of where the science wrote the fiction for me, I can cite the following cases:

In my novel, *Dragon's Egg,* I knew I wanted the action to take place on a neutron star, and I knew that I wanted humans in the story, at least as bystanders. Since all the humans I know are in the solar system, I needed the neutron star near the solar system, so I "moved" the neutron star to where I wanted it. A neutron star has a very strong magnetic field. As the magnetic field does not pass through the center of mass (as it usually doesn't), then this off-center magnetic field flails about in the plasma in the space around the neutron star, and like a magnetic propeller, pushes the star through the plasma and accelerates it along the spin axis. Being resident God in this story, I picked the direction of the spin axis in the direction toward the solar system and got my neutron star delivered to the solar system neighborhood as requested some 500,000 years after the supernova explosion that created the star.

The science thus insists that the solar system has to be above one of the spin poles of the neutron star. I then imagined what it would be like having a very large yellow sun sitting over one of the spin poles. Polaris is an important star in our skies. Sol would be an important star on Egg even if it were small, but Egg is so close that Sol would be large and unblinking. It would be the only star in the sky that remained stationary, while all the other stars rotated about it. It would be, and did become, the God Star "Bright" to the cheela on Egg.

Then, later, I was working out the science for the visit of the humans to the rapidly spinning neutron star. If you are going to all the trouble to send a spacecraft to a neutron star, you want to get close enough to the star to study it in some detail. If you just stand off at a distance, you would be better off spending your money on better telescopes. So you would like to get close enough to the neutron star to at least have it as large in the sky as the sun or moon (about half a degree or one-hundredth of a radian). When you realize that a neutron star is only about 20 kilometers in diameter, this means that you are going to have to get closer than a few thousand kilometers away from that spinning ball. For various reasons, I had the neutron star spinning at 5 revolutions per second. It turns out that "synchronous orbit" for an orbital period of 5 revolutions per second around a neutron star is at 400 kilometers, so I decided to put my human spacecraft in that orbit. There Egg would be almost 3 degrees across in the sky. I could have just assumed that I could do that, but my desire to make the science as accurate as possible led me to calculate the strength of the gravitational tides at 400 kilometers from a neutron star. It turned out that they are 200 gees per meter! That is enough to literally tear you apart. I almost gave up at that point. I would have either to hope that the reader would not do the calculation that I did and go ahead with the story (Larry Niven did so in *Neutron Star* and got away with zooming a spaceship within a few kilometers of a neutron star), or give up and move the humans back where the tides were not so lethal. I then had an idea, and after a week of calculation, proved to myself that six ultradense masses placed in a ring about the human spacecraft would make a counter tide that would cancel the tide of the neutron star. (I later turned these computer calculations into a scientific paper that has since been published in the *Physical Review*. The paper discusses how one might use six 100-kilogram tungsten masses to cancel the tides of the earth.)

The making of these ultradense masses from the asteroidal debris around the neutron star was a vehicle for teaching the reader more about the neutron star, but it also had a significant effect on the plot line down on Egg. For the making of the six-mass tidal compensators, and the placement of them over the west magnetic pole in synchronous orbit would definitely be observable to the aliens on the neutron star below. (They might have missed seeing the seven-meter diameter human spacecraft, but they would not miss seeing the 200-meter condensed asteroids at the 400 kilometer distance.) There would be six of them. They would stay stationary in the sky (being in synchronous orbit) over a pole (only this time it would be a magnetic pole, not a spin pole). Science insisted that the six masses be placed there. The effect of the science in writing the story was almost obvious. Since, like the God Star Bright, these glowing objects remained stationary in the sky, they must be associated with the God Star. They became the "Eyes of Bright" in the story, sent to watch down on the unfaithful cheela on the neutron star below. An example of the science writing the fiction for me.

One of the most amazing scientific features of a neutron star is the strength of the magnetic field embedded in the star. A typical sun is a million kilometers across and has a magnetic field of a few hundred gauss. The magnetic field is trapped in the electronic plasma of the hot gas and is compressed as the mass of the star is compressed in the implosion that takes place before the explosion of the outer layers that makes the supernova so visible. The final magnetic field of a neutron star is a trillion gauss. This magnetic field is so strong that the rapidly moving protons inside the nuclei that make up the neutron star are limited in their motion to directions along the magnetic field lines. That means east-west near the magnetic equator, and up-down near the magnetic poles. The effect is not small. The aspect ratio of the nuclei change from spheres to long cigar shapes. Since the neutron star creatures are made of these nuclei, they, too, experience these effects on their bodies. They are long and skinny near the magnetic equator and compressed and "tall" near the magnetic poles. Would they notice this effect? Or since their eyes are distorted in the same ratio, would their brains compensate and make them think that their shapes are invarient with placement in a magnetic field? I could have chosen either one, but I chose to make them unaware of their physical change in shape. This meant that their world, as measured in body diameters (a "tread length" equivalent to the Roman two-step "pace") took longer to travel across at the poles than it did at the equator. Also, the tendency of the charged particles to move along the magnetic field lines made it difficult for the aliens to move at right angles to the magnetic field lines. In the early parts of the Dragon's Egg story, this reluctance to move across the magnetic lines of force was one of the factors that kept the primitive cheela from crossing over to the southern hemisphere of Egg. Again, if the science had not shown the way, that feature, an essential part of the "alieness" of the story, would never have been thought of. The magnetic field also interacted with the smoke from the volcano. Science said that there would be a belt of smoke along the spin equator. This scientific fact then became a major factor in the culture of the early cheela tribes, keeping them in the northern hemisphere until one "chosen" tribe was able to break through this psychological "barrier."

In my second novel, *Rocheworld*, science also played a significant part in writing the story. *Rocheworld* is set on a twin-planet around Barnard's Star, a small red dwarf. The sun is weak; it is going to be cold. Since the purpose of *Rocheworld* is to teach you that water doesn't always fall downhill, I wanted to have an ocean of water. (Actually it is a conical mountain of water.) To keep the ocean from freezing, I laced it with ammonia and other pleasant gases such as cyanide and hydrogen sulfide. I found an MIT chemistry student (turned out to be Carl Richard Feynmann, son of Professor Feynmann at CalTech) who dug up in an obscure chemistry textbook the phase diagram for a mixture of ammonia and water in equilibrium with its vapor. Lo and behold, there are four forms of ice possible. Pure water ice (floats on pure water, but sinks in a mixture of 75 percent water/25 percent ammonia), an ice of equal parts ammonia and water, another with two parts of ammonia to one part water, and a pure ammonia ice. Little is known about the intermediate ice forms, but you will find them in a very visual scene in the novel where the crew is underwater and sees a two-way underwater snowstorm, ice crystals falling up, and water-ammonia ice crystals falling down. To get that scene in, I had to invent a reason for the human aerospace plane to be under water, and that lead me to the aliens using "body plays" to transmit information, a form of mime. Again, science writes the fiction.

Thus, if you are writing science fiction, don't think of the task of making the science correct as a chore. It is not simply one of those "necessary duties" that you must go through if you are to write in that genre, like looking up a map of New York City to make the streets in your story go the same way as they do in the real city. Instead, look at the new opportunities that the science gives you to make your story, your characters, your world, a new and unique place for your readers. Work out the science faithfully, follow its lead, and the science will write the fiction.

Running Out of Speculative Niches: A Crisis for Hard SF?

David Brin

There is a question that is often heard at science fiction conventions these days.

"Is hard SF dead or dying?"

Certainly from the number of panel discussions devoted to the subject, it would seem that there is some concern out there among the readers, editors, and writers. Whether or not it is true that the subgenre is experiencing problems, it cannot be denied that there is a widespread feeling that hard SF has seen better days.

Of course there is always the question of definition. If by hard SF we mean "boy engineer" stories in which a pair of Aryan-type male heroes—chaste, innocent, and yet wise—come up with a chain of ever more unlikely techno-wizardries to defeat alien bad guys, then few would mourn the loss. But not many modern readers would use such a definition when discussing hard SF.

A more appropriate stab at a criterion to the subgenre might be that in a hard SF story or novel, "science" itself—the body of knowledge which encompasses verifiable, predictable patterns in our universe—is a major character.

In other words, while science or a scientific question need not be all there is to the plot of a hard SF story, it must participate substantially in motivating the characters to do what they do. Also, the science in a hard SF piece must be as consistent as possible with accepted scientific paradigms, straying from what is currently accepted only in purposeful speculation having directly to do with the story. And those departures must be few and rigidly defined.

At its best, hard SF must also be good literature. That almost goes without saying. Well-written hard SF must fulfill the same standards of characterization, setting, plot consistency, drama, and good writing that other varieties of fiction strive to attain. The requirement of having "science as a character" is in addition to all else. It is arguable that the hard SF subgenre can be further divided. For instance, there is clearly a difference between "engineering SF," such as Larry Niven's *Descent of Anansi*, and "scientific SF," such as Gregory Benford's *Timescape*. The two subcategories share a common heritage, but face different problems. We shall speak more of this division within hard SF momentarily. However, for now, let us discuss the goals of hard SF writers themselves.

It is betraying no fraternity secret to say that to some degree hard SF writers write for each other. That is, in addition to wanting their works to be good stories for the sake of the broad audience (and even critics), these writers also tend to be aware of the other hard SF authors as they work out the details of their plots and universes.

There is, at a low, good-natured level, a certain competition among hard SF authors to come up with the most startling and original—yet obvious—possible departures from reality and to present these altered settings or situations in logical and consistent ways.

(Use of the word *obvious* is significant. For, like the writer of a murder mystery, the hard SF author likes nothing better than to have a peer smack himself in the forehead and exclaim, "Of course! Now why didn't I think of that!")

There is some pride in being the first to write about life on a neutron star, or a physically possible world in the shape of a ring, or communications through time in a manner not inconsistent with known physics. Indeed, so many of our recent advances in science and technology were predicted by the hard SF of the forties and fifties that one is compelled to wonder which hard SF speculation of the eighties will be vindicated by history.

Hard SF is, in essence, the portrayal of what "might" happen. In this way it is a little like playing what-if games with the future—excluding what we know to be impossible, but exploring Conan Doyle's range of the improbable in minute detail.

It is even possible that hard SF may someday serve mankind in a critical moment. In its library of well-thought-out situations and plots, hard SF offers a catalogue of scenarios which might shorten our reaction time if and when some truly dramatic event—such as contact with an alien race—ever occurs. The hard SF library has already been influential (e.g. *Brave New World, Fail Safe, 1984, The Andromeda Strain*). Someday it might prove invaluable.

Why, then, all this murmuring over the "death" of hard SF? The hard stuff appears to be well motivated, even useful, perhaps. It remains popular. Yet, talk to the fans, and one might imagine that hardly any is being written anymore.

It may be that what we now call hard SF has begun to suffer from a double-bind. The subgenre seems to have entered new ground where it is simply more *difficult* to write, making many new authors unwilling to chance its slippery surface.

One of the deterrents to dabbling in hard SF might be discomfort with the very same "peer-review" I mentioned above. Few science fiction authors really have substantial educations in science. While in the old days it may have been possible to buy an engineer friend a few beers and come away with the technical details needed for a go-to-the-moon story, the depth of research called for in a truly innovative modern hard SF tale may seem daunting to many writers. Certainly awareness that there is a community of hard SF readers and writers "out there," ready to judge a work by very exacting standards of verisimilitude, may have frightened some away from working in the subgenre. (This seems verified from discussions with several SF authors.)

As Robert Forward discusses in his article, the science often writes all or part of the plot for the author of a hard SF tale. While few carry out this rule with the devotion of Dr. Forward, it is true that hard SF authors must bow to an outside master. They abdicate to Reality some of the storycasting role most writers jealously preserve for their own imaginations. Not all authors can, or wish to learn this partnership.

All in all, it is easier to craft a dragon than a good spaceship.

But there is an additional factor that I believe is having a major impact on hard SF today. It is implicit in the discussion given above. It has to do with the ferocious nature of speculation itself.

Hard SF may face a crisis simply because the knowable universe may be finite, and we may be filling in the gaps faster than we think.

Such a broad statement needs some explaining. I shall try.

In Western civilization we have adopted a number of points of view which are so commonly held that they take on some of the aspect of religious dogma. Yet these assumptions are not labeled dogmatic because they are considered "modern" opinions.

For instance, the famous "Principle of Mediocrity" of astronomy holds that there is nothing special about our place and time—that the earth is a mundane world circling a mundane star among trillions in this corner of the universe alone. The Mediocrity Principle was a daring and revolutionary idea when broached during the Renaissance. It took years to supplant the earlier, anthropocentric, geocentric worldviews and become the bulwark of modern astronomy.

Yet the Principle of Mediocrity is now under assault by an upstart theory called the "Anthropic Principle," which dares to say that the earth may, indeed, be special. (The major evidence given is the total absence of any sign of visits to earth by extraterrestrial civilizations in geologic history. This is a topic getting a lot of attention in certain intellectual quarters today.)

Another example of a major assumption that was once revolutionary, but which now is under attack as "conservative," might be called the Principle of the Endless Scientific Frontier. It proposes that there is no limit to what can be learned about nature, and that natural law has no boundaries. The implication is that there will be generations of scientists without end, and that each generation can stand on the shoulders of its predecessors to learn more.

But will there always be exciting new frontiers of knowledge? Is it possible that we are closing in on the borders of the knowable?

Certainly this was thought to be true around the turn of the last century, when professors of physics actually discouraged new graduate students, stating blithely that everything of real value had already been determined!

Of course we now know that quantum mechanics, relativity, radioactivity, and numerical analysis would blow that contention apart just a short time later. The Principle of the Endless Frontier was reaffirmed in the 1920s.

Yet, we are now beginning to hear the refrain of "limits" once again. Science-philosophers, such as F. W. Atkins and P. C. W. Davies, contend that late 20th-century mankind is on the verge of filling in more than 80 percent of the landscape of physics. If this is so, the other sciences must, perforce, follow.

It is a disconcerting idea to a native of that 20th century. One is tempted to harken back to the failed Cassandras of 1890, and indeed, we might be on the verge of discoveries which will open up the endless horizons once more.

But because the Cassandras of science were proven wrong once doesn't necessarily mean they will be again. Physicists are far more sophisticated today. When they say that the gaps are rapidly being filled, they must, for the time being at least, be taken at their word. If science itself has a boundary, then, must not hard science fiction, as well? We spoke of what almost amounts to a competition among hard SF authors to find thematic gaps where a topic worthy of speculation has not been treated before. The goal is to find and describe such virgin territory—telling a good yarn in the process—before anyone else gets the idea. Once a subject has been treated well by one author, others tend to shy away from covering it again (at least in the same way), seeking to do something original, instead.

Is it possible that this competition is *dangerous* to the profession—almost "Malthusian" in a way? Are hard SF authors gobbling up a finite resource . . . the Possible? If science itself is due to plow its last fallow fields, can hard SF be far behind?

It's a debatable question. However, the appearance of limits is sufficient, perhaps, to cause some SF authors to fear the hard branch, without entirely knowing why.

In this matter of limits to the Possible, we must return to the distinction between "engineering SF" (ESF) and "science SF" (SSF), two branches of hard SF in which, respectively, engineering and science are themselves major characters of the story, having something new to say.

What I have called SSF is the sub-subgenre which faces this quandary of the speculatively possible head on. An author of SSF says "what if?" in a grand way and has to simultaneously satisfy both originality and scientific believability. The muses of SSF are demanding. They don't pay well if the ideas aren't grand, and they are unforgiving if either originality or believability are lacking.

Engineering SF suffers gentler constraints. *Analog* magazine prints no lack of entertaining stories that are, indeed, *hard* SF, and there seems to be no dearth of ideas. The only difference between ESF and SSF is that originality is not so severely judged in ESF. An ESF story does not cover the grand topic of life on the surface of a neutron star, but rather a neat way in which the space shuttle might be used to rescue a doomed cosmonaut. It doesn't worry over the cosmological implications of Black Holes, but plays instead with how to pull off a successful revolt in a space colony with a 98 percent independent recycling system.

Engineering SF faces no shortage of "possibilities" to be exploited. Many SF authors may stay away from it because of some of the other reasons we have discussed here, but not because there are few gaps left to be filled.

However, scientific SF—the hard SF having to do with the very nature of reality—may be entering an era of hard times. It is a common truism that there will never be a dearth of good and original new ideas. But is it wise to count on a truism always being true?

As one who earns his living in part by writing SSF . . . and who enjoys reading it . . . I hope these fears are unfounded. Yet they go a long way toward explaining some of the reluctance many talented SF authors seem to feel toward stepping into the heartland of science fiction—hard SF itself. Not only has the hard stuff become more difficult, with time. But its essence, the idea, also has grown precious and may become more so as time goes on.

It sounds like a tract from some strange ecological exposé. "Will future generations forgive us if we carelessly, thoughtlessly, squander a rare resource . . . the very imagined Possible itself . . . without packing some away for a rainy day?"

It might make a good plot for a story. . . .

Author's Note: Some months after delivering this talk, I saw a piece in *Analog,* entitled "Melancholy Elephants" by Spider Robinson. It was about this very topic of the "mining out" of ideas themselves. I had put off writing my own story on the subject, and there it was. "Melancholy Elephants" won a Hugo Award for best short story. I crumpled my own early draft and threw it away. Rats.

Sturgeon's Law: First Corollary
Frank McConnell

My purpose here is to discuss the distinction between "hard" and "soft" science fiction. Or—to speak in the picturesque if curious terms of the topic as officially announced, we are here to discuss "hard-core science fiction." Now, what can *that* mean, I wonder? My own mind, inelectably Victorian and therefore unreservedly prurient, conjures up for the idea of "hard-core" science fiction any number of titles that, I am sure, you don't want to hear more about: *Deep Transistor,* say; or *The Capacitor in Miss Jones*; or, worst of all, *Beyond the Green Spacewarp.* Consider, as they used to say on movie marquees, the possibilities.

I hope you see my problem. I am driven to discuss a very seriously-conceived topic—the distinction between "hard" or "pure" science fiction and its—what?—*less* hard and pure avatars, and I am driven to discuss it in terms of jokes. Let me be the devil's advocate, and let me suggest that there is *not* such a thing as "hard-core science fiction." Or if there is, let me suggest that we ought to do to it the same thing the present administration has done to the ideal of detente: get rid of it.

Most of us have taught, or talked about, or lectured on, or simply babbled on the subject of science fiction. And that means that we have, most of us, babbled at one time or another about the difference between "hard" and "new wave" science fiction. We have explained, carefully or sloppily, with more or less references to mythology, structuralism, and James Joyce, the difference between *Starship Troopers* and *Nine Princes in Amber, Foundation,* and *Dhalgren,* "Neutron Star" and "I Have No Mouth and I Must Scream." It is one of the great truisms of popular culture criticism, this distinction between mainstream and new-wave SF; like the distinction between the British and the American traditions of detective fiction (Doyle—Christie—Sayers vs. Hammett—Chandler—Mac-Donald, say).

And like all truisms, this one is at least partly true. And like all truisms, it is mainly, boringly, off the point.

The point is this, and let us admit it once and for all: science fiction is *fiction,* no more and no less. Some of the nice-nellying adjectives that well-meaning editors and writers have applied to it—"extrapolative," "speculative," "experimental"—only help point up the *conventionality* of the mode. What fiction, God help us, is *not* extrapolative or speculative or experimental?

If this appears that I am arguing for a deconstruction of our ideas of generic norms, returning us to a primal chaos of fictive forms in which all fictive forms are equally privileged; if this appears that I am arguing for the dismantling of the concept itself, "science fiction," as more a barrier than an aid to reading; if this seems as if I am saying that all fiction worth examining is, one way or another, science fiction; it is because that is what I am doing.

Quite honestly, I can no longer tell the differences among *Mr. Sammler's Planet, V., The Stars My Destination, The Chronicles of Thomas Covenant the Unbeliever* and—for that matter—Bruce Springsteen's "Born to Run." Or, rather, I no longer think it is important to tell the differences among them. All are fictions—and splendid fictions, at that—involving protagonists who *do not understand* the situation into which they are thrown, and whose heroic struggle is to understand, and through understanding to master, a universe of mechanisms that seems set to destroy them.

Mechanisms: either the machinery of the plot itself or the machinery described by the plot itself. Does it make a difference whether the mechanism is more or less explicitly described *in* the story? Dickens's London is, at this point in time, a no less strange technology for living than Alfred Bester's meticulously imagined future in *The Stars My Destination.* What this suggests to me, at least, is that Oliver Twist and Gully Foyle—or Clarissa Harlowe and Paul Atreides, or Emma Bovary and Thomas Covenant—are equally products of the storytelling imagination and equally to be regarded, and honored, as projections of *ourselves* struggling with the impingements of the fictions of the self life wants and tries to impose upon us.

"Hard-core science fiction": what might that be? In the terms I have just suggested for fiction altogether, I suppose that we could define "hard-core" SF as fiction that depends in a specially acute way on a sense of the intransigence of matter and the complexity with which that intransigence tends to manifest itself. A Buddhist, say, for whom such intransigence is mere illusion, or a Taoist, for whom it is sublimely unimportant, could not write hard-core SF. Nor, presumably, could a Franciscan mystic, for whom the intransigence would collapse into a kind of cosmic chumminess (consider the concepts of "Brother White Dwarf" or "Sister Entropy").

But the mainstream Western tradition of thought—the *whole* mainstream—is structured on precisely the sense of the impermeability and the hostility of matter. Herbert Schneidau, in his brilliant study of the Bible, *Sacred Discontent,* argues persuasively that the Judeo-Christian heritage of mythmaking is in fact a heritage of antimythmaking, a narrative tradition whose inmost form blocks the identification of self and world which is at the heart of the mythological imagination. And even more interestingly, Leszek Kolakowski in his book, *Religion,* suggests that "by appointing man the lord of the earth and by subordinating Nature to his needs the Judaeo-Christian tradition encouraged the great thrust of technological and scientific progress on which Western civilization was to be built."

Now what this suggests is, I think, a revision of our idea of science fiction as a genre, or maybe of the idea of fictional genre altogether. Let me draw an analogy. You will remember that in Arthur C. Clarke's *Childhood's End,* when the mysterious "Overlords" arrive from outer space to reorganize earth's society—and eventually lead it toward its own annihilation and self-transcendence—they keep themselves hidden at first. When they finally make their appearance, they are all in the classic shape of medieval devils—leather wings, pointed tails, horns, and complete satanic *ensemble.* The reason for this remarkable coalescence of myth and reality, Clarke hypothesizes, is that mankind, in a sort of proleptic vision of its ultimate fate—of childhood's end—remembered *forward* to the Overlords and placed their shape at the point of an aboriginal, rather than a terminal, catastrophe.

The analogy is this: I want to suggest that we consider hard-core SF, not as a recently evolved form of Western storytelling, but as the form toward which Western storytelling has been tending all along, the perfect antimythological mythology or the perfect technological theology, whose form is implicit in the very roots of our tradition. Hard-core SF, in other words, like the Overlords of Clarke, so frequently looks like a recapitulation of our earliest past because our earliest past was dreaming of it before it became possible.

This kind of formulation will, of course, offend academic intellectuals because it seems to give a kind of evolutionary primacy to a form which is still not officially respectable. And it will offend science fiction fans because it seems to assimilate their chosen and revered imaginative escape to the great tradition of so-called "serious" writing. And this gives me solace, since a formulation that offends nearly everybody cannot, I think, be wholly wrong.

And let us admit, too, that we are all ideological prisoners of Hugo Gernsback, who coined the grotesque term, "scientifiction," in 1926. It is not even *science* fiction: it is technological fiction. If science is the nonintrusionist (*pace* Heisenberg) contemplation of nature, then there can be no real science fiction. But once man does intrude on the environment; once he does begin to use his pure contemplation for impure, acquisitive ends; then technology is possible, and then fiction is possible. From Cain to Genghis Khan to James Watt, despoilers of the landscape have always been the stuff of epic and romance: just because fiction, in the Western tradition, *is* the story of technology and technology is the dynamics of our exile from the primal Garden by instruments of our own devising.

Jules Verne, one of the fathers of the form (did ever a child have so many fathers?) was asked in 1905 to comment on the resemblance of his work to that of H. G. Wells. Verne's testy response virtually encapsulates and exhausts the distinction between "hard" and "other" SF. *Mais,* sputtered Verne, *mais—il invente!*

"But—he *invents!*" And so Wells did, and so Verne did not. Or, rather, so Verne *thought* he didn't. The hard SF writer, from Verne to Asimov to Larry Niven, has always made it a point of personal pride that his work is strict extrapolation from the known, with no—or as little as possible—adulterating admixture from the purely fantastic. This is the boast that produces, among other things, Niven's very funny series of time travel stories, collected in *The Flight of the Horse.* For since time travel is a manifest absurdity in terms of contemporary physics, what Niven's time travellers do—but don't *know* they do—is travel, not into the past, but into fantasy, into the world of the never-was (e.g. the traveller, sent back to find a horse, brings home a unicorn). The journey, for Niven, is not across barriers of time, but across the barriers between genres.

The counter-example to Niven's stories would be, I think, most baldly Isaac Asimov's robot stories: there the fiction is not simply an extrapolation from known laws, but is, really, simply a redemonstration, again and again, of the "three laws of robotics" that are the entire fictive universe of the tales. Reading the robot stories, wonderful as they are, is in fact rather like playing a classic game from the chess column of the newspaper: your interest is not diminished, but is qualified by your sure knowledge that the rules will *always* be established again, in full primacy, at the end. Outside of the romances of Barbara Cartland, this is probably the closest approach fiction can make to playing pinball without using the levers. You just watch the ball take its predestined, gravity-ridden course down the board.

But however hard a hard-core SF writer tries, he cannot help transgressing the artificial generic barriers he may impose upon himself. Not even Asimov can keep his stories from giving delight—and the special kind of delight that belongs to storytelling, not to logical or pseudoscientific demonstration. (Indeed, I would suggest that Asimov's vaunted "hardness" is on a par with the "rationalism" of Arthur Conan Doyle: both men, whether they know it or not, are really involved with creating a *myth* of rationality, not rationality itself.)

To be sure, there is *some* sort of difference between science fiction and fantasy. But I think that difference is only apparent, or obtrusive, when one form impinges ludicrously on the other. Like identical twins, they are easiest to tell apart when their sibling rivalry erupts into fistfights or name-calling.

There is, for example, what I like to think of as the "Princess Aura" syndrome (after everyone's favorite seductress from the *Flash Gordon* serials). A set of technological heroes, full-hardware-equipped space travellers, reach a distant and inhospitable world only to find it populated by venal tyrants, deposed princes, and breathtaking court ladies—all speaking flawless English—straight out of *The Prisoner of Zenda* or, for that matter, *As You Like It*.

But this often-remarked triviality of space opera is, really, not a triviality at all. It is part of the inevitable contamination of technological fiction by romance: because, as I have been saying, technological fiction and romance really are the same imaginative endeavor. And though the discovery of such improbably British aliens is the sort of thing that gives nightmares to the Carl Sagans of the world, a healthy course of reading Rabelais, James Fenimore Cooper, and Edgar Rice Burroughs can work wonders to allay the fright.

To be sure, there are counter-examples, moments when explicit fantasy impinges ludicrously upon the domain of hard SF. In a fantasy I very much admire, Harold Bloom's *The Flight to Lucifer,* a character remarks, early on and offhandedly, "I cross the cosmos through black holes"—prompting one to ask things like, "What time does the next black hole come through?" And when questioned about the nature of his spaceship, this same being laughs, "An illegal borrowing, from your space shuttle perhaps, We will say no more about that." Bloom at least has the wit to see that anything as hardware-rich as the space shuttle *is* an illegal borrowing from one fictive universe into another, and to turn a generic absurdity into a self-conscious joke.

But these, as I said, are instances of the extreme incompatibility of the modes we loosely call "hard" and "soft" SF.

I invoke one of the very greatest theorists of narrative modes. Søren Kierkegaard, in *The Sickness Unto Death,* remarks that there are two elementary forms of despair. "The Despair of possibility is due to the lack of necessity," and "The Despair of necessity is due to the lack of possibility." Or, as he also puts it, the despair of the infinite sense is its hunger for the finite, and the despair of the finite sense is its hunger for the infinite. I do no more than follow Kierkegaard in remarking that these complementary despairs produce complementary narrative modes, the one a fantastic quest longing for the specificity of the limited and the material, the other an exploration of the limited and the material longing for the transcendence of the fantastic. "Eternity is in love with the productions of time," wrote Blake a half-century before Kierkegaard. And the feeling is mutual: the productions of time are in love with eternity. Out of that star-crossed love is generated all our uneasiness with our lives, all our hopes for curing that uneasiness, and, of course, all our storytelling.

Consider the ideas of the quest and the return. They are the prime constituents, the major moments, of any human voyage. And yet how different they are! The quester's journey is always into strangeness, into the unformed or the unformulable, and yet he tends to discover in that inchoate landscape the forms of the familiar. And the journey home, the return after the quest, is always a journey back to the familiar; but what returnee, from Gulliver to Gully Foyle, has not come home only to find the entire universe altered into the strange? "There are two ways of getting home," wrote G. K. Chesterton, "and one of them is to stay there." But even staying there is a kind of voyaging: you don't know you *have* stayed until things begin to look different, perhaps even frightening. And this, very hard-core phenomenological fact is at the heart of two great modern masters of the everyday nightmarish, Samuel Beckett and Philip K. Dick. In a brilliant paper presented at the first Eaton Conference, Thomas A. Hanzo examined "The Past of Science Fiction." All SF, argued Hanzo, is a version of *prolepsis*—i.e. the presentation of future events as if they had already occurred. When you place a ten dollar bet on a horse I *know* is going to lose in the fifth at Santa Anita, and I tell you, "You just blew ten bucks," I have performed a rhetorical act of prolepsis: and, according to Hanzo, I have also just created a very short science fiction story. (Whether "hard" or "soft," I suppose, depends upon whether or not your horse actually wins.)

But this obsession with the past tense, Hanzo suggests, really involves an obsession with two *kinds* of past tense, to which we are all thrall, and within which we all make our feeble gestures toward a human life. There is the primal past, the irrecoverable past before the trauma of the separation of self and other. And there is the historical past, the past of your individual life and mine, and the past of civilization itself. These pasts are irreconcilable. To have a history is not to retain the aboriginal sense of unity, and to return to the aboriginal sense of unity is to abolish history.

And yet we do both, because we must, because we are compelled to do both. "Hard" science can be taken as the architecture of our banishment into time, into the irreversibility of process. And, in fact, one way of imagining the unimaginable Big Bang is *precisely* in terms of this crypto-cosmo-Freudian birth trauma. Fantasy, on the other hand, can be taken as the fiction of the return—the return to that primal scene before action, even before fiction, is possible or necessary. These two possibilities, in fact, are really Kierkegaard's two kinds of creative despair, but articulated with a little more relevance to the business of storytelling itself.

And you see how they implicate, and demand, rather than impinge upon one another. Robert Heinlein's *The Puppet Masters* and *Starship Troopers* must surely be among the most incontestably non-new-wave of SF tales. They are both quest-adventures, inventions of putative future history based on the most cautious extrapolation from present-day technology. In fact, the future culture imagined in *The Puppet Masters*, relying heavily on an extension of contemporary pharmacology and communications-technology, is almost uncomfortably close to the tv-dominated, tranquilized and/or hyped lives many of us lead now, thirty years after the book was written. And *Starship Troopers* may well be the ultimately convincing space-war epic, with weaponry and tactics so precisely imagined that, a generation later, Joe Haldeman could use their details as the basis for his own, anti-Heinlein and antiwar novel, *The Forever War*.

And yet these extrapolations, like so many others, collapse finally into that alternate time, that altenate past which is the myth of our recovery of the primal scene. Sam Nivens and Johnny Rico, the respective heroes of *The Puppet Masters* and *Starship Troopers*, are finally questers for a reunion with their fathers, which is to say questers after the pre-Oedipal paradise that is the landscape of childhood and of pastoral romance. The voyage out—the "hard" SF voyage out—turns in on itself and becomes a voyage inward, into fiction and the stuff of fiction rather than into the inhospitable cosmos. The process is especially clear in Heinlein, but we can remark that the questees in Larry Niven's *Protector* and in his *Ringworld* novels also find themselves impelled backward to a rediscovery of the elder race, to cosmogenesis, and even that Asimov's Second Foundation proves to be the scene that preceded the establishing of the First Foundation.

The process is nowhere better incarnated, though, than in Arthur C. Clarke's *2010: Odyssey Two*. The novel is by no means a towering achievement. It is, in fact, an attempt to reinvent the structure and nature of the universe in less than 300 pages: rather like a disco version of Olaf Stapledon at his profoundest. But it is also an exceptionally clever book. Careful and sometimes even tedious in its attention to scientific detail, it is also packed with references to *The Lord of the Rings,* to the film *Alien,* and, indeed, to the whole tradition of science fantasy. Clarke, in other words, understands—and makes great fun out of—the inevitable interchange between SF and fantasy SF. I will not divulge the mainsprings of the plot for those of you who have not yet read it, but I will observe that in this sequel to the most famous science-fiction story of recent years, voyages out and voyages within are constantly impinging upon one another, and the boundaries between science fiction and fiction itself are constantly on the point—as they should be—of dissipating. Even HAL, that most put-upon of gadgets, finally gets the treatment we all think he really deserves: but only at the expense of becoming *fully* the human being we always knew he was, which is to say only at the cost of crossing the generic border between hard-core SF and psychological narrative.

I once saw a T-shirt at an SF convention that said "Reality is a crutch for people who can't deal with science fiction." The slogan is truer, I think, than the writer of it knew. For what I have been arguing is that science fiction does not and cannot make real sense to us until we understand that it is misnamed, and that it acts out the ancient, and only, task of fiction altogether. It is more "hard-core," to be sure, as it deals more explicitly with the technological facts of the universe we inhabit at the present moment. But precisely as it becomes more hard core, at its best and most valuable it also becomes more and more an approximation of the forms of those ancient modes of storytelling whose natal ground is the subconscious and whose fruits are the strange and lovely and invariant shapes of the racial mythic consciousness.

And, since I have already mentioned that awesome man, Olaf Stapledon, let me conclude with a reference to his work. In *Star Maker* Stapledon invents a situation that is stunning in its coalescence of the matters we have been discussing. The narrator tells us how, musing one night on the place of consciouness in the universe, he suddenly finds himself transported—a "pure viewpoint," he calls himself—into interstellar space, and is there gifted with the power to journey from planet to planet, inhabiting alien mind after alien mind, in his search for the underlying principle of consciouness. Now this is both the most outrageous of fantastic details, and *at the same time* the most satisfying of "scientific" devices: for it allows us to understand that the *real* science fiction deals with is the science of thought itself, and that first human technology, language, which allows us to tell stories about the world and compels us to try and make sense of the world through that language. Stapledon simply does away with, jettisons, the whole clanking paraphernalia of spacecraft, vacuum suits, and life-support systems. And by doing so he reminds us how fanciful, how romantic, those paraphernalia really are: as much so as the shield of Achilles or the lance and sword of Sir Gawain. *Star Maker,* in other words, is the hardest of hard SF stories, because its quest is as unrelenting and as unpicturesque, as single-minded and as pure, as the quest of pure science itself.

And at the heart of that purity there is a terrifying and austere poetry. Early in the tale, the narrator explains to us that it is only with great difficulty and great inaccuracy that he can describe the real nature of his galactic experiences: "Of the less human worlds," he writes, "and the many fantastic kinds of beings which we encountered up and down the galaxy and throughout the whole cosmos, and even beyond it, I shall perforce make statements which, literally regarded, must be almost wholly false. I can only hope that they have the kind of truth that we sometimes find in myths."

"The kind of truth that we sometimes find in myths": it is the only kind of truth, really, that we shall probably ever find to make our lives joyful or habitable. It is the only life-support system we can rely on for very long. And it is the honor, not just of Stapledon, but of the great tradition of mainstream science fiction, to continue unabated the activity of incarnating that lying truth, that most precise of false analogies, that waking dream.

The Unconscious City

Eric S. Rabkin

Writing of the 12th-century birth of the modern city, Henri Pirenne noted that each small community that collected about an ecclesiastical and administrative center was in some sense unprecedented.

> There was nothing in the existing order of things to serve it as a model, since the needs it was designed to meet were new.
> The most pressing was for defence. The merchants and their merchandise were, indeed, such a tempting prey that it was essential to protect them from pillagers by a strong wall. The construction of ramparts was thus the first public work undertaken by the towns and one which . . . was their heaviest financial burden. . . . There were no unfortified towns in the Middle Ages.[1]

The newness of cities continued to define their history, so that, as Raymond Williams notes of the late Victorian era, "Out of an experience of the cities came an experience of the future."[2] Of course, then, as Brian Aldiss observes, "science fiction is a literature of cities."[3] "At the outset," Jean Raynaud says, "science fiction seems an eminently urban literary form."[4] Just as the medieval city necessitated the creation of a protective wall and the simultaneous burdening of the urban population with the debt of the wall's construction and confinement, so the cities of later centuries, down to and beyond our own, have been seen as external, and sometimes ambivalent, technologies by which humanity controls its relationship to the environment and to other predators. The city is "the greater machine"[5] in which we live—or struggle to live.

The city in science fiction has always been a prime locus for invention and for display of such "hard SF themes" as "computers, communications, cybernetics, physics, power sources, [and] technology."[6] One of the most common devices for taking the pulp reader's breath has been the inventive display of "the technological marvels which the urban dweller of the future may expect to enjoy."[7] In a work such as Robert A. Heinlein's "The Roads Must Roll" (1940) with its road cities built on giant interregional slidewalks, the hard SF city becomes the cause and content of the tale. Arthur C. Clarke's Diaspar of *The City and the Stars* (1956) initially represents the culmination of all human science. The SF city is obviously a powerful species of environmental hardware, at least equivalent in its centrality and malleability to the rocketship. Yet Ihab Hassan has asked "what we may conclude about the city, or fiction, or the city in fiction? Nothing conclusive . . . [because the city is] immaterial in its languages, diverse in its desires, projected to some end still obscure to us, which yet menaces the gods!"[8] If we are to have any hope of lifting that obscurity, we must examine the many ways in which writers use the city and seek to discover among them, if possible, some common source for the persistent power of this image.

In science fiction, as in all literature, a city sometimes may be a comparatively inconsequential choice of locale. In tales of world cataclysm, such as Fritz Leiber's *The Wanderer* (1964), or in tales of interplanetary invasion, such as H. G. Wells' *The War of the Worlds* (1898), the city may figure as but one location among many for the manifestation of the general action of destruction or combat. More frequently, however, the city setting represents a narrative choice of major consequence. This is particularly true in works dominated by the images of single cities. Such works have attracted the attention of many scholars.

In his handy, brief survey of city-dominated works, Brian Stableford divides them into three categories. "The first shows up the contrast between the city and a surrounding wilderness, polarizing the opposition between city and country life as we perceive it today. The second shows the city in ruins, decaying and dying. The third is involved with the characterization of the city environment, impersonal and hostile."[9] Examples of these types are, respectively, Arthur C. Clarke's *The City and the Stars* (1953), Clifford D. Simak's *City* (1952), and Isaac Asimov's *The Caves of Steel* (1954). While this categorization is useful in focusing our attention, it does not in itself suggest why there should be these—and only these—three groupings. Indeed, Simak's novel exemplifies the ruined city only after the chapter called "Desertion" in which the glorious escape of humanity to a new life on Jupiter has made the abandonment of earthly cities

seem desirable. In surveying these types together, Stableford rightly
enough concludes that science fiction's general attitude toward cities
is negative; but he himself adds that "there is one remarkable exception to this negative attitude to cities, in which the city becomes the
symbol of escape and freedom rather than the oppressive environment to be escaped[:] James Blish's *Cities in Flight* (1970)."[10] I
believe a deeper understanding of the uses of cities in science fiction
will help explain the relationship of Blish's work to the genre as a
whole.

    Jean Raynaud suggests that "the presentation of cities follows
two major directions—those very ones that orient all SF . . . toward
the clear or the obscure, the dream or the nightmare."[11] What he calls
"SF1" "presents garden-cities, of pleasure or of repose, or space
cities to the glory of a new humanity in which all the "hardware"
signifies before all a vital spirit, the appetite for conquest."[12] Presumably the space-roving "Okie" cities of Blish would fall into this
category. On the other hand, "SF2 puts the accent on the disharmo-
nies, on the superiority of historical determinism over the forces of
reason, and the rules of sociology over those of science,"[13] Raynaud
recognizes that there is in the image of the city the capacity to relate
these two "directions": "The most marked characteristic of the SF
city is its gigantism, which in the first instance was able to be used to
glorify the human species in its works, but which is rather in the
present used to reduce man, to bring him down to the proportions of
an ant. . . . The giant city is also the enclosed city. The image of the
dome, of the cupola, is omnipresent."

    In what is to my mind the most complete and suggestive treat-
ment to date of science fiction cities, Gary K. Wolfe writes that "the
city of tomorrow . . . is hardly representative of anything that could
be called the 'science-fiction mind.' "[15] He then goes on to list "some
of the ways in which the city is antithetical to the traditional attitudes
of the genre, *in no particular order*" (emphasis mine). While Wolfe
himself exemplifies only some of these "ways," and while he does not
present them as a coordinated set, each is, I believe, worth noting:

> "The city is centralized." Thus it highlights by contrast the motive to
> escape that we see in *City*.
>   "The city is collectivistic." Thus it highlights the urge for individua-
> tion that we see in *The City and the Stars*.
>   "The city is xeonophobic." Thus it highlights the need for cross-
> cultural cooperation that concludes *The Caves of Steel*.

"The city is authoritarian." Thus it highlights the significance of the individual that captures our attention in Thea von Harbou's *Metropolis* (1926).

"The city is stable." Thus it highlights the inhibitions to growth that the hero must overcome in William F. Nolan and George Clayton Johnson's *Logan's Run* (1967).

"The city is confined." Thus it highlights the human urge to multiply that dominates Robert Silverberg's *The World Inside* (1971).

"The city is unnatural." Thus it highlights the despoliation of nature that we see in John Brunner's *Stand on Zanzibar* (1968).

"The city is of the past." Thus it highlights the legacy of human culture gone wrong that occupies most of H. G. Wells's *The Time Machine* (1895).

"The city is regressively technological." Thus it highlights the problems that technology itself creates in the diminished future of Frederik Pohl and C. M. Kornbluth's *The Space Merchants* (1953).

"The city is superfluous." Thus it highlights the economic disparity between urban and rural existence that marks even such early locales as the floating city of Laputa in Swift's *Gulliver's Travels* (1726).

"The city is chaotic." Thus it highlights the comparative order of the garden world surrounding the decayed London in William Morris's *News from Nowhere* (1890).

"The city is mythic." Thus it highlights with its walls the boundary between the known and the unknown as in Eugene Zamiatin's *We* (1924).[16]

Although Wolfe does not provide all these examples, clearly they can be found. On the other hand, one can also find counterexamples. For instance, in *We* it is the countryside that is chaotic while the city is ordered—to a dehumanizing fault. In *The City and the Stars,* the countryside is permanently pastoral while the city, though virtually stable, at least has the program for intermittent variation and progress built in as part of its basic structure. Despite such counterexamples, Wolfe's recognition of the city as "antithetical" to science fiction's prevailing ideology at least implicitly suggests a mechanism by which the icon of the city has taken on its narrative importance. My use of the term *highlight* aims to make this suggestion more explicit; however, to move from an exposition of iconography to an understanding of the potential for narrative drama, we must explore not only the visible landscape of the fiction but its more obscure psychological foundation.

Gaston Bachelard, the renowned French phenomenologist, has written that "all great, simple images reveal a psychic state."[17] If a happy child is asked to draw a house, Bachelard reports, the result will be well shaped and firmly rooted on its foundation; if an unhappy child is given the same task, the result will be tilted, cramped, perhaps even doorless. The image of the city, like the image of the house, always potentially embodies an antinomy, opposing meanings that exist always in virtual tension and hence make possible a psychic movement from one aspect of the antinomy to another. In rebuilding one's house, or in becoming master of one's city, psychological needs can be fulfilled, a dramatic trajectory can be traced.

Bachelard has devoted a whole book to one "great, simple image," fire. He elaborates a number of antinomies potential within this image. For example, he calls the tension between disobedience and knowledge gained the "Prometheus complex"; he speaks of "sexualized fire" as both life-creating and person-consuming. Each set of antinomies is a "complex." "In point of fact," he writes, speaking of all emotionally moving art, "a poetic work can hardly be unified except by a complex. If the complex is lacking, the work, cut off from its roots, no longer communicates with the unconscious. It appears cold, artificial, false."[18]

Bachelard does not suggest that all the complexes associated with fire are significant in every work in which fire functions as a unifying image; however, he does suggest that when one part of a complex is activated in a work, the whole of that complex becomes virtual.

Writing of cities, Sharon Spencer reports Michel Butor's observation "that a new *lieu* [place] not only gives us something novel in itself, but enables us, by separation and consequent contrast, to comprehend more clearly the place we have just left behind."[19] What Butor calls "something new," Darko Suvin calls "the novum . . . a mediating category whose explicative potency springs from its rare bridging of literary and extraliterary, fictional and empirical, formal and ideological domains, in brief from its unalienable historicity."[20] Suvin asserts that "the novum is the necessary condition of SF."[21] Since it is already clear from the examples we have mentioned that in science fiction the city can take on the role of novum and through it fulfill the Bachelardian unifying function, I propose to seek in that genre first for the complexes that our culture finds in the phe-nomenon of the city.

John Wyndham's novel *Re-Birth* (1955) is set in a future world long after a nuclear holocaust called Tribulation has largely—but not completely—corrupted humanity's environment and its genetic store. David, the narrator, is one of a small number of telepathic children growing up in an isolated Labrador village that adulates the normal and expunges the abnormal wherever it is found. The story concerns the awakening to telepathic awareness of these children, their secret development into a society within the larger village society, their discovery, and their final flight to claim a life of their own. This is how the novel begins:

> When I was quite small I would sometimes dream of a city—which was strange because it began before I even knew what a city was. But this city, clustered on the curve of a blue bay, would come into my mind. I could see the streets, and the buildings that lined them, the waterfront, even boats in the harbor; yet, waking, I had never seen the sea, or a boat. . . .
> And the buildings were quite unlike any I knew. The traffic in the streets was strange, carts running with no horses to pull them; and sometimes there were things in the sky, shiny fish-shaped things that certainly were not birds. . . .
> I asked my eldest sister, Mary, where this lovely city could be.
> She shook her head, and told me there was no such place—not now. But, perhaps, she suggested, I could somehow be dreaming about times long ago . . . seeing a bit of the world as it had been once upon a time—the wonderful world that the Old People had lived in; as it had been before God sent Tribulation.[22]

This fairy tale beginning associates the city image with what may be traditional symbols of female fertility: the embayed water, the fish. The fish may also call to mind the story of Christ with Mary, here David's close blood relative, and properly with no sexual charge between them. David, perhaps again like Christ, has a vision of a supernatural city that is unshared by normal people, a vision, it is suggested, that speaks of an unfallen world.

The city itself recurs rarely in the novel. When it does, it is a matter of thought-conversation among the telepathic children. As their own sense of danger grows, the city becomes ever more inviting; if only it were real. And then, the youngest of the children, David's little sister Petra (perhaps a female form of Peter, the rock on whom the church is built), manifests the furthest-reaching telepathic powers of all and breaks through consciously to the city. This dream landscape is diametrically opposed to Labrador; it is a habitation in New Zealand full of other telepaths who not only would not kill the children but positively seek them out. The final sequence of actions in the novel begins with the villagers chasing the children in order to kill them. The children, just before the end, are semi-imprisoned in the outlaw camp of some misshapen mutants when the pursuers, including David's father, ride up. "The spider-man" shoots an arrow.

> The shaft took my father in the left of his chest. [David reports no emotion.] . . .
> Suddenly one of the horsemen shouted and pointed upward. . . . As if through a veil, I could make out one of the strange, fish-shaped craft that I had dreamt of in my childhood, hanging in the sky.[23]

A "Zealand woman" operates a machine that sprays out "glistening threads like cobwebs. . . . Involuntarily I closed my eyes. There was a light gossamer touch on my face. When I tried to open my eyes again I found I could not."[24] It turns out that these "plastic threads contract as they dry"[25] and thereby kill. The Zealand woman has dispatched all the pursuers, but her special counterspray has dissolved the threads in time to save all the children. She brings them into the fish-shaped craft and transports them, as the novel closes, to the city where they are joyfully received by "lots and lots of our kind of people."[26]

This is a clear example of symbolic death and rebirth. The emergence from the cocoon accords with the British title of *Re-Birth, The Chrysalids*. While normal parents are death-dealers for the protagonists of this story, a substitute mother of their own kind revives the city associated with the unfallen world, a city now improved in a paradise regained. David, like Christ, is reborn, to be sure, but the city itself, especially as emblematized by the "Zealand woman," is clearly a mother figure.

Psychologically we see that the protagonist makes very little movement in this story. The city represents a refuge from a punishing father. When the father is killed, the city becomes real in the person of a protecting mother. The city from the time of the Old People still exists so that David's infantile regressive impulses may be satisfied. *Re-Birth* is one of the many standard variations on what Freud has taught us to see as the Oedipus myth. There is a clear competition in this novel between father/society/superego and son. The son longs for, dreams of, a city of his own and the chance to be an individual. The father both squelches individuality under the rule of conformity and would kill the son to prevent him attaining his dream of fertility.

When the father in fact attempts David's murder, he is in turn killed by the spider-man, a figure who is, like David, a mutant, that is, an individual, but who is decidedly not David himself. There is thus no need for patricidal guilt. Instead, as soon as the father dies, the mother materializes and David almost instantly receives her enveloping embrace. When he emerges from that darkness, he is re-born, the mother now his, the competitor/father dead and half a world away. In this tale, the city is the manifestation of the fantastic mother/protector.

There is a dark side, too, to maternal protection: maternal imprisonment. In fairy tales, mothers are constantly telling children what not to do and thereby preventing them both from harm and from growth. In *The Caves of Steel*, Asimov presents a vast, future New York all sealed in metal and populated by agoraphobics so extreme that they can barely contemplate the view from the rare, upper-level windows; they cannot ever cross an open field—should they somehow ever find one. A "Spacer" justly criticizes these people, "'all so coddled, so enwombed in their imprisoning caves of steel, that they are caught forever.' "[27] The vision of womb as prison is common to a whole subgenre of city stories often called "hive" stories, a name that suggests the dehumanizing effects of procreative, smothering imprisonment. Protection and imprisonment form one traditional antinomy associated with mothers and clearly possible in the image of the city.

Mother figures have another traditional role in our culture: they nourish us. Diaspar, the city of Clarke's *The City and the Stars,* is another mother figure, this time one associated as much with nourishment as with protection. Here is how the book begins:

> Like a glowing jewel, the city lay upon the breast of the desert. Once it had known change and alteration, but now Time passed it by. Night and day fled across the desert's face, but in the streets of Diaspar it was always afternoon, and darkness never came. . . . It had no contact with the outer world; it was a universe itself. . . .
>
> The last mountains had been ground to dust by the winds and the rain, and the world was too weary to bring forth more. The city did not care; Earth itself could crumble and Diaspar would still protect the children of its makers, bearing them and their treasures safely down the stream of Time.[28]

The city is, in fact, one huge machine, a pyramidal cocoon that houses the leisured, remnant throng of a now decadent humanity.

Diaspar's Central Computer reads each citizen's thoughts and obeys. Our protagonist is a youth named Alvin. Simply by thinking, he "tilted the gravity field, rose to his feet, and walked toward the table he had materialized. A bowl of exotic fruit appeared upon it—not the food he had intended, for in his confusion his thoughts had wandered. Not wishing to reveal his error [to his friends], he picked up the least dangerous-looking of the fruits and started to suck it cautiously."[29] Will it be a poisoned apple? No, not this time.

Max Lüthi has pointed out that the sign of a true mother in the traditional fairy tale is that she feeds the child protagonist. Just as certainly, the sign of the true anti-mother, the witch, is that she would feed the child anti-food, as in *Snow White* or *Sleeping Beauty,* or would even eat the child, as in *Hansel and Gretel.*[30] Diaspar reveals both sides of this antinomy within the "great, simple image" of the mother. As Alvin's teacher explains,

> "our ancestors learned how to analyze and store the information that would define any specific human being—and use that information to re-create the original. . . . This is the way our ancestors gave us virtual immortality, yet avoided the problems raised by the abolition of death. . . . In a little while, Alvin, I shall prepare to leave this life. I shall go back through my memories, editing them and cancelling those I do not wish to keep. Then I shall walk into the Hall of Creation, but through a door which you have never seen. . . . Then one day, perhaps a hundred thousand years from now, I shall find myself in a new body, meeting those who have been chosen to be my guardians. . . . We all have been here many, many times before, though as the intervals of nonexistence vary according to apparently random laws this present population will never repeat itself again. . . . At any moment, Alvin, only a hundredth of the citizens of Diaspar live and walk its streets. . . . So we have continuity, yet change—immortality, but not stagnation."[31]

Diaspar gives birth to its citizens and swallows them back up again; they have something like immortality at intervals, but she, feeding on them, goes on forever.

Obviously a normal child would revolt against such a mother, but where to find a normal child in Diaspar? The teacher continues.

> "You, Alvin, are something that has happened in Diaspar only a handful of times since the founding of the city. Perhaps you have been lying dormant in the Memory Banks through all the ages—or perhaps you were created only twenty years ago by some random permutation.

You may have been planned in the beginning by the designers of the city, or you may be a purposeless accident of our own time. "We do not know. All that we do know is this: You, Alvin, alone of the human race, have never lived before. In literal truth, you are the first child to be born on Earth for at least ten million years."[32]

Obviously Alvin's individuality is confirmed, but now he needs to express it. He can hardly find others of his own kind given the enveloping completeness of the city/mother/womb that knows his every thought and provides for him willy-nilly. What could he wish that she cannot provide? A world outside. Alvin needs to be born. In the course of the novel he discovers a way out in two senses: first, he overcomes the extreme agoraphobia he initially shares with his fellow citizens; second, he discovers an ancient automated tunnel system that runs to the last village on earth, Lys, a bucolic, stable, pacific culture. Unlike the people of Diaspar, those of Lys still reproduce sexually; unlike the people of Lys, those of Diaspar still exercise their minds. Obviously a union is needed. Alvin becomes the agent of that union.

He first approaches Lys through the underground tunnel in a thought-controlled, needle-shaped car, obviously an example of wish fulfillment. He later discovers an ancient, thought-controlled, needle-shaped spaceship. With this, he finds his way to the navigational center of our universe, a location marked by the ancients with a giant needle-shaped pylon. He returns from his voyage of discovery to bring the people of Diaspar and Lys into contact. As the story ends, the shell of Diaspar appears fragile; the possibility of real sexuality in the world has returned.

The nourishment of Diaspar is a drug of Lotus-land, another version of the protection/imprisonment antinomy. In many novels, including Clarke's own *The Lion of Comarre* (1949) and *Against the Fall of Night* (1953), the feeding/drugging antinomy inherent in the image of the city/mother provides the imagistic possibility for the protagonist's drama of discovery. In *The City and the Stars,* this self-discovery necessitates the destruction of Diaspar, humanity's greatest achievement. Such a rejection, like the rejection of one's own mother (or the killing of one's father), is almost bound to create feelings of guilt. However, Clarke is writing a popular romance; his aim is not to force his readers to examine their inner motives but rather to use those motives to provide them a psychologically satisfying experience. How can he allow Alvin fatally to split the womb of his mother/city and not feel guilt? The narrative solution is ingenious. Diaspar is obviously a huge machine built to preserve and pro- tect humanity. As the narrative explains, Diaspar is the creation largely of one mighty ancient engineer, a man named Yarlan Zey. All the potential of Diaspar was designed into it by the supreme father figure. It was he who left the ancient tunnel system and the code that Alvin deciphers to make use of it. It will be remembered that Alvin is unique and that his uniqueness itself was doubtless part of Yarlan Zey's plan. Uniqueness, of course, might just as easily be an attribute of an idiot as of a genius. Near the end of the novel, as Alvin is preparing himself psychologically for infecting/impregnating the cul- ture of Diaspar with that of Lys, he has a sudden thought which he reveals to Hilvar, his friend from Lys: "It's just occurred to me— perhaps *I* am Yarlan Zey. It's perfectly possible. He may have fed his personality into the Memory Banks, relying on it to break the mold of Diaspar before it was too firmly established."[33] With this comforting thought, Alvin forestalls any possible guilt in destroying his mother- culture because he is in fact fulfilling it. He does not kill an Oedipal father; he becomes one. The culture he destroys, the mother/city, is the creation of the father he has become. The city then is rightly understood as the body on which is projected male desire. In the case of this adolescent novel, that desire is to be free. Alvin simultane- ously awakens his world to fruitful sexuality and destroys the womb whence he sprang.

At first glance it may seem strange to treat the city/mother as the body on which male desire is projected, especially when one notices the profusion of skyscrapers in the science fiction city. These sky- scrapers, however, should not mislead us. In most cases, such build- ings are presented as part of a larger city-image. In Fritz Lang's film *Metropolis* (1927) and in Julian S. Krupa's illustration[34] inspired by it (the pun is intentional), we view from above the typical configuration of skyscrapers interconnected at many levels to form a vertiginous cavern into which the eye falls, caught in its descent only by the tiny figures of aircars, spermatozoa in the city/womb. This science fiction image is a projection into the future of the city-scape that Lewis Mumford has already discussed, with its circles and canals, walls, portals, and inner squares, as symbolically representational of the female anatomy.[35] In Leo Morey's depiction of the future city, he brings the viewpoint down to the midlevel so that the lower half of the illustration creates vertigo but the upper half isolates the peaks and upward straining towers. These are perhaps phallic. At eye level, at the point closest to the viewer, Morey's aircars are close and hence large. They are revealed as flying eggs with windows. Inside the closest one we are able to see the occupants clearly: two men.[36] If the towers are phallic, the city itself is still a womb bearing, protecting, and nourishing the seeds of men.

A perfect example of the phallic subsumed within the female occurs in Abraham Merrit's *The Metal Monster*.[37] Seen through the eyes of its first person narrator, the title at first seems to denote "a geometric prodigy. A shining angled pillar that, though rigid, immobile, seemed to crouch, be instinct with living force striving to be unleashed. . . . The Smiting Thing." (40) In the course of his adventures, our narrator learns that "'it is only that which human thought cannot encompass which it need fear.'" (95) The fearsome monster is ultimately revealed as a construction of the same living metal components that constituted The Smiting Thing, a construction so huge that "we were lost within the mazes of this incredible City—lost in the body of the Metal Monster which that City was" (142) and within which are found "Metal Babes" in "the birth chamber of the City! The womb of the Metal Monster!" (142–43). What the male narrator—and perhaps male readers—cannot understand and must therefore fear, at least in this fiction, is the principle of female fecundity. In Merritt's pulp serial, the very force that animates the City causes its ultimate cataclysmic collapse—much to the narrator's relief.

An almost comical example of this inclusion of the phallus within the larger image of the female comes from Hugo Gernsback's archetypal formula story, *Ralph 124C 41 +*. Ralph is a young super-scientist, a world-class almost-everything but still a young, unmarried man for all that. We are in the year A.D. 2660. "His 'house'. . . a round tower, 650 feet high, and thirty in diameter, built entirely of crystal glassbricks and steelonium, was one of the sights of New York. A grateful city, recognizing his genius and his benefits to humanity, had erected the great tower for him on a plot where, centuries ago, Union Square had been."[38] If we take the tower as a metonomy for its owner and treat it as a phallic symbol, it must still be clear that this tower is not the city itself but something quite unusual in the city, "one of the sights of New York," an erection on the place

of Union brought about the gratitude of the populace. The tower
rises within the city; the phallus within the female body. Gernsback's
puns just may have been intentional.

The story of *Ralph 124C 41+* involves us in two ways. First,
there is the constant exposition of the wonders Ralph has invented.
This is the major attraction. Second, and organizing the presentation
of the material, there is the relationship between Ralph and Alice.
Ralph first spots Alice through a long-distance viewing machine. She
is a village girl from Europe who is about to be overwhelmed by an
avalanche. Ralph races half-way around the world, saves her, and
falls in love with her. He takes her back to New York and tours her
and us through it. She is kidnapped into space and he saves her again.
The adventures and the inventions multiply and inflate. Finally, of
course, he saves her once and for all and they return to his tower.
New York is overjoyed. Finally the city has a female at its center.
Ralph, despite the adulation of the masses, "was so thoroughly and
abjectly in love that he . . . knew that unless he could have Alice life
itself would not matter to him."[39] In this eminently uncomplicated
tale, the city is happy to have Ralph and happy to have Ralph take a
wife. There is no competition between city/mother and human consort. This is not deeply searching psychological drama.

Interestingly, this Ralph and Alice are complementary to the
more famous Ralph and Alice portrayed on television by Jackie
Gleason and Audrey Meadows. Their entire series was set in "a
run-down apartment in Brooklyn."[40] Virtually the only room visible
was the kitchen, the place for nourishment, and outside the kitchen
window one saw only other apartment buildings. Ralph was a bus-
driver, a goer-to-and-fro, a driver of groundcars in this lower-class
saga, while Alice stayed home always. Although Ralph threatened to
send Alice to the moon, in fact his love kept her forever at home. She
was the stable center of the city, the body on which he projected his
desire. The show was called "The Honeymooners."

In these two cases, the city is less mother and more consort. Just
as there exist antinomies within the mother image (protecting/impris-
oning and feeding/drugging), there exist antinomies within the consort image. These are quite complex, ranging among the functions of
denying or fulfilling sexual desire, accepting the man within the
female body or rejecting and betraying him, producing children or
thwarting male procreativity. An inadequate but perhaps useful label
for this constellation of antinomies may be that of lover/harlot.

In *We,* Eugene Zamiatin presents the city primarily as lover, the object for which, finally, the narrator and the Well-Doer, a superego father-figure, contend. The story is set in a far future in which humans have become numbers. Our protagonist is D–503, the chief builder of *The Integral,* a rocket ship that is intended to carry the culture of the United State to other worlds. Our view of the United State is confined to one walled city made of glass in which organized masses work in unison according to schedule and may only curtain off their transparent living quarters to copulate. Reproduction is a function assigned by the doctors and social engineers while copulation is everywhere allowed. This city obeys a "Lex Sexualis": "A Number [person] may obtain a license to use any other Number as a sexual product."[41] The term "product" reveals the dehumanization of the role of lover in this controlled state. Such a law, however, has not always been reported in the service of repression. On the sometimes utopian moon of Cyrano de Bergerac's *Other Worlds,* "every man has the right to possess every woman, and a woman, similarly, can take a man to court if he refuses her."[42] A century earlier, Rabelais created the Abbey of Theleme which had as its motto, "Do as thou wouldst."[43] This motto was humanizing—so long as the society of Thelemites met the entrance requirements: basically, good breeding, health, wealth, intelligence, and moral sense. Zamiatin's city-state, on the other hand, is not restricted: everyone is included, like it or not. The resulting frictions must be controlled.

The individual who precipitates D–503's moral awakening is I–330, one of a band of secret rebels. She arouses his sexuality and hence his soul; she would use *The Integral* for escape and counterrevolution. The antinomy of love and harlotry is incarnate in I–330's ambiguous motives concerning D–503 and in the typical rhetoric of the citizens: "Desires are tortures, aren't they? It is clear, therefore, that happiness is when there are no longer any desires, not a single desire any more."[44] The city is the body/tool of the unseen, ubiquitous Well-Doer. When I–330 is finally captured, she is tortured to reveal her secrets. She is publicly placed under a huge glass bell jar and the air is evacuated from it. She faints and is revived. The process is repeated. She never speaks. On the third trial, she is no more. D–503, having already been subjected to an operation for the "removal of fancy,"[45] looks on only vaguely concerned. So is love killed, the potential lover of the builder/son destroyed in an anti-womb created in the harlot/city by the oppressive, Well-Doing father. This

is a true Oedipal conflict fought out for the possession of the city, a
struggle in which, as in the Sophoclean tragedy, we feel with the
stricken son, in this case our narrator.

Perhaps the most famous science fiction city of all is called,
simply, Metropolis. It exists in both a film and a book by that name.
John Pfeiffer writes that its

> plot includes three exciting scenes, an inspiring collection of coinci-
> dences, any number of enticingly mysterious non sequiturs, the satis-
> fying deaths of two profane madmen, a violent rebellion, the destruc-
> tion of the largest city in the world, the moral transformation of a
> megalomanic, a mother reconciled to her son, the fulfilled love of a
> noble hero and virtuous heroine, and the advent of a society of broth-
> erly love for millions of workers. All this takes place in about one week
> of fictional time. The extent to which the novel can be taken seriously is
> questionable.[46]

While this may be true from the standpoint of plot, it is unquestion-
able that the novel plays both sides of a large number of antinomies
and encourages the reader to flow back and forth through them. For
example, the master of this city, again in a tower, is named Joh
Fredersen. The hero is known only as Freder. Who is father to
whom? While biologically Joh fathers Freder, ideologically, Freder
raises Fredersen. The real spirit of the city, parallel to Alice or I–330,
is Maria (Mary again), a parentless paragon who inspires the mecha-
nized masses. Freder, of course, falls completely in love with her. In
order to recapture his son's affections, and eventually raise him to
succeed Joh, Fredersen coerces one Rotwang into constructing an
automaton named variously Parody and Futura. Parody is given
Maria's face and uses the trust of the masses to betray them. At one
point Freder walks in on his father:

> In the middle of the room, which was filled with a cutting brightness,
> stood Joh Fredersen, holding a woman in his arms. And the woman was
> Maria. She was not struggling. Leaning far back in the man's arms, she
> was offering him her mouth, her alluring mouth. . . .
>   "I'll kill you—! I'll take your life—! I'll murder you—!"[47]

Freder shouts. He does not know he is mistaken. This is not Maria.
The Oedipal struggle for the female body is confused here not only by
its dissociation into two bodies but by those incarnating two different
aspects of the consort. Further, Parody's creator, Rotwang, lives in
the house of the ancient magician around which the very city of

Metropolis grew. Rotwang is to Fredersen as Parody is to Maria for they are intimately associated doubles. In fact, Freder's mother, now dead of course, had been Rotwang's fiancee: she had been wooed and won away by Fredersen. Hence Freder's mistaken love for Parody is incestuous, a yearning for the offspring of the man who might have been his own creator. Freder's mother's name had been Hel.

The book is a gorgeous, romantic, lush example of melodramatic symbolism, more florid even than this exposition makes clear. For our purposes, perhaps the key line is this: "Every man-creator makes himself a woman,"[48] a line that recalls W. H. Auden's reference to "Eros, builder of cities."[49] While cities may appear to be simply reflections of social structures, in novels they are not so much male as the creations of males, the feminized expressions of male fears and desires, "the bricks, and the girders, and the faulty wiring and the shot elevator machinery, all conspiring together," in Samuel R. Delany's words, "to *make* these myths true."[50] The examples from science fiction could be multiplied at length.

If the image of the city may express the antinomies of the mother and of the consort, then taken together it seems that the city is expressive of the traditional so-called "female principle." J. C. Cooper defines this as

> the earth and the water; the instinctual powers as opposed to the masculine rational order . . . either beneficient and protective or malefic and destructive; she is both the pure spiritual guide and the siren and seducer, the virgin Queen of Heaven and the harpy and harlot, supreme wisdom and abysmal folly—the total complexity of nature.
>
> The woman is symbolized by all that is lunar, receptive, protective, nourishing, passive, hollow or to be entered, sinuous, cavernous, diamond- or oval-shaped; the cave, walled garden, well, door, gate, cup, furrow, sheath, shield; also anything connected with waters, the ship, shell fish, pearl.[51]

Jung, too, recognized that this suggests the city[52] and that the city may be treated as female.[53]

If we conclude from this examination of science fiction that the city may display in a narrative the antinomian possibilities of the female principle, then we are left with at least three questions. First, when might a fictional city not display these possibilities? Second, why do we not encounter a wider range of uses of the female principle in science fiction? Third, how common is this connection between cities and females outside of science fiction? Let us address these questions in turn.

First, under two sets of circumstances a city seems not to display the possibilities we have been examining. We have already mentioned the first set, those circumstances in which the city has little prominence in the narrative. A city may, after all, be nothing more than a place. As Freud is reputed to have said, "Sometimes a cigar is just a cigar."[54]

Of more importance to our discussion are the circumstances in which cities are prominent but nonetheless seem not to be expressions of the female principle. In this category we may put Stableford's exception, *Cities in Flight*. In this tetralogy the city sometimes seems to express the female principle, as when Amalfi, the mayor of a space-faring New York, greets guests in his sanctum atop the Empire State Building,[55] but at other times, as when a city is called and treated as a "hobo king,"[56] the city seems decidedly male. I believe that any examination of the four novels that make up this series will quickly reveal that when the city is female, it is virtually alone in the action; when it is not female, as when it is just one more Okie worker, it is part of a larger group of cities. Recall that in Cooper's enumeration of the qualities of the female principle, "the total complexity of nature" figured importantly. When there are many different cities, none may map out a satisfying narrative totality. One apparent exception to this is Robert Silverberg's *The World Inside* in which the earth's huge and growing population is housed primarily in "urbmons," urban monads, independent cities each a thousand stories tall. Each city-building is ruled and shaped by men, the plastic body they dominate; each concentrates on procreation; each both feeds its inhabitants and swallows them up—when dead or antisocial—for reprocessing. Each urbmon is clearly an expression of the antinomies of the female principle, both as mother and as consort, yet there are many urbmons. The crucial distinction between Silverberg's novel and Blish's series is that every single urbmon is the same, one stands for all, each a total expression of the fictional totality while in Blish's work we see outlaw cities, worker cities, new cities, old cities, and others besides. The concept of city is stretched beyond the ability of the text to maintain the single city image as the foundation for our psychological engagement. Our main interest in the Blish novels shifts to the problems of the characters among themselves and is distributed among a number of separable, episodic adventures. In Silverberg's book, the different characters only flesh out the varieties of life within the unified city and the unifying city maintains our interest in the episodes.

Given the plasticity of the female in art, we might expect in science fiction other uses of the city than we have found. The city consort shows up occasionally as a virgin (Alice in *Ralph 124C 41+*), commonly as a seducer (I–330 in *We*) and quite often as a termite queen (*The World Inside* and other hive stories). Is the city ever an embodiment of a fully developed and complex lover in science fiction? Perhaps, but no perfect example comes to my mind. A number of factors may help explain this. First, the genre of science fiction is statistically dominated by formula writing. By definition such writing tends to eschew great psychological complexity. Second, the predominant audience for much of science fiction had traditionally been young males "overwhelmingly likely to be nervous, shy, pleasant boys, sensitive, intelligent, and very awkward with people."[57] For these readers, a woman met on full and equal terms is still in their future; their current uses of science fiction are more likely to tend toward refuge from complicated relationships than reflections of and training for such relationships. Third, the dominant ideology of science fiction—reliance on the rational individual to make the unknown known,[58] the alien domestic[59]— runs against erecting a habitation for two equals on the site of Union Square. It is perhaps for this reason, among others, that David Ketterer is correct in observing that "science fiction cities tend toward Babylon rather than toward the New Jerusalem."[60]

The Bible, given its importance for the Western literary tradition, is a prime object for an inquiry into the range of applicability of the hypothesis we have been pursuing. In the Bible—and hence one would expect in the literature that is influenced by it—cities are typically seen either as explicitly female or as incarnating aspects of the female principle.

> *O give thanks unto the Lord, for he is good: for his mercy*
> *endureth for ever.*
> *Let the redeemed of the Lord say so, whom he hath redeemed*
> *from the hand of the enemy;*
> *And gathered them out of the lands, from the east, and*
> *from the west, from the north, and from the south.*

> They wandered in the wilderness in a solitary way; they
>   found no city to dwell in.
> Hungry and thirsty, their soul fainted in them.
> Then they cried unto the Lord in their trouble, and he
>   delivered them out of their distresses.
> And he led them forth by the right way, that they might
>   go to a city of habitation. (Psalms 107:1–7)

Speaking also of the single city, Jeremiah laments: "How doth the city sit solitary, that was full of people! How is she become as a widow!" (1:1).

The biblical city lives, for good or for ill, a body expressing man's desire when she is Babel/Babylon, a body expressing God's desire when she is the New Jerusalem, what St. Augustine called "the most glorious city of God."[61] This opposition is clearest in the last book of the Bible. First Saint John gives us the cause of Judgment: "And there followed another angel, saying, Babylon is fallen, is fallen, that great city, because she made all nations drink of the wine of the wrath of her fornication" (Rev. 14:8). The sensuosity of Babylon endures against all scourging, even in this poem "found" by John Robert Colombo in the Eleventh Edition of the *Encyclopedia Britannica*:

> Be the site
> of Hanging Gardens.
>
> Come practically
> to an end.
>
> Lie on the East bank
> of Euphrates.
>
> Seem not to
> exaggerate.
>
> Receive there
> this crown.
>
> Be the capital
> of Babylonia.[62]

Then Saint John foresees our redemption:

And there came unto me one of the seven angels which had the seven vials full of the seven last plagues, and talked with me, saying, Come hither, I will show thee the bride, the Lamb's wife. And he carried me away in the spirit to a great and high mountain, and he showed me that great city, the holy Jerusalem, descending out of the heaven from God, having the glory of God: and her light was like unto a stone more precious, even like a jasper stone, clear as crystal, and had a wall great and high. (Rev. 21:9-12)

This is not only a female city but quite exactly the source for much of the description of Zamiatin's United State, the New Jerusalem turned upside down.

The city expresses the female principle not only in Hebraic culture but in Hellenic culture as well. Helen of Troy is not *of* Troy in the sense that she is *from* it; she is *from* Sparta. In fact, she maintains her marriage to Menelaus throughout and returns with him to Sparta after the war. She is *of* Troy in the sense that she emblematizes it in the Greek mind. Helen is the quintessential female as expression of fertility and the object of male desire. When Zeus in the shape of a swan raped Leda, the result was Helen, a human hatched from the great fertility symbol, the egg.[63] In Marlowe's famous lines, her face "launch'd a thousand ships,/And burnt the topless towers of Ilium."[64] In other words, she both sent forth the seed of humanity and caused the destruction of its phallic symbols. But she endured. And so does the symbolism.

In John Dos Passos's *Manhattan Transfer* (1925), the title concept refers initially to the city as a location for changing trains, but comes ultimately to stand for the great nexus through which flows all of modern life. Here is a section from that book:

They had to change at Manhattan Transfer. The thumb of Ellen's [sic] new kid glove had split and she kept rubbing it nervously with her forefinger. John wore a belted raincoat. . . .
They got into the parlorcar. . . .
The wheels rumbled in her head, saying Man-hattan Tran-sfer. Man-hattan Tran-sfer. Anyway it was a long time before Atlantic City. By the time we get to Atlantic City . . . *Oh it rained forty days* . . . I'll be feeling gay. . . . *And it rained forty nights.* . . . I've got to be feeling gay.
"Elaine Thatcher Oglethorpe, that's a very fine name, isn't it darling? Oh stay me with flagons, comfort me with apples for I am sick of love. . . ." He put his hand in its yellow glove over her hand in its white glove.
"You're my wife now Elaine."

"You're my husband now John." And laughing they looked at each other in the coziness of the empty parlorcar.

White letters, ATLANTIC CITY, spelled doom over the rainpitted water.[65]

When the great scientist and philosopher of science, J. D. Bernal, dreamed of cities, he too saw them as embodying the female principle, although he did not say so explicitly. He was the first to describe space colonies: "Imagine a spherical shell ten miles or so in diameter. . . . it would be forced to resemble on the whole an enormously complicated single-celled plant. . . . The essential positive activity of the globe or colony would be in the development, growth and reproduction of the globe."[66] Traveling through the heavens, part plant, spreading itself across the sky and fertilizing the universe with humanity, this is almost a science fictional image of Demeter, the Greek goddess of agriculture, fertility, and marriage.

Demeter has within her name the Greek word *meter,* meaning *mother,* and cognate with *metra,* meaning *womb.* These are the words that combine with the Greek *polis, city-state,* to give us a word that literally means *mother-city, metropolis.*[67] The word *city,* too, has a history important to our understanding of it as a "great, simple image." It derives from an Indo-European root, *kei,* meaning *to lie, bed, home, beloved, dear.* In one derivation *kei* produces *civis,* the Latin word for a member of a household; in another it becomes cognate with *home;* and in yet another, with *cradle.*[68] These are the sources in our very language of the image of the city.

In most of the critical treatments of science fiction cities, and of cities in literature in general, we find helpful expositions of topography, of iconography, and of sociology. But something more is needed. As Italo Calvino writes, "Cities, like dreams, are made of desires and fears, even if the thread of their discourse is secret, their rules are absurd, their perspectives deceitful, and everything conceals something else."[69] That is a truth of the unconscious city.

Hard-Core Science Fiction and the Illusion of Science

John Huntington

To its fans and writers, hard-core SF has always seemed to be a clear and unambiguous form. In practice, however, it shows up as more intricate and less pure than the usual theories of the form would allow. The illusion of science which so identifies the form of the hard-core story is, like all other fictional devices, in the service of a narrative fantasy. If we analyse this illusion carefully we discover hard-core SF to be not simply an exercise in scientific rationality, but a psychologically motivated fantasy which can reveal much about the culture that honors it.

The argument I am making moves in three stages. First, I will examine the implications of what the aficionados of hard-core SF see as its defining criterion: its use of the language of science. Second, I will sketch how this criterion can be linked to ideological presumptions which have a historical dimension. Third, I will study closely a classic hard-core SF work from the fifties to show how it employs the hard-core language and conventions to enact a fantasy that it could not otherwise justify.

I

The enthusiastic readers of hard core SF will tell you bluntly when a story fails to meet their criteria for the form. Letters columns filled with belligerent complaints that certain stories are not SF constitute clear evidence of a strong, popular instinct about the genre. That instinct is evident as early as Verne's indignant attempt to distinguish his writing from Wells's:

> "It occurs to me that [Wells's] stories do not repose on very scientific bases. No, there is no rapport between his work and mine. I make use of

45

physics. He invents. I go to the moon in a cannon-ball, discharged from a cannon. Here there is no invention. He goes to Mars in an airship, which he constructs of a metal which does away with the law of gravitation. *Ca c'est tres joli,"* cried Monsieur Verne is an animated way. "but show me this metal. Let him produce it."[1]

Verne's literalness in demanding that Wells produce the metal may sound quaint to our ears, but it addresses a central issue of the plausibility of such SF.

A half century later, in his address at the University of Chicago, Robert Heinlein would propose in much the same spirit that we divide literature into realism and fantasy and that we place SF within the realm of realism.[2] He tolerates fantasy; he even admits to writing it himself (e.g., *Magic, Inc.*); but finally his impatience with the form breaks out:

> It is not enough to interlard an old plot with terms like "space warp," "matter transmitter," "ray gun," or "rocket ship" with no knowledge of what is meant (if anything) by such terms, or how they might reasonably work. A man who provides Mars with a dense atmosphere and an agreeable climate, a man whose writing shows that he knows nothing of ballistics nor of astronomy nor of any modern technology would do better not to attempt science fiction. Such things are not science fiction—entertainment they may be; serious speculation they cannot be. The obligation of the writer to his reader to know what he is talking about is even stronger in science fiction that elsewhere, because the ordinary reader has less chance to catch him out. It's not fair. It's cheating.[3]

What will interest us about this argument is the expectation that SF can play fair."

Behind these two basically similar statements we can see two different criteria for the hard core form of SF. While it usually appeals to an empirical standard of plausibility ("let him produce it"), it also relies on a strong sense of generic conventions. The very idea that a story can play "fair" is a genric one; it implies a set of literary rules. Such SF, like certain kinds of detective stories, is supposed to play in such a way that a reader can hope to "solve" it. As some thought will easily show, one has to be acquainted with the generic rules (not simply empirical reality) before one can even begin reasoning about any story's world. After all, what is so plausible about Verne's cannon? As in the cases in which someone guesses the murderer in a detective story, a correct anticipation of an SF story's puzzle solution is based, not on pure deduction, but on a good knowledge of the probabilities and possibilities of the genre.

Before we try to use these standards to define hard-core SF, we should observe that their combination is common to most literature. And it is especially important to our understanding of the hard-core form to recognize that the language of science itself also succeeds by playing by generic rules of fairness as it appeals to empirical fact.

The generic conventions of scientific discourse become most evident when they are abused. Unscrupulous scientists, by skillful use of the scientific language, can create the illusion of science while in fact promulgating fictions. Thus, a Cyril Burt, while fabricating his data, can create a credible presence that for years can silence completely all critical thought simply by making adroit use of the conventions of scientific discourse. Even more revealing of the conventional generic basis of scientific language are the recurrent instances of self-delusion in science. Stephen Jay Gould's whole book, *The Mismeasure of Man*, may be seen as a study of how investigators of intelligence have used scientific language to validate highly dubious theories about the racial bases of IQ. My point in recalling such notorious instances of the misuse of science is not to debunk science itself, but to remind us that no language is in itself simply *true* or realistic. The language of science has in itself an attraction and persuasiveness. By showing how frequently prejudice and culturally determined expectations have resorted to the language of science to justify themselves, Gould's book testifies to the significant rhetorical dimension of the scientific language itself.

Hard-core SF is a unique fiction in that it has discovered how to put the rhetorical aspect of scientific language to fictional use. Most fiction has allied itself with poetry and has traditionally asserted that it is different from science. Following Sidney, it has excused its lie on the grounds that it never claimed to tell the truth in the first place. But hard-core SF represents a special case; unlike this other fiction, it has asked to be judged by the same criteria we use for science. By laying claim to plausible scientific truth such fiction commits itself to a special rhetorical stance. The assent that hard-core SF compels depends upon its success in rendering an imitation of a scientific language. Heinlein's "realism" and his ideal of fairness boil down to sounding like you know what you are talking about. This is, of course, a familiar observation; what Heinlein neglects to observe, however, is that in hard-core SF this is entirely and only a rhetorical ploy.

We can see how rhetorical the issue is when we see Heinlein's ideas in action. After rejecting as "fantasy" stories "which have the lizard men of Z1xxt cross breeding with human females [and] stories which represent the surface conditions of Mars as being much like those of Earth" (p. 19), Heinlein a little later can allow as "possible" and therefore "realistic" stories which entail "faster than light [movement], time travel, reincarnation, ghosts" (p. 20). For Heinlein some theories (those of biology and astronomy here) designate "fact," while others (Einsteinian physics, psychology) are just "tentative hypotheses." Given the shifting and arbitrary criteria for reality in Heinlein's world, we readers are exactly where we are with Cyril Burt: we accept a fiction, not because it is tested or it has some solid, recognizable empirical basis, but because of the illusion the scientific language itself generates.

II

Once we have agreed that scientific language is used rhetorically, we have not yet arrived at a useful critical conclusion: different authors and different eras use the scientific language differently. For instance, returning to Verne and Heinlein, we can see how what is understood as convincing scientific language changes in time. Historically, as the genre of hard-core SF has established itself, the rhetoric of the scientific language it uses has shifted its appeal away from an empiricist emphasis toward an ideal of generic coherence, and that shift has ideological consequences. To put it bluntly: the shift from Verne's empirical "show me the metal" to Heinlein's generic "it's not fair" signifies an important change in the way the hard-core ideal appeals to its audience.

Intrinsic to Verne's imagination is the refusal to acknowledge the operation of imagination itself. We are in the case of Verne in the same historical-aesthetic situation as we are when Conrad, in the preface to *The Nigger of the Narcissus,* says that his object is to "make you see."[4] Such an empirical ideal results in a fiction which, while it is capable of fantasy, never acknowledges its movement into fantasy. Verne goes to great lengths to obscure the line between the real (scientific) and the fantastic.[5] For instance, in *The Journey to the*

Center of the Earth, the travelog descriptions of Iceland and of the ascent of Sneffels are mundane enough, but at some unmarked point we cross a border and find ourselves in a world capable of producing giant shepherds and an ocean deep in the earth, a world in which you can ride the thrust of an erupting volcano. And even in the midst of such obvious fantasy Verne repeatedly invokes the language of scientific explanation. Similarly, *Twenty-Thousand Leagues Under the Sea* has a regular litany of classificatory rituals which anchor that extraordinary fantasy in a scientific base. Within this tangible world of categorized fact the Vernean heroes shape their monomaniacal private and fantastic destinies.

By the nineteen fifties the genre of the hard core has been established and we find stories, like Heinlein's own future history stories, that casually begin in a mode we might term "plausible fantasy." The generic game consists of playing "fair" according to the agreed upon rules of the genre. In place of Verne's ideology of individualist empiricism we have the ideology of technocracy which, while it may be often overlayed by a philosophy of libertarian individualism, finally tells us to leave moral and social difficulties to the "scientific" experts. The generic perspective often can become so overwhelming that all issues and questions that do not fit the genre's concepts of fairness are seen as trivial and forgotten. This misplaced concreteness, this technological monomania, is then called "realism."[6]

At this historical stage the hard-core genre denies the reality of anything but technological questions. The values implicit in this attitude are bluntly summarized by Heinlein in his 1957 talk. After some lengthy, vigorous, and bad-tempered denunciations of the literary mainstream's concern with psychology, he asks, "Can James Joyce and Henry Miller and their literary sons and grandsons interpret the seething new world of atomic power and anti-biotics and interplanetary travel? I say not" (p. 42). This rejection of psychology in favor of technology is basic for Heinlein. The great accomplishment of SF, for him, is that it has prepared the public to accept space flight.

A literature so passionately committed to denying the psychological and to seeing the future completely in terms of technology asks to be explained psychologically. As a methodological practice, we should begin by questioning the genre's claims to "fairness." Gregory Benford starts such a process by standing the Heinlein idea on its head. He argues that a truly educational pleasure is to be derived from finding the "cheat" in a hard-core story: "There are virtually no cheat-free stories, including my own, and playing the game of finding the error in a story seems to motivate a lot of students to engage in physics who otherwise sit there and stare."[7] Pedagogically, this is probably sound. But insofar as such a debunking is enlisted only as a critique of the "science" of the story, it misses the literary, cultural, and psychological issues.

In most stories the "science," however bogus, is invoked, not to teach science, but to operate a narrative fiction. Frequently, the rhetoric of science is a sop to reason, allowing the reader to indulge in a fantasy which may be entirely irrational. Such an imaginative economy is clearly apparent in works of technological landscaping like *Ringworld*, which after they establish their "ideas," indulge in extravagant, picaresque fantasies. Other stories more subtlely integrate the science and the fantasy. But in all such cases we need to ask, not simply does the science work but what has the author gained by the illusion of science? By discovering the scientific "cheat" we explode the illusion and place ourselves in a good position to see what are the real issues of the fantasy.

III

To explicate these dynamics, let us examine Tom Godwin's extraordinarily popular story, "The Cold Equations" (1954).[8] One of the reasons this story is so popular, I suspect, is that its thesis is a clear reiteration of the hard-core demand that a story play "fair."[9] Also, it is appropriate that the "cold equation" on which the story depends is a ballistic one: to Heinlein ballistics is the epitome of the pure, realistic science, the science of unchallengeable *fact*. It is a sign of the story's success in this respect that Benford can use it in the classroom to teach the objectivity of science: in "The Cold Equations," he argues, we see "society's institutionalized delusions set against the overwhelmingly, absolutely neutral point of view of the universe"[10]

The story, as you may remember, describes the dilemma of the pilot of an EDS (a small, emergency spaceship) which is bringing needed serum to a colony stranded on a distant planet. He discovers a teenage girl stowaway, Marilyn, whose weight has not been calculated in the EDS's fuel allotment. After repeated explanations by the narrator and by the pilot that the craft cannot land with her additional weight, the girl and the reader are convinced that the only solution is for her to be expelled into space, to die. She accepts this fate bravely, and we are impressed by the logic of the "cold equations" of physics that "killed with neither hatred nor malice." (p. 569)

Since in what follows I will be challenging a number of aspects of the story, let me here make clear that I do not at all disagree with the argument that the universe is "neutral." I also agree that what is now called "triage" may well be a necessary and regretable consideration in some circumstances. I will thus not be questioning the truth of the story's thesis, but I will be asking what purpose that "truth" is being made to serve in this case.

Until its end the story hovers between two incongruent ideas of SF: one promises liberation by means of an ingenious solution to what seems an irresolvable problem. The other promises a rigorous holding to the rules of plausibility. The story line is completely clear. Yet by repeatedly insisting on its unavoidable end, the narrative raises the reader's hopes for a more humane solution. All of us are familiar with fiction which uses repetition of difficulty as a way of heightening tension and rendering the anticipated "solution" all the more amazing and relieving. Yet here such repetition constitutes a lecture designed to make absolutely clear and unambiguous that there is no way out and to insist on the essential hard-core point that science and nature are "neutral." Because we have faith in the genre, we persist—in a way we might not were we reading another genre—in waiting for an invention that never arrives. At the end we realize (perhaps with some dismay) how extraordinarily hard core the story is: this is playing "fair" with a vengeance!

But while the story plays "fair" scientifically, it also raises the possibility of a different criterion of fairness and thereby directs our attention to the very standards that the scientific illusion obviates. At one point, just after the pilot discovers that his stowaway is a "girl," the story allows him to consider an alternate, more melodramatic formula:

> Why couldn't she have been a man with some ulterior motive? A fugitive from justice, hoping to lose himself on a raw new world; an opportunist, seeking transportation to the new colonies where he might find golden fleece for the taking; a crackpot, with a mission—
>
> Perhaps once in his lifetime an EDS pilot would find such a stowaway on his ship; warped men, mean and selfish men, brutal and dangerous men—but never, before, a smiling, blue-eyed girl who was willing to

pay her fine and work for her keep that she might see her brother. (p. 548)

This conventional figure of the man of resentment could relieve the fiction of the need for any more complex analysis by supplying a completely sufficient object of hatred and violence.[11] Yet the story invokes this figure only to reject him. Thus, the fiction raises as a real question something that has no place in "science": how can the murder of the stowaway be morally justified? And the story then solves the problem it has raised by rejecting the "moral" criterion of fairness and by appealing to the criterion of absolute hard-core SF: to play "fair" is to obey the scientific formulae, no matter what morality and emotion demand.

But let us step outside the generic game for a moment to ask if the girl really has to die? The equations are certainly cold, but do they really justify the pilot's behavior? Throughout the story items have been mentioned on the spaceship that are dispensable: there is the door of the closet, the blaster, the people's clothes, the pilot's chair, the closet itself, its contents, the senser that registers body heat, the bench she sits on . . . Do they need the radio any more? Once one's mind gets on this track, the story becomes quite frustrating. In stories of sinking ships and of falling balloons, the *first* thing anyone thinks of is what can be thrown out instead of a human. But in "The Cold Equations" no one even begins to consider such possibilities. These "scientific" men, tragically wise about the "cold equations" of physics and space, immediately take a favorite SF stance: they feel greatly, but they master those feelings and go on to do "what they have to do."[12]

Of course the story doesn't want such piecemeal and conventional solutions as I am here suggesting. I am being a spoilsport. But am I really? Am I not holding up to the story the very kind of standard that is always held up to soft-core SF by hard-core addicts? The fact that most critics accept the story's conclusion is ample testimony to the hard-core illusion, but we have to admit now that it is an illusion. This quintessential hard-core story, a story that even appears to regret its own rigors, its obedience to the "cold equations," can be shown to be just as much a "fantasy" as the soft-core stories it rebukes.

It might be objected that my unsympathetic complaint is trivial and that we could easily rewrite the story in such a way as to answer it.

Perhaps. But let us first admit that such a rewrite amounts to a concession that the story *as it stands* is seriously blind. And I suspect that in the process of such a rewrite we would lose more than we would gain. As we "purify" the story we would deprive it of its imaginative texture. Without the blaster, the clipboard, the heat senser, and so forth, what do we have? Surely, the effect of the story depends in part on the sense of the wonderful technological cornucopia implied by these casual details. Without them the EDS is just another sinking ship.

And as we "purify" the story we come up against another hard-core contradiction: if the story insists on the "realism" of the equations, it nevertheless participates in a fantasy about machines. As we try to make it more hard core we will have to account for the idealization of technology that dreams of a space ship so precise, so perfect, that it has no margin of safety, no reserve fuel, no back-up system. Curiously, elsewhere in the story's universe machines can be cranky and undependable—the EDS cannot contact Marilyn's brother in his helicopter because "some printed circuits went haywire" and the radio won't work (p. 560). But on the EDS itself the machine matches the equation exactly. This is, if you will, a fantasy of utopian technology.

The important thing for us to realize at this point is, not that the story has faults, but that its details are not inevitable. Once we have rid ourselves of the illusion of inevitability, we are in a position to see its details in a new way.

Marilyn is a particularly helpless scapegoat. In the passage we looked at describing the kinds of vicious man the pilot expected and hoped for, it becomes clear that in the moral economy of this story a woman cannot be guilty; only a man can be guilty. It is remarkable that once he sees she is a "girl," the pilot never thinks, and the story certainly supports him in this, that she might do something desperate to save her life (seduce him, grab his gun, become a creature of resentment herself). No. She is a pure innocence, a pure victim, an object incapable of self-defense.

Paradoxically, this pathetic innocence, this state of defenseless "object" who has no guilt except weight, may be instrumental in making us accept Marilyn's death even as it increases the sense of injustice. She herself invokes the proper analogue when she recalls the kitten which her brother replaced after it died. Rhetorically, this little anecdote is a complex parable, and I don't here claim to do it

justice, but at least one of its implications is that for certain innocent
but expendable and replaceable creatures death is not real. At one
level the anecdote raises our hopes by suggesting that a competent
man, inspired by crisis to the point of violence, can overcome death
(her brother threatens to beat up the pet store owner if he doesn't
open his shop at three AM and sell him a new kitten). But such hope is
illusory, and the final force of the parable is to suggest that Marilyn is
expendable. Perhaps she, like the kitten, is renewable, but only by
replacement.

The pity that such a creature inspires may hide a more basic rage
at innocence and incompetence. The moment when Marilyn, unaware of the cold equations of the situation, cheerfully and smugly
asks, "I'm guilty, so what happens now? Do I pay a fine, or what?"
(p. 546) seems designed to elicit anger. She is, after all, guilty of
trespassing: the sign said clearly in extra large letters, "UNAUTHO-
RIZED PERSONNEL, KEEP OUT!" (p. 547). Women, so this
stereotype goes, expect to get away with things. They think they can
cruise along, doing what they want, seeing whom they want, never
really taking responsibility, paying token fines when they get caught.
But, while such rage is certainly generated by Marilyn's act, the story
never acknowledges this emotion as such. Instead its anger is concealed by an elaborated pity. But the anger, however hidden, is acted
out, and Marilyn is killed. The story is, thus, an exercise in punishing
a woman, but at every conscious level it tries to hide that real activity
and avoid responsibility by claiming deep sympathy with the victim.

The issues of responsibility and irresponsibility figure promi-
nently in an important later passage describing the tornado that
destroyed one of the camps on the planet the EDS is approaching.
The passage needs quoting in full, for the contradiction at work is
here embedded in the prose:

> It had been in the Western Sea that the tornado had originated, to *strike*
> with such *fury* at the camp and destroy half their prefabricated build-
> ings, including the one that housed the medical supplies. Two days
> before the tornado had not existed; it had been no more than great
> gentle masses of air out over the calm Western Sea. Group One had
> gone about their routine survey work, unaware of the *meeting* of the air
> masses out at sea, unaware of the force the union was *spawning*. It had
> *struck* their camp without warning; a thundering roaring destruction
> that *sought to annihilate* all that lay before it. It had passed on, leaving
> the wreckage in its wake. It had destroyed the labor of months and had

> *doomed* six men to die and then, as though *its task* was accomplished, it
> once more began to resolve into gentle masses of air. But for all its
> deadliness, it had destroyed with neither malice nor intent. It had been
> a blind and mindless force, obeying the laws of nature, and it would
> have followed the same course with the same fury had men never
> existed. (pp. 558–59, italics added)

The assertion that the tornado is "blind and mindless" is surely true,
but certainly the vocabulary used to describe the storm (*fury, sought,
doomed, its task,* etc.) suggests just the opposite, that the tornado
was conscious and intentional. In the very process of denying motive
to nature, the prose personifies and thus motivates nature. We have
here an act of destructive malice for which all responsibility is denied
by an appeal to an inanimate, neutral nature.

The disavowal of responsibility that takes place here is a version
of the disavowal that pervades the whole story. After it has been
made abundantly clear that "there could be no alternative" (p. 545)
to Marilyn's death, the story announces repeatedly and extrava-
gantly that no one can change things. It is worth quoting the most
prominent of these disavowals just to make it clear how insistent the
story is about this point:

> "I'm sorry," he said again. "You'll never know how sorry I am. It has to
> be that way and no human in the universe can change it." (p. 550)

> "It's not the way you think—it isn't that way, at all," he said. "Nobody
> wants it this way; nobody would ever let it be this way if it was humanly
> possible to change it." (p. 552)

> "Everyone would like to help you but there is nothing anyone can do."
> (p. 553)

> He swung around to face her. "You understand now, don't you? No one
> would ever let it be like this if it could be changed." (p. 555)

A little later we are told that even Marilyn's brother, an experienced
man "of the frontier," "would know there had been nothing the pilot
could do" (p. 561). We have already seen how hasty is this conclusion
that nothing can be done, but we can also ask whether the voice
repeatedly denying responsibility here is accurate even if there were
no other solution possible. After all, there is one person "in the
universe" who could change things, and that is the author himself.[13]
Let us here recognize that this pathetic story of unavoidable death is a
completely gratuitous exercise, chosen by the author and engineered

by him. It is he, after all, who has worked so hard to try to make sure there is no way to save Marilyn, and it is he who has created men who, obedient to the cold equations, never try to improvise some mode of salvation for her.

All through the story, from Marilyn herself with her pathetic cry, "but I didn't do anything," to the tornado whose "fury" is declared to be unmotivated, to the pilot and the other men in the story who easily accede to the equations' conclusions, to, finally, the author who has made up the story, we find people disavowing responsibility for what is happening. And it is science and its neutral mathematical language which justifies such evasion. The victims and the victimizers adjust themselves to their roles of passivity and irresponsibility by appealing to the cold equations.

Thus, in our paradigmatic story, behind the unchallengable assertion of the "neutrality" of the universe lies a fantasy about punishing a woman who tries to use her innocence to get away with things. As the passage which contrasts her presence to that of a man shows, the author faces a problem in justifying her punishment. The "scientific" explanation comes to the rescue in two ways. It says she *must* be severely, fatally punished even for a minor violation of the law. And at the same time it allows all the men in the story and the fantasizing author himself (and perhaps the fantasizing reader) to assure themselves, even as they perform this rationally satisfying act of obeying the equations, that they don't *want* it this way, that they would change it if they possibly could. As a way of hiding the blame attached to the murder of such innocence, the scientific equation has all the brilliant efficiency of dream.

IV

Let me in conclusion try to place this kind of analysis in its proper critical context. Our goal is not an "appreciation" of a work in the conventional sense. Rather, it is to see what purpose, laudable or not, it serves. Hard-core SF becomes particularly interesting in such an enterprise because the language of science, which so identifies the form, functions both to enable and to conceal the psychological and social basis of the story. It has become a commonplace of modern criticism to assert that one of the major functions of literature is to deal with taboo subjects without naming them and with contradictions without admitting them. An important purpose of criticism is to make these unacknowledged presences visible. Fredric Jameson's conclusion to "Metacommentary" remains a classic statement: "Metacommentary . . . aims at tracing the logic of the censorship itself and of the situation from which it springs: a language that hides what it displays beneath its own reality as language, a glance that designates, through the very process of avoiding, the object forbidden."[14] Terry Eagleton makes a similar case for the analysis of the ideological suppression that fiction performs: "The task of criticism, then, is not to situate itself within the same space as the text, allowing it to speak or completing what it necessarily leaves unsaid. On the contrary, its function is to install itself in the very incompleteness of the work in order to *theorise* it—to explain the ideological necessity of those '*not-saids*' which constitute the very principle of its identity. Its object is the *unconsciousness* of the work—that of which it is not, and cannot be, aware."[15] Our brief examination of "The Cold Equations" is the beginning of a critical process whose end is to describe the unconscious of the culture.

What Makes Hard Science Fiction "Hard?"

David Clayton

Addressing the subject of hard science fiction, I find myself in a somewhat awkward, if not an altogether false position, that, let us say, of a guest at a banquet honoring someone he knows of only by second-hand report. Nothing would please me more than to offer a paean to the past and present heroes of "hard" science fiction; unfortunately, my background, which is that of a student of literary history and not that of a science fiction aficionado, has not adequately prepared me for such a task. What arouses my attention is less the subgenre possibly designated by the label "hard science fiction" than the label itself, a label whose self-proclaimed solidity contrasts with a certain conceptual flaccidity. The literary historian, confronted with a process in which formerly peripheral genres push older, once dominant ones to the periphery, must constantly reexamine the generic categories that have been passed down to one by one's predecessors: does such-and-such a label meaningfully characterize a well-defined body of texts? Does the label accurately point up the salient traits of the genre—or here subgenre—under discussion? Should several apparently unrelated genres or subgenres be combined under one classification? In our case, however, the problem begins with the label: how can a quality serve to define a genre? If its conventions primarily define a genre, what kind of conventions might the adjective "hard" properly designate? At this point some helpful soul might justifiably reply that there is no problem, that "hard" in this context simply means "hardcore." This answer, far from eliminating the difficulty, only displaces it elsewhere, from the familiar, if provincial domain of literary studies out into the shifting sandy wastes of cultural values. Instead of trying to determine the limits of a fictional subgenre, we must look into the highly ambivalent connotations of the expression "hardcore" in contemporary American English, connotations evident to anyone unfortunate enough to have seen the wretched motion picture that bears this expression as its title.

In fact, we may not be able to avoid such an excursion, but before rushing into it, let us pause to take stock of an interesting peculiarity of this label. "Hard science fiction" carries an inescapable aura, the aura not only of a certain kind of writing, but also of certain writers: Heinlein, Asimov, Hal Clement, and, more recently, Larry Niven, Jerry Pournelle, and Robert Forward. Without a doubt, there are works in which scientific discourse as such plays a more or less restricted role, in which no scientific "novum," to use Darko Suvin's term, occurs—for example, most of Bradbury, as well as novels such as Bester's *The Stars My Destination,* Philip K. Dick's *The Man in the High Castle,* or even Delany's *Dhalgren*—works which, although clearly science fictional, lie outside the realm of "hard science fiction." Conversely, there are works in which scientific discourse plays a crucial role—in Delany's *Triton* or Le Guin's *The Dispossessed*—that we would not ordinarily think of as examples of "hard science fiction"; hence we cannot describe "hard science fiction" as simply science fiction more than usually saturated with scientific discourse—scientific discourse properly speaking, and not just pseudoscientific jargon. Let me make a preliminary hypothesis: perhaps "hard science fiction" does not so much generically label a body of texts as it designates a period, one marked by the ascendence of writers who produced "hard science fiction."

Nevertheless, we still find ourselves stuck where we were before, since until we know what makes "hard science fiction" "hard," how are we to recognize its texts if we see them? Are we not in the same predicament as the anonymous narrator of Samuel Beckett's *The Unnameable* who begins by exclaiming, "Where now? When now? Who now?" Not necessarily. If this term "hard" allegorically fulfills its semantic destiny by blocking our access to the body of texts we believe to lie beyond it, we can always try an alternative, more literal route. In other words, while the hardness of the label "hard science fiction" might prevent us from immediately picking out a group of texts to which the label would be applicable and interrogating them in order to find out what could be the sense of the designation, we can instead question the obstinate signifier itself in the hope it will eventually yield to our entreaties and point us in the right direction. What then might be the possible relevant significations of "hard" in this context?

Thinking back to the expression "hardcore" that we took notice of a moment ago, we might be tempted to envision, in a parody of structuralist procedures, a paradigm in which the complementary term would be "laid back" or "mellow." But this is already too figurative, as well as too facetious a level of discourse. Should not "hard" suggest first of all the material resistance of the natural environment, a resistance that must be overcome in order for scientific research to take place? And overcome by what, if not correspondingly "hard" traits: tenacity, resolve, fortitude? We need only think of the vital connection between metallurgy and technological progress to see what relevance this meaning of the word might have for our discussion. Such a "hardness" of the material world, Gaston Bachelard speculates in *La Terre et les rêveries de la volonté,* can evoke its characterological equivalent in the individual, developing in him or her the imaginative stance he or she needs to counter its resistance:

> Thus matter reveals our forces to us. It suggests a transposition of our forces into dynamic categories. It not only gives a durable substance to our will, but well-defined temporal schemes to our patience. Moreover, matter receives from our dreams a complete future of work: we want to conquer it in working. We enjoy in advance the efficacity of our will. One should not be surprised that simply dreaming of material images— yes, simply dreaming—has the effect of "toning up" the will. Impossible to be distracted, absent, indifferent, when one dreams of a clearly defined resistant material. One could not gratuitously imagine a resistance. Different materials, placed between the dialectically opposite poles of *hard* and *soft,* designate numerous types of adversity. Reciprocally, all the adversity that one believes profoundly human, with its sordid or cynical violence, its shock or hypocrisy, comes to find its realism in actions directed against particular inanimate materials. Better than any other complement, the material one specifies hostility.[1]

Already we find ourselves forsaking a material for a psychological variety of "hardness," which, present in all of us to some degree, could supply the criterion for distinguishing between different personality types—a possibility foreseen by William James when he contrasted the "tender-minded" thinker who goes by "'principles'" with the "tough-minded" who goes by "'facts.'" Admonishing us that "the history of philosophy is to a great extent that of a certain clash of human temperaments," James goes on subsequently to observe that:

> Historically we find the terms "intellectualism" and "sensationalism" used as synonyms of "rationalism" and "empiricism." Well, nature seems to combine most frequently with intellectualism an idealistic and optimistic tendency. Empiricists on the other hand are not uncommonly materialistic, and their optimism is apt to be decidedly conditional, tremulous. Rationalism usually considers itself more religious than empiricism, but there is much to say about this claim, so I merely mention it. It is a true claim when the individual rationalist is what is called a man of feeling, and when the individual empiricist prides himself on being hard-headed. In that case the rationalist will usually also be in favor of what is called free-will, and the empiricist will be a fatalist . . .[2]

Approaching our problem in this way, we could see our task as that of decomposing this nominally irrefrangible term into its possible constituent significations, producing a semantic spectrum at one of whose ends stand the "hardness" of the physical environment, and at the other the psychological "hardness" of James's "tough-minded" thinker, with the "hard" traits elicited by the former lying between the two. In addition, we could make a ready transition to the subject at hand, since aren't James's "tough-minded" values the ones which stand out so conspicuously in works of "hard" science fiction? Isn't the hero typically an engineer, a problem solver who delights in facing the facts and triumphing over them? (It might be interesting in this connection to count the number of times the phrase "jerry-rigged," an indefatigable stigmata of this attitude, crops up in the novels of Heinlein or Niven.) If this account were true, our semantic spectrum would also resemble a causal chain: just as the material world promotes the growth of "hard" values necessary to bring it under control by the resistance it offers human beings, so science fiction, or at least its hard variant, would complete this process by demonstrating the symbolic success of these same values in works of literature.

Let us turn our attention to a specific example which seems to suitably illustrate all of these senses of "hardness" at once, to an incident from John W. Campbell's story "The Invaders." In this story mankind, fallen into a Rousseauistic state of decadence with more than a passing resemblence to that which Wells ascribes to the Eloi in *The Time Machine*, succumbs to the Tharoo, a hostile, technologically superior race compelled by the decay of their sun to search out a new home. Jan, the main character, and his girl friend Meg, are taken prisoner and separated; inside the Tharoo spaceship Jan manages to break loose and discovers Meg, surrounded by aliens, anaesthetized on a table:

> One of the strangers had something in his hand, something bright like the mirror-metal, and he was bending over Meg now. He made a swift movement, and even the fear of the guard's tube could not quiet Jan as he cried out desperately. For suddenly he saw Meg's smooth warm skin split open all along her abdomen, and the carmine-red of her blood welled out suddenly. Her body changed in an instant from something slim and beautiful and bronzed to a horrible thing of red.[3]

Interestingly, we encounter—as we might not expect—"hardness" first of all in a literal, if implicit sense: in the "mirror-metal"; Campbell has previously used this phrase to describe the Tharoo spaceship when it first arrives, "gleaming with the hard sheen that those rare bits of mirror-metal which they found in the Ancient Places had."[4] As the last quotation should make clear, this epiphet has a more than descriptive significance: metal functions here as a cultural metonym indexing the technological capabilities mankind has forfeited—these people only know metal from the ruins around them, they no longer know how to work it. Why? Because, as Campbell does not fail to inform the reader, the race has "gone soft." "For two thousand years no human being had had to think, to work, or escape danger. . . . Man had had no need of intelligence. There was nothing to drive man, so he had fallen easily, gently down."[5] But no one could accuse the Tharoo, whom Campbell characterizes as "great and bold, men of fine ideals and high courage,"[6] as lacking in hardness; in fact, the role Campbell assigns them is less that of malevolent aliens than that of teachers, providentially despatched to cure man of his inherent slothfulness. After "the inevitable disintegration that follows in every case in all history where man has been allowed indolence," Campbell explains in the following story, "Rebellion," "The Tharoo came . . . and mankind received such a lesson in labor, work and productivity as the race had never before experienced. Even Mother Nature, in creating the harsh world of evolution, had never equalled the efforts of the Tharoo. It was an excellent course."[7]

In this incident we thus find all of the senses of "hardness" we have so far discussed, from the literal "hardness" of the metallic instruments to the psychological "hardness" of the Tharoo, who do not recoil from any extreme in fulfilling their role as humanity's self-appointed disciplinarians. Yet the incident hardly seems a satisfying illustration—doesn't the behavior of the Tharoo, as Campbell presents it, more resemble cold-blooded brutality than scientific objectivity? Wouldn't a race as advanced as the Tharoo is supposed to be have a more sophisticated method for investigating the internal anatomy of humans than that of carving up a young girl? Up to this point, "hardness" has had predominantly positive connotations, even in James's characterization of the "tough-minded" thinker; in this passage it takes on a new, less agreeable tone, one that suggests a high degree of sadistic aggressivity only thinly masked by the purportedly disinterested aims of the Tharoo. Involuntarily, God only knows, Campbell's story clearly manifests the link postulated by Freud between sadistic impulses and man's quest to gain mastery over the environment. At the earliest stage of our development, Freud argued, since we resent our dependence upon the external world, we experience it as an antagonistic rather than an attractive force, a possible source of frustration and thus a goad to aggression: "The object, as we have heard, was brought to the ego from the external world by the survival instincts, and one cannot deny that the original sense of hate signifies the relation to the foreign, stimulus transmitting external world. . . . The outside, the object, what is hated, would have been identical at the very beginning."[8] Such a theory, which asserts that aggressivity marks and mars our primordial relation to the world, necessarily implies that even under our most civilized attempts to organize the world—for example, in scientific research— a current of sadistic aggressivity flows, an implication that Freud made explicit when he stated that "From the desire for knowledge in particular one frequently gets the impression that it could replace sadism in the mechanism of the compulsion neurosis. Fundamentally, this desire is a sublimated offshoot of the desire for possession, raised to an intellectual level. . . ."[9] In "The Invaders," it is, oddly enough, the earthlings who take on the role of the "foreign object," and the "aliens" who come to bring back to them the knowledge they have lost; but in doing so they reveal the aggressive sources from which that knowledge derives.

Some could well object at this point, justifiably, that I have loaded the dice; the person might argue that my example is an isolated one, that "The Invaders" is not representative of "hard" science fiction, if it is such at all. A more devious interlocutor might remind me that Campbell was a notorious reactionary who in this story has fashioned a science-fictional soap box from which to propound his own personal views. Such an objection does not lack merit: we could read "The Invaders," published in the 1930s, as the paranoid fantasy of a militant proponent of "rugged individualism," trying to come to grips with social and economic disorder of the Great Depression. This interpretation, however, would not bring us any closer to understanding what "hard" science fiction might be; we need to approach our problem from a different perspective—an historical one. What would, I think, immediately strike any knowledgeable reader of science fiction upon reading Campbell's story is its indebtedness to Wells. The Tharoo are clearly modeled after the Martians in *The War of the Worlds,* of whom Wells tells us that they studied man "perhaps almost as narrowly as a man with a microscope might scrutinize the transient creatures that swarm and multiply in a drop of water."[10] And does not Wells also present the Martian invasion as ultimately beneficial to the human race?

> It may be that in the larger design of the universe this invasion from Mars is not without its ultimate benefit for men; it has robbed us of that serene confidence in the future which is the most fruitful source of decadence, the gifts to human science it has brought are enormous, and it has done much to promote the conception of the commonweal of mankind.[11]

Unfortunately, the comparison, far from sanctioning Campbell's treatment of his material, can only serve to discredit it: apart from his vastly superior ability as a writer, Wells possessed a subtlety utterly lacking in Campbell, who frequently blunders into a story like a hell-fire-and-damnation revivalist laying down the law. We can measure the difference by juxtaposing the heavy-handed pronouncement about man's justly deserved fate at the hands of the Tharoo, with a similar statement in *The War of the Worlds:* " 'We have to invent a sort of life where men can live and breed, and be sufficiently secure to bring the children up. . . . We can't have any weak or silly. Life is real again, and the useless and cumbersome and mischievous have to die.' "[12] Wells shrewdly puts these lines into the mouth of one of his characters, the artilleryman whom the narrator encounters after earth has apparently fallen to the aliens. This device has a double function, both allowing Wells to absolve himself from the responsibility of presenting these ideas in propria persona, and to limit their validity by attributing them to a character whom he subsequently places in a somewhat unfavorable light.

More importantly, Wells, like Swift whom he admired, dialecticizes oppositions. The "hard/soft" duality which figures so blatantly in "The Invaders" has an evident counterpart in *The War of the Worlds:* like the Tharoo, the Martians easily conquer the human populace because of their "hardness"—their high degree of scientific development and their lack of moral scruples—and because of the "softness" of the earthlings—in this case, less indolence than complacency. But Wells complicates things when he exposes the—doubly—"soft" side of his invaders. First, as a result of their peculiar evolution, the Martians have paid for their high intelligence with a loss of physical organization: "They were heads—merely heads. Entrails they had none."[13] Secondly, of course, they suffer from a fatal lack of resistance to terrestrial bacteria. Enormous ambulatory brains, radically cut off from nature and sexual division, the Martians represent, morphologically at least, a regression to primitive forms of life; in spite of their great intelligence, they, unlike the Tharoo, cannot be held out as a model for humans to emulate. Wells, here using as he does in *The Time Machine*, evolution both as scientific given and metaphor, gives us in the Martians, who combine the physical degeneracy of the Eloi with the cunning and viciousness of the Morlocks, a possible future of the human race.

Nevertheless, we can readily discern an evident structural continuity between the texts of Wells and Campbell: ideas present in Wells's novel in a latent form precipitate out, so to speak, in Campbell's story—and harden. The affinity becomes all the more evident when we notice the indebtedness to *The Time Machine* as well to *The War of the Worlds;* in a strange way, "The Invaders" seems like a fusion of both novels, in which the Martians instead of the Time Traveler arrive in the future to straighten out the Eloi or in which the Morlocks have a benign and not a demonic role. The influence of *The Time Machine* appears not only in the obvious parallel between the Eloi and the earthlings, but also in the grandiose time scale which both stories employ, although for different reasons. Wells, having proposed an identity of time and space at the beginning of his novel, uses time much as he uses space in *the War of the Worlds*—as an antidote to man's overweening pride. In "The Invaders" the situation is somewhat different. This tale forms the middle section of a group of three stories which trace mankind's history from the arrival of the Machine—a kind of supercomputer which ends man's enslave-

ment to natural forces and thus brings about his ruin—to its liberation from the Tharoo several thousand years later; here we find a
temporal framework which appears even more emphatically in later
works of science fiction, one in which the writer presents future
history as a drama unfolding over eons.

Not without reason, we ordinarily associate this device with such
"classic" examples of "hard" science fiction as Heinlein's *The Past
through Tomorrow* or Asimov's *Foundation* trilogy, and its persis-
tance in later novels such as *The Mote in God's Eye*, prefaced by a
"Chronology" that commences in 1969 and extends to 3017, gives it
the status of a hallmark, if not an indispensable feature of "hard
science fiction." While Robert Scholes and Eric Rabkin see in this
device the influence of Vico and Spengler,[14] a more likely candidate, I
think, would be John Calvin, of whom Roland Bainton wrote that
"he envisaged not the speedy coming of the Lord but a considerable
time span in which *le Seigneur* could unroll the drama of the ages and
set up *le royaume de Dieu*."[15] Do we not catch a glimpse in these
"time charts" and thousand-year sagas of a return of the repressed
Calvinistic background of the modern sciences? Without a doubt
Calvin would be horrified, could he return from the grave, to see
where his ideas have led, yet we could hardly underestimate the
significance of his role in undermining the sacramental world picture
which had prevailed throughout the middle ages and thus laying the
ground for a rational investigation of natural phenomena. Motivated
by a deep conviction of the utterly fallen nature of the creation,
Calvin saw in medieval religion, in which God constantly exhibited
Himself in the world through wonders, a delirious parody of true
piety. Although he did not deny the veracity of scriptural miracles,
God, Calvin asserted, had used only one channel of communication
to deal with man in more recent days: the Word. "It is clear," he
wrote in *The Institutes of the Christian Religion*, "that God has
provided the assistance of the Word. . . . because He foresaw that his
likeness imprinted upon the most beautiful form of the universe
would be insufficiently effective."[16] To protect the creator from being
contaminated by His depraved creation, Calvin chose to demytholo-
gize that creation.

The final result of Calvin's efforts was, of course, quite different
from what he had anticipated: later thinkers, at once stimulated by
the rationalistic aspect of Calvinsim and repelled by its irrational
dogmatism, found that the world, so thoroughly cut off from its

maker, could get along quite well without Him. Historically, however, Calvin may have had his secret revenge, for do we not discern in the concept of determinism, which has hung so balefully over the growth of modern scientific thought, the secularized prolongation of one of the most notorious of Calvinistic dogmas, the doctrine of predestination? Scientific laws which ultimately exist only for a human consciousness that formulates them and acknowledges their validity, take on, interpreted in this way, an alienated existence, imposing themselves on the human subject with the irresistable fatality of the Calvinistic deity. Such an interpretation clearly belongs not to science but to ideology, to "false consciousness"—and yet does not this conception underly the "time schemes" we have been discussing? What do we find in all of these works except "scientific laws," so conceived, guiding man to his destiny just as Calvin's God had done before? Lest I give a false impression, my purpose here is not to detect the existence of a closet Calvinism in science fiction, much less in scientific discourse itself; Calvin's relevance for our discussion lies in the way he so aptly illustrates what Max Horkeimer and Theodor Adorno called "the dialectics of the enlightment"— enlightment here referring not to the specific period in the 18th century but to the process by which humans rationally analyze and thus master their environment. Enlightenment, Horkheimer and Adorno argue, derives from man's fear of a world he needs to control so that it will not threaten his survival: "The gods cannot take away fear from man when they bear its petrified cries as their names. He fancies himself free from fear if there is no longer anything unknown. This determines the course of demythologization. . . . Enlightenment is mythic terror become radical."[17] To the extent that this process occurs in a constitutively unfree society, one still governed by the economic struggle for survival, enlightenment itself takes on the guise of a "natural" force outside of human control. "Each attempt," Horkheimer and Adorno write, "to break natural constraint, while nature is broken, only leads deeper into natural constraint. . . . Abstraction, the tool of enlightenment, acts upon its objects just as did the fate whose concept it eliminates: as liquidation."[18]

We can see this process vividly enacted in later—i.e., post-Campbell— works of "hard" science fiction: for example Heinlein's *Starship Troopers*. Heinlein's novel, denigrated by Samuel Delany for "its endless preachments on the glories of war, and its pitiful founderings on repressed homosexual themes,"[19] harks back to a privileged genre of the Enlightenment, the *conte philosophique*, in which the hero's adventures are accompanied by a commentary that they illustrate at the same time the commentary explains the adventured; in this case, the story recounts the experiences of Johnny Rico as he rises from enlisted man to officer in the Mobile Infantry. In what may be the novel's crucial episode, Johnny, still undergoing basic training, must witness the execution of another recruit—named Dillinger, appropriately—who has killed a little girl; perplexed, Johnny cannot decide how to react to this event until he recalls in detail a discussion in a high school class on "History and Moral Philosophy" taught by Mr. Dubois, a retired officer who plays Imlac to Johnny's Rasselas. In the course of explaining "the breakup of the North American republic, back in the XXth century," Dubois poses the question: "What *is* 'moral sense'?" To which he replies:

> It is an elaboration of the instinct to survive. The instinct to survive is human nature itself, and every aspect of our personalities derives from it. Anything that conflicts with the survival instinct acts sooner or later to eliminate the individual and thereby fails to show up in future generations. This truth is mathematically demonstrable, everywhere verifiable: it is the single eternal imperative controlling everything we do.[20]

The key phrase here is certainly "mathematically demonstrable"; unlike a conventional spokesman for "law and order," Heinlein's *advocatus diaboli* appeals neither to traditional nor to religious but to scientific authority: the theory of evolution projected onto the moral universe assumes the rights of a none-too-benevolent despot who severely punishes any infractions of his rules. Again, as with "The Invaders," someone might reply that Heinlein has arbitrarily imposed these ideas on the material, that they have nothing to do with "science"; nevertheless, the book draws upon perfectly coherent and rationally acceptable concepts to support its picture of the world. According to the argument which emerges from dialogues interspersed throughout the narrative, each individual exists only for the sake of the social organization—" 'The basis of all morality is duty,' " Dubois states, " 'a concept with the same relation to group that self-interest has to individual,' "[21]—and each individual can be exchanged for another since " 'a human being has *no natural rights of any nature*,' "[22] and each individual must render payment for having existed with his life. (Significantly, Heinlein uses an economic metaphor—"to buy the farm"—to describe the deaths, of which there are many in the novel, of various characters.) To accept this argument is to fall prey to the dialectic of the enlightenment such as Horkheimer and Adorno have outlined it, granting to purportedly scientific laws the blind authority of natural forces they are deemed to overcome.

Here we reach the furthest point in our investigation of "hardness," a point at which "hardness" becomes ideology and doubles its force, reinforced by the hardness of ideology. Our previous models, those of the semantic spectrum and the causal chain, give way to a new model, that of a series of concentric circles in which the innermost, the aggressive libidinal investments that characterize our primary relation to the world, discharge energy to the outermost, ideological and socially mediated, and are in turn supported by it. "If the lion had consciousness," Adorno wrote in *Negative Dialectic*, "then his rage at the antelope he intends to eat would be ideology."[23] The importance of the texts I have been discussing, however, is to have manifested this "hardness" so relentlessly; ideology is not a discourse but a force which shapes discourse, and one cannot eliminate it by simply exchanging "good" humanistic ideas for "bad" reactionary ones. Replacing the Mobile Infantry in *Starship Troopers* with the Peace Corps would not make it less ideological, just as in *Foundation*, the humanistic answer to Campbell and Heinlein, fatality does not vanish with the triumph of the Second Foundation, it only becomes less conspicuous: Asimov changes the gloomy Calvinistic *deus absconditus* for the benign watchmaker god of the Deists. The "harder" science fiction becomes—the more it offers us the vision of alienated scientific laws governing human life—the more it strengthens ideology. It was necessary for this to happen during one period of the history of science fiction; the alternative, which could not have come into existence otherwise, is represented by works such as *Solaris* and *Triton*.

The Readers of Hard Science Fiction
James Gunn

Criticism developed to deal with mainstream literature has difficulty dealing with science fiction. One reason is put forward by Robert Scholes in the introduction to the Oxford University Press series of one-author studies: "As long as the dominant criteria are believed to hold for *all* fiction, science fiction will be found inferior: deficient in psychological depth, in verbal nuance, and in plausibility of event. What is needed is a criticism serious in its standards and its concern for literary value but willing to take seriously a literature based on ideas, types, and events beyond ordinary experience."

Another reason may be that most traditional criticism (there is, to be sure, "reader response" criticism) looks at the artist and science fiction looks at the reader. Traditional criticism holds that it is the reader's responsibility to understand, science fiction, by and large, that it is the author's responsibility to make the reader understand. I would like to consider here the readers of hard science fiction, why they read it and what serious critical standards can be suggested for it, but first I must deal with some problems of definition.

From the point of view of the science-fiction magazines, where contemporary science fiction was born and nurtured, fiction is an emotional experience for the reader induced by the author's persuading the reader to invest concern in the plight of a character, to care about what happens to him or her, and to obtain a release of concern, identified as pleasure, when the character resolves his situation. Satisfaction is produced when the situation of a story is resolved in a way that the reader has not foreseen but recognizes as appropriate, even inevitable. This view does not insist that readers cannot look for and obtain other rewards—as indeed they do in science fiction and in hard science fiction—but that the fictional response is basic. Science fiction obtains its unique fictional response by dealing with characters whose situation has been created by change, and usually scientific or technological change. The reader's involvement is dependent upon his intellectual recognition of the change, and his emotional satisfaction is dependent upon the character's rational response to the situation, or upon the reader's recognition of the character's failure because the obstacles are too great, because the character did not know enough to achieve the correct response, or because the character's response was irrational. Mary Shelley's *Frankenstein*, for instance, seems more like a gothic novel than science fiction because the experienced science fiction reader keeps wanting the tormented scientist to behave rationally, and he doesn't even behave like a scientist when he shrinks in revulsion from his creation; instead, it is the monster who behaves rationally when he asks about the responsibility of the creator to his creature.

The insistence that emotion derives from the intellectual in science fiction often confuses the discussion, as if the heart and the mind actually were the location of the humors attributed to them rather than part of a gestalt. An emotional response often is irrational, but a rational response is not always dispassionate. As an example we need only think of Archimedes shouting "Eureka!" and leaping from his bath to streak the streets of Syracuse.

The difficulty of defining science fiction is basic. Every critic has tried his hand at one or several definitions. Damon Knight finally gave up and said, "Science fiction is what I mean when I point at it," but even this criterion is subject to questions about the difference between the kinds of fiction pointed at.

I've tried a few definitions myself, and I think the problem is that science fiction, unlike other genres, has no characteristic action or location; instead it is more like an attitude toward experience, an attitude that can be applied to almost any subject. We might compare the attitude of the mainstream author that man is a fallen creature placed on earth to refine his soul (or find salvation) through misery and despair to the attitude of the hard science-fiction author that man is here to understand the universe and discover his place in it. The first attitude makes suffering the central fact of the human experience and uses the mind only to find acceptance; the second insists that understanding is central and that not only is misery not inevitable but that understanding can change human behavior. The late John W. Campbell used to say that science fiction encompassed mainstream literature, because science fiction covered everything from the origin of the universe to its end, and the mainstream covered only a small range and a tiny space within that longer and larger literature. Although this is mostly intellectual goading on Campbell's part, nevertheless, it makes the point that almost anything can be written as science fiction—and often is. It is hospitable to all the other genres: one can have a science fiction western, for instance, or a science-fiction detective story or love story or gothic or sports story, or a fantasy, or even a mainstream story of character. Most common, of course, is the science-fiction adventure story. Much of the confusion about science fiction is created by this fact. Readers who view science fiction as escape are usually attracted by a non-science-fiction element, the adventure, say, or the wish-fulfillment fairy tale, like that of *Star Wars*. If one removes the elements of the other genres, what one has left is the irreducible quality that makes the work science fiction. Sometimes, of course, nothing is left, and we conclude that the piece wasn't really science fiction after all.

The irreducible quality is change. In science fiction the situation in which the characters find themselves is significantly different from the here and now; nevertheless, the events, though they can be considered fantastic because of the significantly different situation, take place in a universe that is recognizably our own.

The only example I wish to present here is "The Cold Equations," Tom Godwin's influential story. In *The Road to Science Fiction* I call it a touchstone story because if readers don't understand it they don't understand science fiction. The intellectual point made by the story is that sentimentality divorced from knowledge and rationality is deadly. "The Cold Equations" could have been told only as science fiction, not because the point of the story is science fiction but because every other situation retains an element of hope for rescue. In a contemporary lifeboat story or a story about wagon trains crossing the plains, the sacrifice of an innocent stowaway to save the lives of the remainder brings up images of the Donner party: the point of those stories would be the survivors' lack of faith and their love of life above honor. Science fiction gave Godwin an unparalleled opportunity to purify the situation in such a way that there was no hope left for last-minute salvation, no possible sight of land or rescue ship, no company of soldiers to ride over the hill. The girl is to blame for her own predicament, her innocence is irrelevant, the universe doesn't care about her motives, and the others would be as guilty as she if they compounded her fatal mistake by dying with her.

The reader who does not understand this has not read the story correctly. The intellectual perception that the girl must die produces the emotional response the reader gets from the story. Perhaps the point of the story is science-fictional after all; where else would such a point be made; by what other audience would it be understood? And considered satisfying?

Still we are not yet to our discussion of hard science fiction, although "The Cold Equations" is one example of the form. First we must contrast the reader's reaction to science fiction with his reaction to fantasy. On the basis of the fact that everything in science fiction is fantastic, Damon Knight has denied that a difference between science fiction and fantasy exists. Other writers, such as Brian Aldiss, refuse to use such science-fiction conventions as faster-than-light travel because they are impossible and thus elements of fantasy rather than science fiction. Where we must begin in differentiating between science fiction and fantasy is with the reader's response.

Because science fiction takes place in a universe recognizably our own, when we read science fiction we are continually comparing the events of the story to reality. That is why plausibility ranks so high in the qualities necessary to science fiction, and why H. G. Wells, in his famous advice to science-fiction writers, though he speaks of tricking the reader, stresses the need for a "plausible assumption." "Possibility" is another key word. John Campbell made use of it when he called for a science-fiction story that was "interesting and good and possible," but a fantasy story that was "interesting and good." "Possibility," of course, suggests subjectivity: one reader's possibility may be another reader's ridiculous fantasy. By "possibility," however, I mean that which is presented plausibly and which the reader is supposed to accept as real for scientific reasons, not as a willing suspension of disbelief. Faster-than-light travel, for instance, may be considered "possible" if we assume that Einstein's theory, like Newton's, was only an approximation, or that ways have been found around the limitation of the speed of light. Where it is used only as a convenience, as a way of getting on with the story, readers accept it as a convention rationalized in earlier stories.

Plausibility and possibility lead the reader to question the text: "How did we get there from here? What does that mean? Did it come about through human decision? Was that decision good or bad? Are people responding to the changes around them rationally or emotionally? What is the right course of action for them? What does that mean?" All of these questions are intellectual, comparisons of the changed environment of the story with the environment of the here and now and judgments about the relationships of people to environment and proper responses to it. The science-fiction story demands that we ask these questions and make these judgments.

So-called science-fiction stories and novels that do not tell us how we got there from here seem much more like fantasy, for fantasy does not tell us these things—or, if it tells us, does so only by a wave of the wand that changes a closet into the portal to another world or a rabbit hole into a passageway to wonderland. Our reaction to that, as readers, is to accept if we wish, but not to question. At its best, fantasy leads us to psychological insights; at its least, to mindless adventure.

Which brings us—finally—to hard science fiction. By hard science fiction we mean that science fiction in which the story turns around a change in the environment that can be understood only scientifically and generally through what are known as the hard sciences, usually the laboratory sciences such as chemistry, physics, and biology, and the observational sciences such as astronomy, geology, and geography. Mathematics and computers are two of the tools used by all the hard sciences. These sciences are considered hard because they deal with objective data, and predictions can be made from these data that are verifiable. The soft sciences—the behavioral and social sciences—are considered soft because their data are at least partially subjective and because they deal with theories and general statements rather than predictions on whose truth the validity of the theories must rest. But the soft sciences can become the substance of hard science fiction if the story revolves around them and if the story imagines a situation in which the soft sciences have become hard sciences.

John Campbell, the long-time editor of *Astounding/Analog* who did more than anyone else to give meaning to hard science fiction, wrote in the 1947 symposium *Of Worlds Beyond*:

> To be science fiction, not fantasy, an honest effort at prophetic extrapolation of the known must be made. Ghosts can enter science fiction— if they're logically explained, but not if they are simply the ghosts of fantasy. Prophetic extrapolation can derive from a number of different sources, and apply in a number of fields. Sociology, psychology, and para-psychology are, today, not true sciences; therefore instead of forecasting future results of applications of sociological science of to-

day, we must forecast the *development* of a *science* of sociology. From there the story can take off.

Implicit in the scientific method is the provisionality of all truths, the questionability of all facts, the falsifiability of all theories. In fact, a test suggested to distinguish between scientific theories and non-scientific theories, such as creationism, is that scientific theories are falsifiable, that is, can be proved wrong. So the hard sciences are not truly hard in the sense that their current interpretations of data are final, and one science-fictional technique, similar to assuming that some soft science has been turned into a hard science, is to assume that new discoveries and theories have turned current hard sciences, at least partially, into soft sciences.

Norman Spinrad believes that there are discernible differences between stories based on the hard sciences and those on what he calls the "rubber sciences." There is, he says in his article in *The Craft of Science Fiction,* a hard science fiction "feel": "a sense of hard black vacuum and cold pinpoint stars, a universe filled with hard-edged metallic artifacts and a reality whose rules are all of a piece, fixed, seamless, and invariant." Its "hard-edged, materialistic, deterministic reality," he says, "admits of no fuzziness in locus, no blank spots, no indeterminacy, no multiplexity—more Newtonian than Einsteinian." But when the soft sciences are treated as hard sciences, rather than material for what Spinrad calls "visionary science fiction," the universe in which the fiction takes place is rational and ruled by law, not arbitrary. And it should be pointed out that Einstein rejected indeterminacy with his "God does not play dice with the universe."

We might make one last comparison: that of hard science fiction with "New Wave" speculation fiction. All New Wave fiction was not the same, any more than all hard science fiction, but New Wave fiction characteristically was anti-science, even anti-science fiction. The events encountered in the fiction that represented the heart of the New Wave, J. G. Ballard's catastrophe fiction, for instance (though much of it, to be sure, appeared before Michael Moorcock took over as editor of *New Worlds*), discouraged reader curiosity: the catastrophes clearly were arbitrary—they had no discernible cause and the characters either knew this or were incurious, and the reader's intellectual desire to know how we got there from here was deflected in a manner similar to that of fantasy.

What hard science fiction worked upon, then, was the same

motivation that produced science: the desire of the reader to understand the universe, and himself and the human species in relationship
to that universe. Hard science fiction, like science, took as its first
premise that the universe could be understood by an organized
application of observation and thought. The use of accepted scientific
theory or, where necessary, the theory that, in a rational manner,
superseded accepted theory focused the reader's attention on rational explanation. Often the fiction dealt with rational people moving into the unknown, most commonly by spaceflight and the future;
once having reached the unknown, the characters do not simply
experience it but try to understand it. The reader of hard science
fiction embarks on a voyage of discovery not unlike that of Charles
Darwin aboard the *Beagle*. In fact, one collection of stories, in which
A. E. van Vogt made hard sciences out of education and history in
order to shape adventure stories and fairy tales into hard science
fiction, is called *The Voyage of the Space Beagle*. To observe what the
impact would be without the sciences, without the search for explanations, one need only view the film *Alien*—all terror and no
effort to understand, no rational behavior.

Ultimately the attempt to deal rationally with change, whether it
is change created by people or change encountered during exploration into the unknown or change that comes to humanity out of the
unknown, produces a reader not only prepared for change and
prepared to deal with it rationally, but one who reads science fiction
about aliens or alien environment realizing that it is really talking
about the influence of environment on people.

Mission of Gravity, Hal Clement's masterpiece, is considered
one of the hardest of hard science-fiction novels. Its scene is an alien
world whose gravity at the poles is five hundred times what it is on
earth, but, because of the equatorial bulge, only two or three times
earth's gravity at the equator. Its dominant race has evolved from
caterpillar-like creatures, built low to the ground and with many legs
in order to cope with gravity, but inside they are a great deal like
humans. The reason for this is not only that the reader will care about
the Mesklinites but will understand their problems, when, at the
equator, they must conquer the normal fears and precautions that
their polar environment has bred into them. If the reader reads the
novel correctly, he asks himself at the end how gravity—a physical
fact he has seldom considered—has created in him uninspected responses, including fears and prejudices.

On a different level but in an almost identical process, Ursula K. Le Guin's *The Left Hand of Darkness* explores the influence of bilateral sex on human history, politics, psychology, social status, myth, and many other aspects of existence by studying alien androgyny on an alien world. This makes hard science fiction seem cerebral, and it is, but it also can work as fiction, and the standard of critical judgment is how well the message of the work is matched by the means: a good hard science-fiction piece is one in which the story is completely integrated with the idea. *The Left Hand of Darkness,* though it displays a bit of what I call the idiot plot (that is, the events of the novel would not have happened if the major characters had displayed normal levels of intelligence), proceeds through a journey of discovery in which Genly Ai is continually educated in the facts of Gethenian sex (and, by contrast, his own) until he at last accepts Estraven as a person. Using this criterion, it seems to me that Le Guin's *The Dispossessed* is a lesser novel; as a utopia, ambiguous or otherwise, it does not present politics as a hard science but as an exploration of a wish. What Theodore Sturgeon calls "if only" stories (an addition to the conventional wisdom that divides science fiction into "if this goes on" stories and "what if" stories) tend to develop through the less convincing strategies of lecture and parable.

Ringworld displays another way in which hard science fiction can be softened. Larry Niven is considered a leading hard science-fiction author, and *Ringworld,* one of his finest achievements of this type. In fact, it has often been described as a novel that might have been written by Hal Clement. What is "hard" about it is a concept of staggering scope: a world or worlds that have been fashioned into a gigantic ring spinning around its sun; on its great surface thousands of races and different civilizations can live out their lives with no knowledge of each other. This is the image that defines and sustains the novel (a concept derived from the speculations of astronomer Freeman Dyson), but the novel turns vaguely disappointing when Niven chooses to explore only a tiny fraction of the Ringworld and plays the ring for adventure rather than making the magnificient artifact the heart of his work. A sequel written much later, *Ringworld Engineers,* to be sure, answers a number of the questions left open at the end of the first novel without exploring the Ringworld image much more significantly.

On the other hand, Bob Shaw's *Orbitsville,* which also was based on Dyson's speculations about advanced civilizations converting planetary matter into a sphere about a sun and utilizing all that star's energy and all the converted planet's area as living space was not as spectacularly popular as *Ringworld* but kept the concept of the Dyson sphere at the center of the novel. Shaw's world turns out to be an alien construct intended to consume the time and energy of ambitious spacefaring creatures and delay their further expansion into the galaxy.

Perhaps the best way of illustrating the differences between hard-core science fiction and other kinds is to look at some classic examples. Van Vogt's most famous early novels, *Slan* and *The World of Null-A*, seemed at the heart of the hard science-fiction magazine *Astounding* when they were first published in its pages, probably because they treated not soft sciences but even softer concepts like telepathy, telekinesis, teleportation, general semantics, and the entire bundle of concepts collectively known as superman as if they were hard sciences. But even then they read more like myths. Some critics call them power fantasies, but this seems pejorative, and I prefer to call them fairy tales—fairy tales of science such as Tennyson referred to in "Locksley Hall." And Van Vogt's stories had all the innate power of fairy tales to structure the dreams of its readers— witness the fans who built a Slan Shack in the 1940s as an early experiment in communal living.

To compare another famous pair of books, Isaac Asimov's *I, Robot* seems consistently more "hard" than his *The Foundation Trilogy. I, Robot* projects the development of a robot industry and its social and technological consequences, as well as the problems of dealing with individual robots due to conflicts between the famous three laws of robotics. *The Foundation Trilogy,* on the other hand, does speculate about the creation of a science of general social prediction, psychohistory, but—important as psychohistory is in preserving civilization—psychohistory is not truly central, and, in fact, becomes virtually irrelevant throughout the second half of the *Trilogy.* What is central is the concept of the Foundation, which halfway through the series becomes Foundations in the plural. And even though the Second Foundation makes an exact science out of psychology, the uses of that science remain more mysterious than rational. The heart of the stories, moreover, is the struggle of determined men against great difficulties—the greatest of these being the fall of a galactic empire and the shortening of thirty thousand years of dark ages to a thousand. Asimov has described the series as adventure stories, and so they are, even if the adventure is almost totally cerebral.

The Caves of Steel is Asimov's best example of a novel in which the theme of environment is central and in which fiction and theme are skillfully integrated. *The Gods Themselves,* however, is Asimov's best-developed "hard" novel, in which he used his knowledge of chemistry and of scientists to speculate about the kinds of universes that might have developed where the "strong force" in the atomic nucleus had different values.

All John Brunner's ecological novels—*Stand on Zanzibar, The Jagged Orbit, The Sheep Look Up,* and *The Shockwave Rider*—are hard science fiction in that each is clearly extrapolative from present to future conditions and in each of them science plays a central part in trying to cope with the conditions. Robert Silverberg has written a number of hard science-fiction works, but his *Dying Inside,* in which telepathy was used as a metaphor rather than an exploration, was a mainstream novel that was unappreciated and probably misunderstood by science-fiction readers—and probably by mainstream critics as well.

Religion can be the subject of hard science fiction, as in James Blish's *A Case of Conscience,* which considers with great rigor the efforts of a Jesuit priest to deal with the fact of an alien race born without sin. C. S. Lewis's *Perelandra* trilogy, however, as a retelling of Christian beliefs rather than a critical consideration of them, does not come close.

Another soft science turned into a hard science is linguistics in Jack Vance's *The Languages of Pao* and Samuel R. Delany's *Babel-17.* Vance's novel is "harder" because of its more rigorous and more central use of linguistics. In another well-known Delany novel, *The Einstein Intersection,* the initial reaction of the science-fiction reader is bewilderment because he never learns "how we got there from here." The novel is more profitably read as fantasy.

Often, of course, novels are mixtures of hard and soft. *Dune,* for instance, leaves readers with conflicting reactions because the ecology is hard, the anthropology and the psychic abilities are soft, and the structure is palace intrigue. This may be the reason for its success, and that of its sequels—readers attracted by the structure can enhance their enjoyment with richness of other kinds.

If the writer wishes to make a point in what he or she writes, a point that the reader is intended to consider rationally and perhaps be convinced of its merits, the writer might well consider the potential of science fiction, particularly hard science fiction. If the writer wishes to describe behavior or analyze character, either non-judgmentally or in terms of social or religious morality, then the writer does better to couch the fiction as fantasy or mainstream literature and stay away from science fiction. That is why science fiction, at least of the hard variety, is primarily didactic; rational consideration of how we got there from here and how we can cope with the process or the end result is necessarily judgmental.

Writing hard science fiction has its difficulties. The major one is knowing the science, at least enough to know what questions to ask or what sources to search, and how to place the information into some reasonable context of how science works. Even if the writer's only desire, as it often is, is to make the science sound plausible, research is usually essential, although too much knowledge of a science can be inhibiting to the imagination.

A related problem is how to explain the science to the reader, and to explain it in such a way as to enhance, not distract from, the story's narrative flow. Sometimes this problem is solved with epigraphs, sometimes with discussions between the characters or with descriptions or explanations worked into the action. Brunner, in *Stand on Zanzibar,* accomplishes this expository purpose in a variety of ways but partially through chapters of fragmented clues; Le Guin, in *The Left Hand of Darkness,* inserts entire chapters of anthropological reports or accounts of myths and Gethenian stories.

Authors whose works are truly hard also run into the problem of readers who spend long hours trying to catch the authors in a scientific or logical inaccuracy, like the general criticism of Ringworld (the artifact) for basic instability, or the even more embarrassing criticism that the author made the sun come up in the wrong direction. The committed "hard" author, however, enjoys the game, and like Niven, admitting his errors in the foreword to *Ringworld Engineers,* turns it to his own didactic advantage.

It may be instructive about the reader's response to hard science fiction to ask this question: what reader ever worried about these kinds of questions concerning a fantasy or mainstream work? On the other hand, writers who deal in turning soft sciences hard, like the fantasy writer, are limited largely by psychological plausibility.

Recent developments have created what seems to me an ideal mixture of fiction and science at this moment. In a pair of introductory essays in *The Road to Science Fiction #4* entitled "Fiction and Science" and "Science and Fiction," I held up two stories as illustrations of what I have been trying to describe. One author approached his subject—a solar nova (or solar flare)—from the viewpoint of the mainstream writer seeking metaphor, but the science seemed accurate and the human relationships were revealed and made meaningful by the science. The other author approached his subject from the viewpoint of science; he made his science believably human and his protagonist made sense of his scientific decisions by connecting them with human experiences. The first story was Ed Bryant's "Particle Theory," and the second was Gregory Benford's "Exposures." Benford also provided an instructive blend in his award-winning novel, *Timescape,* where his scientists had human problems but seemed like real scientists doing science.

Hard science fiction does not have to mean an ignorance of literary values, nor do literary critics have to remain invincibly ignorant of science and its influence on our lives. At its best, hard science fiction brings together the two cultures in a way achieved by no other dialogue, no other art.

Is There a Technological Fix for the Human Condition?

Gregory Benford

People don't read science fiction to learn science any more than others read historical novels to learn history. There are easier ways to go about it.

Yet the most simon pure breed of SF, that based on the physical sciences, somehow seems to be the core of the field. Its practitioners command SF's share of the bestseller markets. The gritty detail and devices of the "hard" brand form the background reality of many SF films. To many it seems more true, less wishful, and more hard-nosed than works based primarily on the social sciences. Certainly it seems to many more probable than that broad area of SF which copies jargon or emblems from the sciences without understanding them.

Why? What makes hard SF the center of the field? Answering this goes beyond literary criticism into realms of sociology, Zeitgeistery and political theory. I shall attempt a bit of all those in the process of mapping hard SF—detailing what I think it does, what its primary modes are, some voices it naturally adopts, and what personalities are drawn to read or write it. My bias is that of a scientist, so I shall first classify and later on attempt some theorizing. First comes botany, then genetics. I shall tell you how this remarkable region of SF looks to me, as one who has worked and socialized in it for decades.

My minimum definition of hard SF demands that it highly prize fidelity to the physical facts of the universe, while constructing a new objective "reality" within a fictional matrix. It is not enough merely to use science as integral to the narrative; thus I rule out the works of C. P. Snow, Sinclair Lewis's *Arrowsmith,* etc. SF must use science in a speculative fashion. The physical sciences are the most capable of detailed prediction (and thus falsification by experiment), so they are perceived in fiction as more reliable indicators of future possibilities, or stable grounds for orderly speculation.

Science and Its Roles

Using science in fiction introduces tools not generally available to ordinary fiction. The most relevant of these is *constraint*—defining what is possible or plausible. H. G. Wells admonished us to make one assumption and explore it; a world of infinite possibilities is uninteresting because there can be no suspense. In the same way that the iron rules of the sonnet can force excellence within a narrow framework, paying attention to scientific accuracy can force coherence on fiction.

This rigor creates a fundamental tension between dramatic needs and the demands of accuracy and honesty. It is this which underlies the pleasures many seek in hard SF. Those rewards occur even when hard SF types write what is by strict definition fantasy. Consider, for example, Niven's stories about the era before magic (mana) was used up on earth ("When the Magic Went Away," etc.). These regard magic as a piece of technology we have lost, and the plot logic follows the rules as strict as a chess game. Heinlein wrote early stories ("Magic, Inc.") celebrating this same sense, rationalizing territory previously thought to be beyond the realm of "hard" method.

The fidelity to an external standard of truth makes hard SF resemble the realistic narrative, in that it becomes a realism of *possibilities,* guided by our current scientific worldview. Variations are allowed, since the same facts can be explained by new theories. Thus time travel and faster than light journeys slip by, since they are probably impossible but difficult to disprove. Indeed, various notions of both spring from the speculative end of physics—Wheeler's "wormholes" which allow tunneling "through" the geometry of spacetime, or an intriguing result from black hole dynamics, which allows rapid travel forward in time by tangential trajectories in highly curved spacetime.

Rigor can have drawbacks, of course. Stories can turn on as trivial a point as whether a match will stay lit in zero gravity. This is the danger of overdoing the constraint imperative, while ignoring the dramatic requirements of all powerful fiction. In the hands of a writer sensitive to the tension between drama and fidelity, epics such as

Herbert's *Dune* can move the reader while retaining the internal cohesiveness imposed by building the planetary ecology correctly.

Hard SF authors call this fidelity "playing the game"—by the rules, of course. Veering from the facts of science runs the grave danger of losing the audience. As Robert Frost said of free verse, much SF is playing tennis with the net down. At first a netless game has an exciting freedom to it, a quick zest, but soon you find that no one wants to watch you play.

A reasonable standard, generally shared by hard SF writers, is that one should not make errors which are visible to the lay reader—keeping in mind that the usual hard SF reader is sophisticated and not easily fooled. (Hard SF types love to catch each other in oversights; Heinlein once snagged me on a matter of the freezing point of methane at low pressures, and I was mortified.) More important than the factwork, though, is an understanding of science, its methods and worldview. Hard SF types will deride fiction which misrepresents how scientists think, too. A novel such as Fred Hoyle's *The Black Cloud,* which realistically depicts scientists as they grapple with problems, revealing their styles and quirks, will be forgiven its sometimes stiff characters and clumsy prose.

This demand for imaginative realism imposed by scientific constraint provides a foundation for a second major function of science in SF: *verisimilitude.* SF must imbue fantastic events with a convincing reality, aided by a reader's willing suspension of disbelief. The piling on of well-worked-out details, derived from firm science, is a valuable tool. One can pursue C. S. Lewis's "realism of presentation" by working out names, geography, maps, titles of nobility or government, etc., as in *Out of the Silent Planet.* This is a well-known technique in both fantasy and SF, used by authors, as diverse as Tolkien and C. J. Cherryh.

A method strongly identified with hard SF, pioneered by Heinlein, is to fix upon a few surprising but logical *consequences* of a society or technology. The more unexpected the implications, the better. The surprise of an unanticipated facet of the future, implicit in the author's assumptions, instills wonder and convinces the reader of an imaginary world's "truth." Often the best effects come from noticing how human beings will use physical laws in delightful ways. The moon colonists of Heinlein's "The Menace From Earth" notice that low gravity doesn't merely mean you can carry more on your back—you can *fly*. In his *The Rolling Stones* the basic fact that Mars is sandy and has light gravity is used to make the Stones a nifty profit, because they realize that bicycles would be a logical, cheap, but overlooked method of transport. They set about importing them, their ingenuity reaffirming the self-sufficiency of so many hard science heroes.

In employing science's third role, as *symbol*, SF distinguishes itself from fantasy most clearly. In roughly the 19th century, science became widely perceived as a better way to understand our world than either religion or myth—two elements which, used at face value in fantastic fiction, typically yield fantasy. In SF, science appears as impersonal, not man-centered. Tom Godwin's "The Cold Equations," for all its wordiness and melodrama, still retains its effectiveness because it so clearly states this case. Science in hard SF is often a reality deeper than humanity's concerns, remorselessly deterministic, uncaring of our personal preoccupations, and yet capable of revealing wondrous perspectives. It can either encase us in the indifference of the universe, or liberate us.

These two reactions to external reality are called forth in Poul Anderson's *Tau Zero*. A runaway starship cannot brake itself and has no choice but to go on, leaving our galaxy. Boosting ever closer to the speed of light, relativistic effects cause time to slow on board. The ship witnesses the entire outward expansion of our universe, during which whole species rise and fall. Here the science of cosmology paints for the crew a majestic vision outside the ship, including the cyclic collapse inward of all matter and the universe's rebirth into the next expansion.

In direct contrast, inside the craft the crew breaks under the strain of their isolation from any enduring human context. They retreat into endless rounds of sexual misadventures and self-pity. Science is the infinite here, and man falters before it. Yet some of the crew persists, retains its values and wins through to a fresh start on a new planet, in a new phase of cosmic evolution. Hard SF is particularly good at revealing the stark contrast of these two attitudes; I cannot recall a non-SF work which so clearly dramatizes this.

Interestingly, Anderson achieved this symbolic substance while violating the constraint of fidelity to physics. He needed his starship to travel through the remaining 30 billion years of outward expansion, in order to preserve an Aristotelian dramatic unity—keeping the central characters alive. This implied an enormous rate of acceleration, far above what the ship could attain by scooping up interstellar hydrogen and burning it in the onboard fusion reactors.

He was forced to make the ship dive directly through stars themselves, to get more reaction mass. But this would destroy the ship!

How to get around this? He finesses the issue, using an argument from relativity which he knew to be wrong, but hoped was convincing to most of his readership. The hocus-pocus of it sounded quite all right, as long as you didn't think long and hard about it. He succeeded, I believe. Few readers noticed the deft way he slid it by.

This is a clear example of a contradiction between the constraints of hard SF and other, literary aims. Such quandaries arise occasionally in any realistic fiction, but in SF they appear at every turn, powerfully shaping the narrative.

Voices From Above

There are several narrative tones often adopted by hard SF writers, giving part of the "hard feel." They contribute to the reading protocols Delany has pointed out, providing the reader with immediate hints about possible postures toward the material.

1. *Cool, Analytical Tone.* This is commonly used by Clarke, Blish, Clement, Niven, etc. (In Clarke the narrator is often an historian-chronicler, deliberately removed from the action by time.) It mirrors the scientific literature, where precision and clarity are paramount. The true language of the hardest sciences is mathematics; some narratives seek to reflect this pure, dispassionate statement of facts and relationships, without placing an overt human bias on them.[1] This is also the origin of introductory quotations from histories written in the far future, the "Britannica Galactica," etc. James Gunn used this voice in a novel in his most scientifically "hard" novel, *The Listeners,* by inserting lengthy quotations from the scientific literature, wherein radio astronomers debated the philosophy of listening for extraterrestrial intelligence. Of course, there is an esthetic content to science which is also conveyed by this tone. I used this effect myself in a chapter of *Timescape,* in which a physicist keeps on working on the mathematical structure of a theory, rapt in intellectual beauties . . . not noticing that the airplane in which he is a passenger is about to crash.

2. *Cosmic Mysticism.* (Examples: Clarke again in *Childhood's End* and the 2001 novels; Blish's Cities in Flight series; Zebrowski's *Macrolife;* Anderson in *Tau Zero* and elsewhere; Stapledon in *Star Maker* especially, where the disembodied point of view explores and exhausts myriad subuniverses.) This tone is an amplified form of the cool voice and dispassionate overview science affords. Here the objectivity is the viewpoint of a (usually unnamed) higher entity, often Godlike. The progress of physical law, often on a cosmological scale, is seen as the exemplar of a higher logic and scheme, to which humans would be well advised to respond with a mingling of scientific interest and mystical devotion. The emotional impact comes from the search for order (and perhaps meaning) in the universe, and confirmation of the role of reason in doing so. I suspect such vast perspectives fight feelings of powerlessness by putting the reader at one with a universal scheme. We might describe this voice as appropriate for a problem story in which the "problem" the reader needs resolved is, What is the underlying meaning to the apparent indifference of the universe? Is there some purpose to intelligence, to tenacity and curiosity?

3. *The Wiseguy Insider.* This tone appears often in Heinlein, Pohl (*Gateway,* "Day Million"), Haldeman (*The Forever War* and rather more coolly elsewhere), Varley, and Pournelle. It provides a way for initiates to recognize each other, with a kind of boot-camp tone suitable for instructing the raw recruit. There is a conspicuous ease with large matters—the aphorism expanded into social wisdom, a wisecrack relegating whole political views to oblivion, kernels of truth blown into a kind of intellectual puffed rice. I believe this tone appeals to adolescents particularly, who need to extend their sense of personal power—often gained by their knowledge of science and technology—into larger areas, where they may be more uncertain. This tone often carries an air of the newly arrived, and is beloved by those whose first introduction to SF was through the Heinlein 'juveniles' (variant forms of which have since been written by Alexei Panshin, Joe Haldeman, John Varley and myself).

Mainlining the Sci/Tech Fix

Martin Bridgstock[2] has applied the existing analysis of psychologist Liam Hudson[3] to the notions of Brian Stableford[4] and others that fiction, including SF, serves for its readers a maintenance func-

tion—not to instruct, but to reinforce existing assumptions and ideas.
People who become addicted to a particular genre or subgenre, then,
read to get their "fix."

Bridgstock uses two basic categories of reader:

The Convergent Personality, committed to order and rationality
in understanding and controlling the world. This type must still deal
with irrationality and chaos from outside (other people) and from his
inner, subconscious self. We might say in the context of this
paper that he seeks a rational or "technological" fix for the human
condition.

The Divergent Personality, according to Bridgstock, "specializes
in the arts and humanities, is verbally fluent, good at 'creativity' tests,
and perfectly at ease with a world—and a self—that is not fully
rational or controllable." Hudson[5] suggests that in the divergent
personality, "The alien is not eluded, or slain at the boundary wall,
but assimilated and—more or less effectively—defused."

This leads immediately to the suspicion that perhaps we can
usefully relate the hard SF reader to the convergent personality. This
would mean that the primary signature of hard SF is an *attitude*.
Perhaps so; I suspect Godwin's "The Cold Equations" became so
popular precisely because it articulated an attitude many felt but
were unable to express clearly. I personally resist relying solely on
such an easy classification, though it does have a partial validity, a
ring of truth. Yet hard SF does not always take such simplistic views
of the alien, for example—and as I shall argue later, the alien may be
a core issue in hard SF. I myself have argued before[6] that fusing with
the alien is literarily possible, yet I am clearly regarded as a hard SF
author.

We must be careful to note that convergent does not imply
authoritarian, and divergent is not necessarily more "creative" than
convergent. These arts graduates simplifications ignore that scientific
creativity is of a different sort than artistic creation, but no less
difficult or original. In 19th-century literature a romantic equation of
scientist with artist was common, and some SF retains this odd
shibboleth.

Such habits are probably based on both unconscious motivation
and ignorance. Scientists have become collaborators, even team
players, in this century. After all, for writers it is difficult to deal with
figures who do not dominate the foreground, as would the lone
investigator, without slipping automatically into the reverse—the
cliché scientist who is narrow, specialized, alienated, a cog in the

machine (a New Wave staple). Literature has few depictions which do not lapse into these ritual roles. Authors who are perhaps wary but basically supportive of science usually unconsciously choose the first posture, the scientist as noble pseudo-artist.

Thus romanticizing typically seizes on the few figures who stand outside this trend—notably Einstein—and ring the same changes upon this character as did the conventional fictions. At basis this is a failure of imagination or even of simple observation; few scientists work that way. Attitudes, craft, intuition, sociology—in these and other ways art differs from science profoundly. Fiction has so far had little to say about this. Further, by equating the moral issues of science with those of art we lose the special, powerful role science plays in society. Thus in LeGuin's *The Dispossessed*, Shevek did not need to be a scientist at all, and indeed the novel itself is marginally science fiction.

There are prevalent glib generalities about hard SF and the divergent personality—that readers prefer little characterization or stylistic sense—which have obvious exceptions. Although Tom Disch's brilliant essay in *Science Fiction at Large* anticipated much of Bridgstock's argument, I think Disch overgeneralizes with his assessment that hard SF disbars "irony, aesthetic novelty, any assumption that the reader shares in, or knows about, the civilisation he is riding along in, or even a tone of voice suggesting mature thoughtfulness."[7] An obvious counterexample is Clarke, who is often reflective. There is also Lem, who commonly writes not true hard SF, but something closely allied—narratives about the structure of science and its limitations as a man-centered activity—reflecting a familar, ritual Eastern European skepticism which owes more to Hume, I suspect, than Gödel. Typically, those who have used irony or aesthetic novelty widely are the occasional writers of hard SF, such as Pohl, Gunn, James Tiptree, Jr., Greg Bear, Algis Budrys, or Brian Aldiss in the Helliconia trilogy. An odd variant of this is Barry Malzberg's *Galaxies*, a commentary on Campbell and hard SF itself. Its science is dead wrong, but its heavily ironic points are interesting.

Consider the flip side of this argument. Do those SF writers concerned with "soft" sciences, "inner space," stylistic experiments, or even outright fantasy all fit into a single divergent personality category? Here the polarity of the argument is obviously simplistic. With an eye toward keeping the essential argument intact, I suggest we split the divergents into two subgroups: First, the moderate middle who are not threatened by rationality, though they may be disrespectful toward science, thinking it has too many unanticipated side effects, that its mind set leads to rigidity in real-world problem-solving, etc. Second, the far wing—whose genuinely fearful of sci/ tech, unable to cope with a society demanding more rationality and the expertise it implies. These people flee to the glades of fantasy, where *human will* can command powers, bending the universe to our will. The emotional refuge sought by such readers harkens back to an earlier time when the perceived world was smaller, more cozy. (Little fantasy deals with events outside the earth, for example, though the existence of other planets has been apparent throughout modern times.)

The qualities which distinguish the convergent-personality hard SF writers enable them usefully to contemplate "a future which is urban, diverse, technology-driven, and packed with ambiguities."[8] Recently, SF has seen a fusing of the values in this convergent vs. divergent spectrum. I think that blending the two results in inferior literature, for the most part.[9] The convergent/divergent dichotomy can be fruitfully explored further, though our task here is to use its broad concept to map the territory of hard SF, and particularly its readership.

Fixing a Whole: Hard SF as a Class Expression

In an outline of his general overview of SF, as seen from a French Marxist perspective, Gérard Klein stated: "The great charac-teristic of recent SF is a distrust of science and technology, and of scientists, especially in the exact or 'hard' sciences of physics, chemis-try, biology and genetics."[10] He maintains that SF mirrors a social class—the "sci/techs," I shall call them—which sees itself as losing power from the 1960s on, thus confirming the pessimistic writers of the 1950s (Vonnegut in *Player Piano,* Wolfe in *Limbo*). For them "the appearance of imperialism was no longer so benevolent. For SF there followed a period of skepticism, illustrated by the appearance of a new kind of magazine such as *F&SF* and *Galaxy.*"

If Klein were correct, we would expect hard SF to show increas-ing pessimism. Overall, I think it has not. Hard SF is replete with the evocation of the ever-outward movement of mankind, of the majes-tic image of the frontier, of disasters averted by knowledge and hard work. As individuals, I have not found hard SF writers to be more pessimistic about the future than the norm. Quite the opposite, as their strong support for the L–5 Society and scientific research in general attests. Indeed, even when considering such intractable problems as American urban decay, Niven and Pournelle offered a high tech fix with genuine thought behind it in *Oath of Fealty.*[11] Even Ian Watson's occasional hard SF work shows a transcending of the barriers of language, and technical means for communicating with the alien, overcoming our own cultural and specist biases.

Klein holds that "literary works are attempts to resolve through the use of the imagination and in the aesthetic mode, a problem which is not soluble in reality." The problem here is *who* is expressing the worldviews of the sci/techs? Increasingly, outside hard SF, the influx of humanists and arts graduates, Clarion writing-school types, etc., has altered the tone of SF. I fear many of these people are largely antiscience from ignorance. (Though the most prominent Clarion graduate, Ed Bryant, wrote the remarkable hard SF story, "Particle Theory.")

There is also a basic rule about SF: *It is always easier to see problems than propose solutions.* This makes the unforeseen-side-effects story the easiest to write, and the ingenious problem-solving ones much harder. We should expect to see more of the former as arts graduates enter the field, particularly if we ignore that citadel of hard SF, *Analog.*

Hard SF's central mode is the problem story. These appeal to convergent personalities, the true class that fits Klein's description. His error lies in assuming all SF readers are members of his newly oppressed sci/tech class. His examples of writers who have "recognized the advent of tyranny based on monopolies" are Zelazny (*The Isle of the Dead*) and Spinrad (*The Men in the Jungle, Bug Jack Barron*). Yet these are not hard SF writers. (Though Spinrad's atypical *Riding the Torch* is an eloquent hard SF work.) Indeed, I suspect the alienation besetting some regions of SF arises from the usual sources—not the familiar whipping boy of capitalism, but the same forces that operate on all technological societies: the onslaught of fast communications, economies of scale, demographic shifts, and the multinational homogenizing that follows.

Politics In Two Dimensions

Many hard SF writers are described as politically conservative—on the face of it, a surprising classification for people writing the "literature of the future." To study this, I propose a different way of plotting the political spectrum. Keep Right and Left on the horizontal scale (though I feel they are virtually useless terms), perhaps denoting by the Right a desire to retain or return to traditional values, while the Left desires to bring into being new values (Socialist Man, for example). Perpendicular to this, add a scale with Statist at the top (those believing in concentration of power in the hands of a state), in opposition to the Anti-Statist.

I prefer such a two-dimensional scheme to the usual one-dimensional view because it separates people who otherwise get lumped together. Thus the Fascists are Rightist Statists, while Stalin was a Leftist Statist. The striking similarity of Soviet and Nazi architecture, for example, is then not surprising. The Leftist Anti-Statists are Anarchists, while their Rightist brethren are the Libertarians. I have also placed Mao, Hubert Humphrey (HH), Ronald Reagan (RR) and Mitterand where I think they fall. I've also included myself, GB, in the spirit of full disclosure. Of course, this choice of axes may not be the best for clarity; after I advanced this diagram Jerry Pournelle showed me a two-dimensional scheme he had proposed, with Left-Right replaced by "attitude toward planned social progress."[12] Other choices are possible.

Still, my sketch, aside from its possible utility in political theory, does bring up a striking fact, indicated by the circle in the Rightist, Anti-Statist quadrant. This circle, I submit, contains a great majority of hard SF writers. I believe Pournelle, Heinlein, Anderson, Niven, Clement G. Harry Stine, James Hogan, Spider Robinson, Dean Ing and several others fit in. Why, then, should so many hard SF writers end up near the Right Wing Libertarians?

I have no clean answer to this. Writers are lonely types, individualist by nature; this alone may draw them toward the Anti-Statist end. But why should they gravitate to the Right? Ursula LeGuin, not a hard SF writer, occupies a position I would take to be that of Leftist, Anti-Statist. Ian Watson—mostly a soft science fiction writer—is, he tells me, a Trotskyite. Clarke betrays little clear political orientation, other than a desire for cooperation, regarding politics as transient and not what the human race is basically "about."

Hard SF types may reflect the innate conservatism of science itself, building on an edifice of accumulated facts and the provisionally accepted theories which explain them. The scientist's habits of mind—painstaking accuracy, constant rechecking, carefully proceeding from what's proved true, individual verification vs. authority, wariness of ungrounded speculation—may militate against the "leaps of faith" often required by revolutionary social doctrines. But these are only guesses. I submit that, in the spirit of doing botany, this is a curious grouping which a socioliterary theory of hard SF should explain.

It is worth noting that if we include the Stapledon of *Star Maker* as a hard SF writer, then to my knowledge he and Ian Watson are the only left-wing statists on the chart. *Star Maker* is notable in that it attempted to span the physical sciences *and* the social. Stapledon invoked a Marxist dialectical evolution, even on worlds inhabited by insects and sea-creatures, depicting such diverse creatures undergoing schematic evolution, through the rise of a proletariat to the eventual triumphant communism. Despite the vast changes in cosmology and cosmogony since, this strikes me today as the most dated

STATIST

Stalin   Fascists

Mao

Mitterand

HH

Trotsky

LEFT _____|_____ RIGHT

RR

Hard
SF ?

GB

Anarchists   Libertarians

ANTI-STATIST

and naive feature of *Star Maker*. The impulse to be "hard" and mechanistically scientific can merely make one seem naive.

Hard Scientists

"The great simplicity of science will only be seen when we understand its strangeness." (John Wheeler)

Though he lurks in hard SF from the beginning, the scientist has gotten rather unfair, two-dimensional presentation. Discounting the earlier mad scientist cliché, present since Mary Shelley, we confront the lab-smocked cardboard figures who thronged SF stories and films of the 1930s through the 1950s.

Yet many hard SF authors were scientifically trained to some degree (Asimov, Clarke, "Robert Richardson," Pournelle, Hoyle, Anderson, Hogan, Brin, Sheffield, Forward, Stanley Schmidt, Vernor Vinge, Rudy Rucker, G. Harry Stine, Clement, myself). They have direct experience, yet seldom give us deep portraits of scientists. Most of them have been concerned more with problems than with style or character, and so chose as handy conveniences the spaceship captain or savvy lab administrator as natural pivots of their fictions. They subscribed to the conventional wisdom that, in hard SF, things were more important than people, intellect dominates over the heart, and that ideas, rather than experience, will play the leading role in setting, character and plot.[13] This view is still common, but fading, as more sophisticated authors seek to use the traditional territory of hard SF.

Scientists actually *doing* science are boring unless the narrator can get deeply inside them. Conventional literature seldom depicts them.[14] Only devotees, such as the *Analog* readership, will sit still for extended technical discussions between pieces of decorated cardboard. There are some examples of solid SF characterization of scientists—Richardson's stories, some works of Poul Anderson, Paul Preuss's *Broken Symmetries,* others—but not many. A major hurdle in depicting scientists is the lack of science education in our society as a whole. I feel that by showing scientists dealing with a *new* problem—not simply showing a historically validated study under way, as in Eleazar Lipsky's *The Scientists*—we see them most realistically. When the reader can understand the problem he is more involved. What's more, in fiction the reader can know *more* than the scientists, via narrative devices such as the two points of view at different times, which I used in *Timescape*.

My own instinct is that the problems confronting hard SF as it attains a larger audience lie not merely in better characterization or smoother prose, but in integrating *all* the facets of narrative. The constraint of scientific truth must be balanced against aesthetic imperatives. The scientific world view, its methods and unfolding discoveries, calls into question many of the assumptions of conventional fiction. E. L. Doctorow has remarked that for him, "the great root discovery of narrative literature" is that "every life has a theme, and there is human freedom to find it, to create it, to make it victorious." He wonders whether "the very assumption that makes fiction possible, the moral immensity of the single soul, is under derisive question because of The Bomb." By merely substituting the larger canvas of science for The Bomb, we can state the problem SF presents. Though science is a human creation, it casts doubts upon the primacy of humankind in the larger perspectives of time and space. Inevitably, then, SF's goals are sometimes at odds with traditional methods and aims. We cannot expect that a major work of hard SF will read more of less like a conventional novel, but with dollops of science stuck in for reasons of background, plot or atmosphere. That would be a subversion of the potential of the field. SF, by bringing to literature the elements of science, inevitably creates fresh tensions between content and form, character and ground. The resolution of these tensions must be evaluated by critical standards which simply do not yet exist, because the problems are new.

We occasionally hear calls for higher standards in SF which hark back to the bourgeois novel of characterization (Le Guin, in *Science Fiction at Large*). This oversimplifies the difficulties, because one of the prime tasks of SF is conveying strangeness. Portraying people living in a different future is harder than, say, getting into the mind of a 19th-century mayor of Casterbridge. SF presents genuinely new challenges. Should the reader even be sympathetic toward such people? Does making a character "real" for our readers subvert the very strangeness SF strives to convey? How much of what we "know" about character is in fact conventional wisdom of the times, and when is it necessary to destroy these preconceptions before proceeding?

Surely we can say that the use of aliens who live in *outré* environments but talk like 20th-century middle-class Americans undercuts the elements of strangeness in Clement's *Mission of Gravity* and Forward's *Dragon's Egg*. In contrast, Terry Carr's deceptively simple short story, "The Dance of the Changer and the Three," attains an eerie sense of alien character without sacrificing its sense of a different perspective. In non-SF, William Golding's *The Inheritors* and Richard Adams's *The Plague Dogs* strive in this direction. There are a variety of strategies possible; I myself have used some of the techniques of modernism to imply *outré* perspectives, perhaps best illustrated by portions of *In the Ocean of Night* and in a novella, "Starswarmer." Though of course we know that we cannot escape human categories wholly—a point Lem makes repeatedly, often with elephantine humor—the depiction of people or aliens outside our culture represents an aesthetic challenge central to hard SF. Regrettably, it is a challenge seldom met. Although science can give us strange vistas, merely reciting this is not enough; the Cool, Analytical Tone is a limited method. Different, perhaps totally new literary techniques must be developed.

There are tensions between the known and unknown, as Gary Wolfe has discussed, that present unique problems in SF characterization. We must face the fact that our notions of character are themselves ethnocentric, and indeed, so is the assumption that character is central. The perspectives science allows will not always assume that human values or human interactions reign supreme. Characters will be molded by the universe in ways which will not pay even lip service to "humanistic values"—which are often simply the prejudices of Western Europeans inherited from the last few centuries, and sometimes merely those of people working in English departments. Hard SF attempts to face this fact squarely, though not always adroitly or even consciously.

One of the charms of Pohl's short "Day Million" is its street-wise expression of human values shifted by advanced technology. He makes a bizarre technical future appear more understandable, and far less ridiculous, than our own times. Of course, some hard SF authors prefer to stress our continuity with the future, probably because this is a safer narrative strategy. Poul Anderson's moody, reflective and historically knowledgeable hard SF tales often show how certain elements of human behavior will continue into distant, bizarre settings.

Pursuit of the technically complex and aesthetically unfamilar limits the hard SF audience. We might ask ourselves: what maintenance function does the mainstream provide for its readers? In part, I think, it reinforces their perception of humanistic values. Doctorow's assumed "immensity of the single soul" is personally reassuring, and its comfortable, human-centered world far less threatening.

SF, on the other hand, cannot guarantee to support these. It cannot limit itself to the cozy confines of humanism. Thus, its message is unwelcome in some quarters. (Often, people who cannot abide SF do respond to books or shows like *The Hitchhiker's Guide to the Galaxy,* which poke fun at SF clichés, undermining the unsettling strangeness of it all. An alternate, highly successful strategy, is to use the props of SF to retell a sentimental, human-centered story, a la *Star Wars.* These are all evasions of the core of the field.) Given its close association with the sciences which yield the largest vistas in space and time, hard SF will remain inherently difficult—indeed, almost opaque—to many.

This is unfortunate. For I do agree with Gérard Klein that hard SF, at least, is the underground literature of a usually silent class— not merely technology hounds, but men and women who have seen the genuinely strange territory that lies beyond the slick finish of popularized science. It is an underswell of our remorselessly complex age, often fixated by futuristic technology and drawn forward by unfolding vast perspectives.

These people are not mere facile technophiles, as some critics (divergent types themselves, no doubt) imagine. They have a certain ingroupishness, I suppose, and within the small garden of hard SF sometimes loyally mistake a rutabaga for a rose. A minority may seem to propose technological fixes for genuinely irreducible features of life—note, for example, the repeated avoidance of death in Heinlein's work, and the frequent treatment of preservation through cryonics by several hard SF writers (including me). But overall the writers and their natural audience, the scientists themselves, know that science is not a mere stack of facts to be memorized, or an authoritarian structure, or the province of Strangelovian fanatics.

High quality scientists are remarkably diverse, broadly educated, and by no means narrow victims of Snow's polarized two cultures. They usually have read hard SF; sometimes, despite a crammed schedule, they still do. SF uniquely displays the tension between realism and imagination, using fresh materials. And hard SF, they know, plays with the net up. Indeed, this creative constraint is so apparent in hard SF that, like a sonnet, it can bring fresh angles and surprises, intriguing new ways of looking at our consensus reality.

This is, I think, the primary pleasure scientists themselves get from hard SF. They see it not as a literature of hardnosed technophiles and adolescents—though of course there are some—but as an expression of the bittersweet truths emerging in our century, an echo of man's progressive displacement from a God-given center of creation, so that mankind's perspective is now forever, like science, provisional and ambiguous and evolving.

Thomas Burnet's *Sacred Theory of the Earth* and the Aesthetics of Extrapolation

Paul Alkon

The 1983 Eaton Conference call for papers poses the question "Is fiction a medium capable of intelligently using and presenting science?" No problem is more basic to our concerns, but we might also reverse the terms of that question and ask whether science is a medium capable of using fiction. I believe the answer is "yes." Accordingly I want to suggest that in seeing why that is so, in what sense it is true, and when it is the case that science uses fiction, we can find more complete answers to questions about the history of science fiction. We can also thus answer questions of the kind raised by the conference invitation to consider, too, those methods by which science fiction can "appear to create future worlds and situations that are imaginatively yet accurately extrapolated from a series of probable conditions that purport to function according to known laws of science." Without such methods of extrapolation there could be no science fiction nor in some cases, arguably, any science.

Consider geology. Its concern is more often with the past than with the future, but outside of physics, extrapolation to a remote past is very like extrapolation to the distant future, and indeed much science fiction since *The Time Machine* exploits the past imagined by geology no less than its projections about the earth's future: Brian Aldiss's *Cryptozoic,* for instance, or Robert Silverberg's *Hawksbill Station.* For geology, it is in the late 17th century that the interface between science and fiction is especially conspicuous, and perhaps nowhere more revealing than in Thomas Burnet's *Sacred Theory of the Earth:* a work of the 1680s whose first two parts provide a scientific explanation of Noah's flood as well as of differences between pre- and post-diluvian geology, and whose last two parts attempt a scientific explanation of the earth's final conflagration and the ensuing millennium as foretold in the Apocalypse of St. John.[1] In this essay I want to show how extensively Burnet worked out not merely a science of extrapolation but also, and more significantly for the history of science fiction, an aesthetics of extrapolation.

I

Although historians of science grudgingly acknowledge *The Sacred Theory of The Earth* as too influential in its own day to ignore in accounting for the rise of scientific geology, it is usually dismissed rather curtly by them for reasons that should arouse our interest. Thus Frank Manuel notes its primacy among the works known as *physica sacra,* books attempting scientific explanation of biblical allusions to natural events and written mostly by scholars under Newton's influence whose "enthusiasm for harmonizing Scripture and science led to the proliferation of bizarre literary fantasies bearing the trappings of science."[2] This could be a detractor's definition of science fiction. Toulmin and Goodfield are even more explicit in their classic study *The Discovery of Time,* where they concede that Burnet's book "attracted as much attention as Newton's *Principia* itself" but complain that the *"Sacred Theory* reads more like science fiction than serious geology"—as indeed it does to our eyes, and in ways that also caused uneasiness long before the invention of science fiction. Toulmin and Goodfield note, too, that "the French naturalist Buffon described it . . . as 'a fine historical romance.' "[3] Burnet had to deal with similar charges of fictionality brought against the book in his own lifetime, even though Newton himself took it seriously enough to correspond at some length with Burnet about *The Sacred Theory of the Earth,* exchanging speculations about geological realities apparently alluded to by the account of creation and deluge in the Book of Genesis.[4]

To Newton *The Sacred Theory of the Earth* was more science than fiction, and doubtless appealing, too, on account of its attempt to grapple scientifically with the Book of Revelation. Newton also had a profound interest in the nature of apocalypse, as we know from surviving manuscripts of his "Treatise on Revelation" as well as from his posthumously published *Observations Upon the Prophecies of Daniel, and the Apocalypse of St. John* (London, 1733).[5] If David Ketterer is right in arguing for close affinities between the apocalyptic imagination and science fiction, then we should look more carefully than we have at this moment during the late 17th century when the interest of Newton and his circle converged on scientific and apocalyptic extrapolation. Whatever the influence of that convergence on Newton's scientific thought, a matter that has increasingly challenged his biographers, the outcome in Burnet's case was a book of speculations about the distant past and future that has for three centuries suffered the curious fate of provoking many of its readers to reclassify it from science, its intended genre, to fiction. That response suggests that historically at least the borderline between these areas may not be so firm as we are inclined to suppose. Certainly, too, there is much support for those who would go further and agree as I do with Arlen Hansen's assertion that "Scientific theories . . . are functional fantasies, not absolute truths. As products of human inventiveness and creativity, they are as rich a subject for the critic and analyst as is science fiction or any other form of verbal art."[6]

For purposes of defining science fiction, David Ketterer is right to blur the line of demarcation between scientific and fictional modes of writing by insisting as he does that "apocalyptic literature"—presumably of any kind, whether fictional, theological, or even scientific—"*is concerned with the creation of other worlds which exist, on the literal level, in a credible relationship (whether on the basis of rational extrapolation and analogy or of religious belief) with the 'real' world in the reader's head.*" Ketterer stresses *credible* rather than necessarily rational relationships because he thinks "visionary and science-fictional worlds should be understood as performing essentially the same apocalyptic function"—the same function, that is, for their readers of juxtaposing familiar and unfamiliar mental worlds with the result that perspective on the familiar world is altered.[7] Whether or not Ketterer's insight applies quite so widely as he thinks it does to science fiction, reaction to Burnet's *Sacred Theory* at least bears out the idea that for readers similar effects can be elicited by scientifically or religiously extrapolated new worlds.

The possibility of arousing similar responses to extrapolations that we usually regard as having a quite different basis is notable during the 17th century because for Newton, Burnet, and most of their contemporaries science and theology were not only compatible in the sense of coexisting peacefully in ways less possible after Darwin, but mutually reinforcing. In his preface to *The Sacred Theory of the Earth* Burnet insists that "We are not to suppose that any Truth concerning the Natural World can be an Enemy to Religion; for Truth cannot be an Enemy to Truth, God is not divided against himself."[8] Far from only constraining science by setting doctrinal boundaries that inhibited enquiry, theology was more often taken as an inducement to scientific speculation because the Bible provided premises inviting construction of explanatory hypotheses by a process of what we would call thought-experiment. Thus Burnet's theory of how and when mountains first arose on our planet, and indeed all his speculations about planetary geology, stemmed initially from his attempt to account for the amount of water that would have been necessary for Noah's deluge. Given the size of the earth and the height of those flood waters, Burnet reasoned, there must have been "a quantity of Water eight times as great as the Ocean" (I, 17). But this contradicts the other inevitable consideration that if heavy rainfall accumulates at a rate of at most four feet every twenty-four hours then forty days and nights of rain could only result in one hundred sixty feet of water at best, hardly enough to cover mountains or even respectable hills. Assuming no miraculous contravention of the laws of nature, where then did the water for Noah's flood come from? When Burnet turns to the distant future, he confronts the equally vexing question of how (again assuming no miraculous contravention of the laws of nature) the final conflagration will get started given the apparently incombustible nature of so much of our planet. How will all the oceans, rocks, and sand ever catch fire?

Burnet's answers to these and similar questions are less relevant to the history of science fiction than his response to charges that his theories are wrong and his book accordingly no more than a mere work of entertaining fiction. Joseph Keill, for example, wrote that Burnet's "lofty and plausible stile may easily captivate any incautious reader, and make him swallow down for truth, what I am apt to think the Author himself . . . designed only for a Philosophical Romance, seeing that an ordinary Examination thereof, according to the laws of Mechanisme cannot but shew, that . . . in reality none of these wonderful effects, which he endeavors to explain, could have proceeded from the causes he assigns." After more than one hundred pages given to refutation of Burnet's ideas about the earth's geological past, Keill ends on a note of commiseration for anyone whose pleasure at reading *The Sacred Theory of the Earth* may be destroyed by finding out that its theories are wrong: "Perhaps many of his Readers will be sorry to be undeceived, for as I believe, never any

Book was fuller of Errors and Mistakes in Philosophy, so none ever abounded with more beautiful Scenes and surprising Images of Nature; but I write only to those who might perhaps expect to find a true Philosophy in it. They who read it as an Ingenious Romance will still be pleased with their Entertainment."⁹ Keill takes for granted an absolute distinction between true and false writing, between science and fiction, and above all between the pleasures appropriate to each.

In Keill's view neither beautifully described scenes of earth's paradisal state before the flood nor striking descriptions of a drowned world or an earth aflame will redeem a work of speculation whose science is wrong. Nor, conversely, will erroneous theories matter in the least to readers who do not look for a "true philosophy" in their fiction but are content to accept any "Ingenious Romance" as a clever fantasy whose scientific accuracy is irrelevant. Keill assumes in a perfectly Coleridgean way that science and literature are distinct because works of science have for their sole object truth whereas literature, which may be indifferent to scientific accuracy, has for its primary object pleasure. It follows that while there is no harm in enjoying well-written fantasy intended and accepted as such, there *is* something wrong with allowing literary pleasures to sway or even accompany judgment of a scientific hypothesis. For Keill and others like him then and now aesthetic properties are an attribute of litera-ture and the other arts but not of science, which displays only truth or falsehood, not beauty or ugliness.

Burnet denied that proposition. Although he defended his theories at every point where they came under attack, thus claiming for his book the virtue of scientific accuracy, Burnet was not content to rest his defense on the issue of whether his extrapolations were true or false, probable or improbable, as accounts of the distant past and future. Nor was he content to accept the idea that aesthetic considerations are irrelevant to a judgment of whether a scientific hypothesis is properly framed. In short Burnet refused to accept any absolute dissociation of science and aesthetics. He insisted that there is an aesthetic dimension to any theory and also insisted that we should not treat this artistic aspect of science as merely a kind of irrelevant side-effect.

Burnet first characterizes opponents like Keill as people too "apt to distrust every Thing for a Fancy or Fiction that is not the Dictate of Sense, or made out immediately to their senses" and who are therefore inclined to "call such theories as these [in his book] philosophick Romances, and think themselves witty in the Expression; they allow them to be pretty Amusements of the Mind, but without Truth or Reality" (I, xxi). Far from admitting either the charge of falsehood or its implied confinement of all science to induction from observable cases and experiments that may be repeated in a laboratory—conditions impossible for (among others) the cosmologist and historical geologist—Burnet retorts that "If an Angel should write the Theory of the Earth, they would pass the same Judgment upon it" because "where there is Variety of Parts in a due Contexture, with something of surprizing Aptness in the Harmony and Correspondency of them, this they call a Romance; but such Romances must all theories of Nature and Providence be, and must have every Part of that Character with Advantage, if they be well represented" (I, xxi–xxii). Here Burnet's response takes the extraordinary tack of admitting the charge that his theories read like and in fact are like a romance. They are, Burnet concedes, exactly like an entertaining fiction that offers the aesthetic pleasure of variety along with harmonious correspondence of parts that do cohere as a pleasing whole but are not at first perceived to hang together—hence the quality of *surprising* aptness in a properly written ("well represented") theory or romance. For Burnet, however, their likeness is not to be mistaken for identity. While conceding that all skillfully explained theories will indeed have the aesthetic attributes of a good romance, and have those attributes moreover to an even more perfect and pleasing degree than the best fiction can hope to attain ("Must have every Part of that Character with Advantage"), Burnet denies that his or any theories are on that account necessarily false.

Quite the contrary. Because scientific theories reflect nature, which Burnet takes to be harmonious and well-contrived by its great Artificer, it follows that the more accurate a theory is, i.e. the more truthfully it describes the properties of nature, the more such a theory will necessarily have the aesthetic properties that we expect in well-designed fiction: "There is in them [i.e. all theories of nature], as I may so say, a *Plot* or *Mystery* pursued thro' the whole Work, and certain grand Issues or Events upon which the rest depend, or to which they are subordinate; but these Things we do not make or contrive ourselves, but find and discover them, being made already by the great Author and Governor of the Universe" (I, xxii). Thus far from admitting that a theory is rendered suspect to the extent that it offers aesthetic satisfactions like those afforded by fiction, Burnet counters with an argument that such pleasures are more likely to be a sign of accuracy. He winds up this part of his defense with an eloquent assertion that when the laws of nature "are clearly discover'd, well digested, and well reason'd in every Part, there is, methinks, more of Beauty in such a Theory, at least a more masculine Beauty, than in any Poem or Romance; and that solid Truth that is at the Bottom gives a Satisfaction to the Mind, that it can never have from any Fiction how artificial soever it be" (I, xxii). Burnet's conviction that valid scientific theory offers better "satisfaction to the mind" than fiction can ever provide does not lead him to renounce the pleasures of poetry and romance. Instead he appropriates them for science.

If Burnet had foreseen the rise of science fiction he might have argued that its artistic appeal, its early attraction for a male audience, and conceivably even its climb to equality with other genres, may have owed more to the "masculine Beauty" of its science than to its fictive trappings of character and story. Even now we do not sufficiently consider the possibility that science may contribute as much artistry to the genre as do the techniques of fiction. H. Bruce Franklin, for example, in his excellent discussion of Edgar Allen Poe's contribution to American science fiction correctly takes *Eureka,* "Mesmeric Revelation," and "The Fall of the House of Usher" as exemplifying three forms which "may be called pure speculation, pure speculation in a dramatic frame, and dramatized speculation." Neglecting the potential aesthetic attraction of science itself, however, Franklin concludes that a work like *Eureka* "might lose its interest as imaginative fiction if it were to be regarded as serious scientific theory" because for him, as for most of us too much of the time, a thoery is only judged as a statement of fact: "one can reject it as unbelievable, accept it as believable, or dismiss it as already believed."[10] Of course any reclassification from fiction to science or vice versa will in some ways alter response to a work so transformed, as Burnet discovered; and Franklin is right to think that it does make a difference whether we take a work for science or literature.[11] But such a change would not necessarily rule out response to imaginative qualities because, as Burnet understood very well, even a pure scientific speculation may seem appealing or unappealing according to current aesthetic tastes *as well as* true or false according to current canons of verifiability. Mathematicians still describe their proofs as not only valid or invalid but as elegant or inelegant, and prefer the

most elegant as the best mathematics. Conversely and even more
significantly for science fiction, aesthetic qualities apparent in pure
scientific speculation may contribute to the success of a fiction in
which such speculation plays an important role. Viewed from our
present perspective, Burnet's defense of his theories as both true and
beautiful should suggest in the first place the possibility that "hard
science" embedded within a work designed for some nonscientific
purpose may not only contribute to verisimilitude or provide the
attraction of ideas interesting on their own account as extrapolations
to a possible future, but sometimes also determine the underlying
aesthetic appeal of the narrative to which they give shape.

II

Throughout *The Sacred Theory of the Earth* Burnet scatters
many other observations on the aesthetic affinities of scientific
theories and fiction. Thus after some two hundred pages explaining
his view of planetary formation from the original chaos mentioned in
Genesis through those geological changes that resulted in transformation of a smoothly spherical earth to the mountainous postdilu-
vian world that we inhabit, Burnet pauses to anticipate the potential
objection that he has indulged in a bit of fictionalizing. Again as in
defending himself against Keill, Burnet admits the charge but denies
its power to discredit theories which by the nature of all theories *must*
be like fictions:

> How fully or easily soever these things may answer nature, you will say,
> it may be, that all this is but an *Hypothesis;* that is, a kind of Fiction or
> Supposition that Things were so and so at first, and by the Coherence
> and Agreement of the Effects with such a Supposition, you would argue
> and prove that they were really so. This I confess is true, this is the
> Method, and if we would know any Thing in Nature further than our
> Senses go, we can know it no otherwise than by an *Hypothesis.* (I, 201)

Burnet is willing to recognize that any hypothesis is "a kind of
Fiction" and face the fact that scientists must invent such fictions in
order to perform the imaginative exercise of extrapolating from the
very narrow sphere of what we can observe to the circumstances
governing other realms whose conditions are beyond direct observation on account of their remoteness in space or time:

> When Things are either too little for our Senses, or too remote and
> inaccessible, we have no Way to know the inward Nature, and the

> Causes of their sensible Properties, but by reasoning upon an *Hypothesis* . . . if you would know the Nature of a Comet, or of what Matter the Sun consists . . . you can do this no otherwise than by an *Hypothesis;* and if that *Hypothesis* be easy and intelligible, and answers to all the *Phaenomena* of those two Bodies, you have done as much as a *Philosopher* or as *human Reason* can do. (I, 201-202)[12]

To this admission that scientists must often resort to "a kind of Fiction or supposition" made to fit all the known facts and account for them as easily and clearly as possible, Burnet adds (in "A Review of the Theory of the Earth" printed by way of summation after the fourth part) further clarification of the relationship between the form and content of theories: "As to the Form, the Characters of a regular Theory seem to be these three: *Few and easy Postulatums; Union of Parts; and a Fitness to answer, fully and clearly, all the Phaenomena to which it is to be apply'd"* (II, 327). This is not merely a restatement of the familiar principle of Ockham's razor in its stress upon economy of explanation ("few and easy Postulatums"). It is also a definition that includes a logical principle of formal unity ("Union of Parts") that for Burnet is also an aesthetic virtue in scientific theory no less than in any other "kind of Fiction."

Accordingly Burnet finds it necessary to warn his readers against the fallacy of mistaking such unity, which is the mark of a well-designed theory no less than of a well-designed story, for proof of validity: "bare coherence and Union of Parts is not a sufficient Proof; the Parts of a Fable or Romance may hang aptly together, and yet have no Truth in them: This is enough indeed to give the Title of a just Composition to any Work, but not of a true one; till it appear that the Conclusions and Explications are grounded upon good natural Evidence, or upon good Divine Authority" (II, 328). If truth is beautiful and if scientific theories should be no less well-composed than romances in point of unity, it does not in Burnet's view follow that beauty is a proof of truthfulness. This issue would be less problematic for him if he thought there were no aesthetic response elicited by scientific theories. But since in Burnet's opinion all such theorizing will elicit pleasure to the degree that it satisfies the formal requirement of "Coherence and Union of Parts," it becomes especially important to guard against accepting merely attractive extrapolations as valid without some external basis for judging their probability.

For Burnet the Bible is one such basis providing "good Divine Authority" for many of his premises, as he notes again in reminding his readers that "The Matter and principal Parts of this *Theory* are such things as are recorded in Scripture: We do not feign a Subject, and then discant upon it, for Diversion; but endeavour to give an intelligible and rational Account of such Matters of Fact, past or future, as are there specified and declared" (II, 324). Here and elsewhere Burnet is so very careful to draw the line between fiction and science in terms of intention because of his acute awareness that from the standpoint of how scientific writing affects readers no such distinction is necessarily apparent. There would be no need for him to insist so much upon biblical and other evidence for the veracity of "the principal Parts of this *Theory*" if it were not that theory—his *Sacred Theory of the Earth* or any well-designed and well-written theory—provides the very same kind of entertainment ("Diversion") that results when writers of fiction simply make things up ("feign a Subject"). Paradoxically, Burnet distinguishes so often between science and fiction because he realized better than most that they differ in the claims they make upon our assent but not necessarily in the pleasures they afford.

Where the Bible is silent and cannot be taken for a source of facts serving as a basis for extrapolation, there are for Burnett especially acute problems in separating the incidental pleasures afforded by science from the application of logical tests for veracity. The difficulty is that such tests often may be measures of that "coherence and Union of Parts" within a theory which, while testifying to its proper scientific economy of explanation, also account for its resemblance to "the Parts of a Fable or Romance" that "may hang aptly together, and yet have not Truth in them." Thus when Burnet considers possible natural causes for the future conflagration that will destroy the earth as we know it and usher in those geological changes necessary for establishment of the millennium as it is described in the Revelation of St. John, two theories are dismissed: Burnet rejects as unsatisfactory extrapolations both the idea that the earth will move closer to the sun, thus scorching the planet's surface, and the idea that central fires will erupt from the earth's core with the same result. He concedes that the sun and the fires burning within the earth "are potent Causes indeed, more than enough to destroy this Earth, if it was a thousand Times bigger than it is." But he then applies a test that is at once aesthetic and probabilistic:

> For that very Reason, I suspect they are not the true Causes; for God and Nature do not use to employ unnecessary Means to bring about

> their Designs. Disproportion and Over-sufficiency is one sort of false
> Measures, and 'tis a Sign we do not thoroughly understand our Work,
> when we put more Strength to it than the Thing requires. . . . This
> Supposition of burning the Earth, by the Sun drawing nearer and nearer
> to it, seems to be made in Imitation of the Story of *Phaeton,* who driving
> the Chariot of the Sun with an unsteady Hand, came so near to the
> Earth, that he set it on Fire. (II, 66)

This shrewd guess that the myth of Phaeton underlies one common
theory explaining the future destruction of the earth is further evidence of Burnet's sensitivity to the role of fiction in the formation of
scientific extrapolations.

His objection is not so much to the fictive origin of that theory in
the Phaeton legend as to the resulting scientific fallacy of postulating
a stronger force than is necessary to account for the phenomenon in
question. "Over-sufficiency" of causation is equated in Burnet's
phrase with "Disproportion"—presumably disproportion between
cause and effect, which is to say imbalance between their respective
sizes. While such disproportion implies a lack of symmetry that could
be equated with ugliness of a kind absent from God's well-
proportioned universe, Burnet's use of "disproportion" as almost a
synonym for "over-sufficiency" here evokes a standard for measur-
ing theories that is more logical than aesthetic. It is a standard,
moreover, that Burnet applies to discard a theory derived from a
famous myth that is rejected as the basis for a scientific hypothesis not
because it is a fiction but because it is a fiction that leads to an
implausible extrapolation about the future.

III

For Burnet the aesthetic affinities of science and fiction create
also a blurring of the borderline between rhetorical effects due
primarily to stylistic choices and those effects elicited in readers by
the very nature of scientific theory. For Burnet as for other good
critics the boundary between style and content often dissolves. Thus
he explains that for both the scientist formulating theories and the
reader apprehending them there will be a two-stage pleasure inherent in the process of discovering a problem and arriving at a solution
however provisional:

> There is a double Pleasure in Philosophy; first, that of Admiration,
> whilst we contemplate Things that are great and wonderful, and do not

yet understand their Causes. . . . Then the second Pleasure is greater and more intellectual, which is that of distinct Knowledge and Comprehension, when we come to have the Key that unlocks those Secrets, and see the Methods wherein those Things come to pass that we admir'd before: The Reasons why the World is so or so, and from what Causes Nature, or any Part of Nature, came into such a State." (I, 196–97)

In this and related comments Burnet switches his focus from the aesthetic properties of well-framed theories to the closely related issue of accounting for those pleasures that reward the activity of proposing—or reading about—such theories. He assumes that only if our sense of the problematic nature of some phenomenon is aroused will we feel the delight of arriving at an explanation. The greater our sense of initial bafflement at an apparently inexplicable event the greater will be our initial response of "Admiration," in its then-current sense of surprise, awe, and wonderment—a response which Burnet legitimizes by remarking, too, that although "Admiration proceeds from Ignorance, yet there is a certain Charm and Sweetness in that Passion" (II, 196). In literary criticism admiration was then the accepted category of appropriate response to the sublime, that is to the awe-inspiring whether in nature or in such lofty kinds of writing as the epic.[13]

In a scientific treatise admiration may be heightened by inviting particular attention to the apparent difficulties that stand in the way of formulating an adequate explanation of the phenomena in question, and by delaying to the latest possible point in the text a statement of the hypothesis that will resolve the reader's perplexity. Burnet not only resorts to both strategies but he invites readers to notice that he is doing so, thereby explicitly attempting to enhance their pleasure still further by making them acutely aware of the suspense they are intended to feel, and in his view *should* feel, while awaiting the relief of an explanatory hypothesis. After promising, for example, "a double Satisfaction to the Mind, both to shew it a fair and intelligible Account of the general Deluge . . . and likewise to shew it how the Mountains were brought forth," Burnet announces that he "must beg leave to draw a Curtain before the Work for a while, and to keep your Patience a little in suspense, till Materials are prepar'd" (I, 44–45). Instead of merely getting on with his exposition to arrive in due course at an appropriate hypothesis after first setting out the relevant facts, Burnet, by invoking an image of drawing the curtain while his audience waits "in suspense" for the ensuing performance, creates an implied metaphor of the author-scientist as impresario.

So too in considering the problem posed for geologists by Noah's flood, Burnet first states the dilemma confronting anyone who seeks a scientific explanation of how there came to be so much water as he has just proved to his satisfaction must have been necessary: "Either there must be new waters created on purpose to make a Deluge, or there could be no Deluge as it is vulgarly explained; there not being Water sufficient in Nature to make a Deluge of that kind" (I, 28). Some such statement is necessary to Burnet's argument. What is not necessary to the argument itself but only to ensure that readers appreciate the aesthetic dimension of it and all such attempts to identify a problem before resolving it is Burnet's next sentence defending his decision to state a difficulty so sharply: "We do not tie this Knot with an Intention to puzzle and perplex the argument finally with it; but the harder it is ty'd, we shall feel the Pleasure more sensibly when we come to loose it" (I, 28). Instead of arguing only on logical grounds that no theory is likely to be valid if there is insufficient enumeration of the facts which it is to account for, Burnet here stresses the heightened *pleasure* that will result from first tying the knot tightly by starting with a thorough statement of all the obstacles to a satisfactory explanation.

Elsewhere Burnet uses the same metaphor of tying a knot when he concentrates more on the sheer logical necessity rather than the aesthetic advantages of attending to difficulties instead of ignoring or minimizing them. Upon surveying potential natural causes of the final conflagration, for example, Burnet remarks that "The Difficulty, no doubt, will be chiefly from the great Quantity of Water that is about our Globe; whereby Nature seems to have made Provision against any Invasion by Fire." The problem cannot be avoided, however, because "To state the Case fairly, we must first represent the Difficulty of setting the Earth on fire; tye the Knot, before we loose it; that so we may the better judge whether the Causes that shall be brought into View, may be sufficient to overcome so great Opposition" (II, 61). Here Burnet stresses the importance of first tying the knot in order to allow assessment of any theory's explanatory force. If as Burnet is so careful to explain, any "regular Theory" must have "a Fitness to answer, fully and clearly, *all* the Phaenomena to which it is to be apply'd," it follows that all relevant phenomena must be noted to assess any theory. What Burnet's metaphor adds to this almost tautological point is a sense that the scientist is not merely someone who responds, however ingeniously, to problems set by nature. Nor is the scientist a kind of brutal though efficient Alexander cutting the knot which he could neither tie nor untie. Instead Burnet's metaphor figures the scientist as a creative inventor of the knots which as impresario he deals with at the moment calculated to make his audience not only understand nature more fully but in doing so "feel the pleasure more sensibly."[14]

If the detective story had existed in the 17th-century Burnet might have remarked that scientists no less than mystery writers may best heighten their readers' pleasure by employing a narrative sequence that reverses the order of cause and effect: first the crime, then identification of the criminal; first an account of the scientific mystery of baffling phenomena to be accounted for, then a theory explaining the causes that brought about or will bring about those phenomena. This expository structure of mystery-followed-by-solution, of effect followed by explanation of its causes, underlies much science and mystery writing despite their other obvious differences. To Burnet's credit he recognized this structure as accounting for literary pleasures in addition to enhancing scientific validity. When the same expository structure of creating for readers a problem and then outlining its solution is adopted in science fiction, the resulting pleasures will be potentially common to both science and fiction, not necessarily only pleasures grafted onto a scientific idea by embedding it within a fictional narrative.

Whether a particular scientific problem (or group of related problems) is initially set and then resolved, as in so many of Hal Clement's novels, or whether there is set initially the more general problem of introducing readers to a strange future or past world and then accounting for its attributes by scientific explanations, the aesthetic situation for readers is precisely that explained by Burnet: the harder the knot is tied by presenting a challenging world whose outlines are at first apparently inexplicable in scientific terms, the greater will be the pleasures when credible scientific explanations are provided. Works like *Solaris* or *The Investigation* that present a problem but withhold a satisfactory scientific solution show what may be done by departing from the "hard-core" pattern of scientific exposition whose aesthetic dimensions Burnet so clearly recognized. Of course I do not claim that he foresaw the structure of science fiction or anticipated its existence so long before there was any such genre. I do suggest that throughout *The Sacred Theory of the Earth* Burnet was not only speculating as scientifically as he could about the distant past and future but also working out explicitly for such extrapolation an aesthetics that could serve perfectly well for much science fiction. I suspect, too, that the existence of such an aesthetic "in place" as it were, and available to accomodate new forms by the beginning of the 18th century, is one of the conditions favoring (though not necessarily causing) the birth of science fiction.

IV

For viable science fiction there had to be available not only an appropriate aesthetics along with, of course, enough scientific activity to provide ideas and encourage speculation about their further applications in a changing world, but there also had to be at hand credible ways of dealing with the future. Astrology was being discredited.[15] Religious prophecy was not easily displaced by secular methods of extrapolation, as Newton's preoccupation with apocalyptic visions of the future may remind us. His attempts to explicate the Book of Daniel and the Apocalypse of St. John had for him if not for us almost equal standing with his attempts to work out predictive laws of planetary motion. In that 17th-century context of scientific and religious concern with the shape of statements about the future, Burnet (like Newton) is conspicuous for his acceptance of both prophecy and science as well as for being remarkably attentive to the problem of choosing an appropriate style for each of these modes of dealing with the future.

Establishing credibility is, as Burnet was keenly aware, the fundamental difficulty for any writer who invites us to imagine things to come: "We are naturally heavy of Belief, as to Futurities, and can scarce fancy any other Scenes, or other State of Nature, than what is present, and continually before our Eyes" (II, 130). One way to "cure our Unbelief" about accounts of the future, Burnet notes, is simply to "take Scripture for our Guide, and keep within the Limits of its Predictions" (II, 130). This way of dealing with the future is appealing on account of its certainty because the Bible can be relied upon as a repository of true, not fictitious, accounts of the future: "We must not imagine," Burnet insists, "that the Prophets wrote like the Poets; feigned an Idea of a romantick State, that never was, nor ever will be, only to please their own Fancies, or the credulous

People" (II, 243). The catch, however, is that even if prophecy is
taken as truth, not fiction, and accorded a higher degree of certainty
than the best scientific extrapolations, "the limits of its Predictions"
are notoriously hard to determine because the prophetic style of
writing is vague: "though the Sum and general contents of a Prophecy be very intelligible, yet the Application of it to Time and Persons
may be very lubricous. There must be Obscurity in a Prophecy, as
well as Shadow in a Picture" (II, 59). This creates for the writer of
science (or fiction) attempting to stay within the limits of scriptural
predictions the interpretive problem, with which Burnet like Newton
and many others wrestled extensively, of clarifying what in the Bible
is obscure. One result apparent throughout *The Sacred Theory of the
Earth,* though most striking in its chapters on the conflagration and
millennium, is what might be called hermeneutic extrapolations:
predictions about the future and speculations about the past whose
content is determined exclusively by principles of biblical interpretation rather than by such interpretation in conjunction with principles
of natural science.[16]

There are several places where Burnet momentarily abandons
scientific speculation and resorts to biblical interpretation alone for
dealing with matters such as "the Time of the *Conflagration*" which
"no Foresight of ours, or Inspection into Nature, can discover to us"
and where consequently the "Method . . . of Prediction from natural
Causes" must be "laid aside as impracticable" (II, 35). It is only in
Book Four, however, where Burnet probes the most "dark and
remote Futurities" of the postapocalyptic millennium that he almost
totally renounces the role of scientist in favor of turning for guidance
to prophecy. That book, "Concerning the New Heavens, and New
Earth, and Concerning the Consumation of all Things," opens with a
"Preface to the Reader" urging those unwilling or unable to make
such imaginative leaps into the distant future to stop reading: "rest
here, and be content with that Part of the Theory which you have
seen already" (II, 177–78). Burnet assumes a kind of absolute temperamental distinction between those future-oriented (or obsessed)
readers willing to engage in such mental time-travel as he proposes to
wind up with, and those who refuse to see any value at all in such
exercises: "To whom . . . such Disquisitions seem needless, or
over-curious, let them rest here; and leave the Remainder of this
Work, which is a kind of PROPHECY concerning the STATE of
things after the Conflagration, to those that are of a Disposition

suited to such Studies and Enquiries" (II, 178). He recognized what I believe is still the case, that speculation about the distant future is not only a matter of finding appropriate methods, whether scientific or religious, and choosing a suitable style of writing, but of addressing an audience for whom the very possibility of such speculation seems worth pursuing. Many who accept other topics with at worst indifference angrily resist visions of the future. Burnet saw what the hostility so often aroused by science fiction still painfully demonstrates, that even the right aesthetics of extrapolation will never work for the wrong readers. All genres must find a sympathetic audience, to be sure, but that quest has perhaps been hardest for those concerned with envisioning the future.

If not the first, Burnet is surely among the earliest English writers to draw a sharp and necessary distinction between those for whom extrapolation *may* succeed because they accept the legitimacy of probing the distant future, and those for whom extrapolation can *never* succeed no matter how it is done because the very activity is suspect. What aroused Burnet to the unusual step of warning off the latter class of readers—a warning that he did not find necessary when writing the first three books of *The Sacred Theory of the Earth*—is his awareness that when dealing with the post-apocalyptic millennium and what lies even further into the future it is most often the case that *"natural Reason. . .* sees no Track to follow in these unbeaten Paths, nor can advance one Step farther." That leaves only the writer's imagination aided by ability to interpret the hints provided in "Holy Scriptures, the Oracles of God . . . and where *Human Faculties* cannot reach, a seasonable Help and Supply to their Defects" (II, 202). But turning to scripture for such help and providing extrapolations based upon interpretation of it does not resolve the aesthetic problem of how to find an appropriate style for what Burnet calls "the Remainder of this Work, which is a kind of PROPHECY"—but a kind very different from the Bible itself. The fourth book of *The Sacred Theory of the Earth* shows Burnet's view of the stylistic options available to a writer dealing with the distant future in a transitional form that is neither pure religious prophecy, nor primarily science (taken as application of "natural Reason" to the "method of prediction from natural causes"), nor yet outright fiction in the sense of storytelling on an apocalyptic theme.

One possibility for dealing with the past as well as the future was to mimic the obscure style of prophecy itself. Thus in commenting on

the difficulties of squaring with the Bible his or similar scientific
extrapolations far backwards in time to the period of planetary
formation Burnet notes:

> The Reflections that are made in several Parts of the divine Writings,
> upon the Origin of the World, and the Formation of the Earth, seem to
> me to be writ in a Style something approaching to the Nature of a
> prophetical Style. . . . The Expressions are lofty, and sometimes abrupt,
> and often figurative and disguis'd. . . . And it commonly happens so in
> an enthusiastick or prophetick Style, that by reason of the Eagerness
> and Trembling of the Fancy, it doth not always regularly follow the
> same even Thread of Discourse, but strikes many times upon some
> other Thing that has relation to it, or lies under or near the same view.
> (I, 124)

This prophetic way of writing about the distant past is in Burnet's
view also the style of apocalyptic visions of the future, for as he goes
on to remark it is a style of which "we have frequent Examples in the
Apocalypse, and in that Prophecy of our Saviour's, *Math. xxiv* concerning the Destruction of *Jerusalem* and of the World" (I, 125).
After the meaning of such biblical passages about the past or future
has been detemined, there would be disadvantages to adopting an
equally apolcalyptic style of lofty, abrupt, figurative, disguised, and
digressive writing when attempting to explain in scientific terms as
Burnet does "the Origin of the World, and the Formation of the
Earth," or its future destiny. More desirable for such works, as the
Royal Society had recognized in urging all scientists to adopt a plain
style, is clarity achieved by sticking to the point at hand in straightforward prose that avoids the obscurity of figurative language.[17]
Seventeenth-century science encouraged expression of even the
most visionary apocalyptic imaginings in a totally secular prose style.
Hence Burnet's attempt to reassure readers that "As to the Style, I
always endeavour to express myself in a plain an perspicuous manner; that the Reader may not lose Time, nor wait too long, to know
my Meaning" (II, "Preface to the Reader," n.p.).

At odds with the scientific pressure to adopt such a plain style
throughout any work dealing with the future, however, is Burnet's
conviction that everyone is more resistant to such speculation than to
accounts of the past or present. Convinced as he was that "we are
naturally heavy of Belief, as to Futurities," Burnet remarks of his
own style, and by way of advice to other writers, that "especially
when Things future are to be represented, you cannot use too strong

Colours, if you would give them Life, and make them appear present to the Mind" (II "Preface," n.p.). Thus in accounts of the future particularly vivid descriptions are called for in a way that may clash with the requirements of a plain style. Attempts to envision the apolcalypse even in its scientific aspects, moreover, cannot be altogether separated from moral concerns or a tendency to arouse terror, and accordingly in Burnet's view must be designed to express as well as elicit some emotion: "For to see a World perishing in Flames . . . one must be very much a Stoick, to be a cold and unconcerned Spectator of all this. And when we are mov'd ourselves, our Words will have a Tincture of those Passions which we feel. Besides, in moral Reflections which are design'd for Use, there must be some Heat, as well as dry Reason " (II, "Preface," n.p.). Clarity in scientific writing about the future did not for Burnet imply cold detachment.

Far more problematic than the intrusion of some emotion-laden prose, however, is Burnet's disturbing thought that the more success-ful he or anyone is in painting a vivid picture of the final conflagra-tion, the less credible that picture will seem to its audience: "If one should now go about to represent *the World on Fire,* with all the Confusions that necessarily must be in Nature, and in Mankind upon that Occasion, it would seem to most Men a Romantick Scene: Yet we are sure there must be such a Scene" (II, 155). Of the writer's problem with such apocalyptic events Burnet also remarks ruefully: "He that comes nearest to a true Description of them, shall be look'd upon as the most extravagant" (II, 144). Burnet thus confronted the paradox that where an apocalyptic future is concerned, what on the basis of accepted assumptions may be the closest possible approxima-tion to "a true description" will *seem* more fantastic the more fully its implications are portrayed in passages of vividly rendered detail. There will be constraints upon verisimilitude posed by the difference between such remote future possibilities and everyday reality as it is experienced in the reader's present life.

Burnet not only admitted this difficulty more candidly than most writers who face it, he responded by winding up his book of scientific and religious extrapolation in a way justified neither on scientific nor religious grounds but instead by aesthetic considerations arising from the need to provide an appropriate sense of an ending that does not go beyond what readers will accept as credible. Limits are set by the literary test of versimilitude, not by religious doctrine or by the scientific laws of probability. Instead of closing *The Sacred Theory of the Earth* with a portrait of the postconflagration millennium based on details suggested by the Bible, Burnet takes up the even more highly conjectural matter of the earth's final fate: "The last Thing that remains to be considered and accounted for, is the Upshot and Conclusion of all; namely, what will become of the Earth after the thousand Years expir'd?" (II, 316). Because Revelation is silent on this topic "all Parties are equally . . . free, to give their Opinion, *What* will be the *last State and Consummation* of this Earth" (II, 316–17). Burnet tells why he believes "that the Earth after the last Day of Judgment, will be chang'd into the nature of a Sun, or of a fix'd Star, and shine like them in the Firmament" (II, 317). But this theory is more appealing on account of its pleasingly harmonious vision of a world ending as it began than on account of the hard scientific evidence in its favor, as Burnet concedes:

> I have no direct and demonstrative Proof of this I confess, but if Planets were once fixed Stars, as I believe they were, their Revolution to the same State again, in a great Circle of Time, seems to be according to the Methods of Providence, which loves to recover what was lost or decay'd . . . and what was originally good and happy, to make it so again, all Nature, at last, being transform'd into a like Glory with the Sons of God. (II, 318)

In the last paragraph of Book Four Burnet reiterates that this idea cannot be proposed "otherwise than as a fair Conjecture" (II, 319–20). But he invites readers to join him in imagining this final transformation of the earth into a sun, and on that note bids farewell both to our planet and to his survey of its past and future: "There we leave it; having conducted it for the Space of seven thousand Years thro' various Changes, from a *dark Chaos to a bright Star*" (II, 320).

That eloquent final sentence with its evocative juxtapostion of planetary beginning and ending is surely intended to linger in the reader's mind. The antithetical clause is a striking departure from Burnet's usually more plain style. More revealing of the aesthetic principle that prompted his conclusion, however, is Burnet's earlier explanation of just why he refrained from beginning *The Sacred Theory of the Earth* with what might have seemed an even more neatly balancing account of the earth's original state as in fact a bright star too, not a dark chaos: "We took our Rise no higher than the Chaos, because that was a known Principle, and we were not willing to amuse the Reader, with too many strange Stories; as that, I am sure would have been thought one, TO HAVE brought this Earth from a fixed Star, and then carried it up again into the same Sphere; which yet, I believe, is the true Circle of natural Providence" (II, "Preface" to Book Four, sig. N2ʳ). Burnet's scientific conviction about the earth's ultimate origin as a fixed star thus gave way to an aesthetic consideration that set limits on the backward reach in time of his book.

Rather than begin its discussion of plantetary formation "higher," that is earlier, than creation from the chaos mentioned in Genesis, Burnet chose to start with that "known principle' not primarily because of its authority or truthfulness (which he accepts) but on account of its familiarity. Burnet hoped thereby to avoid the danger of straining credibility by providing *too many* strange stories. Again the interchangeability of terms such as *story* and *principle,* as elsewhere of *fictional* and *hypothesis* is telling. Burnet does not evade the resemblance of hypothesis and narration so far as concerns their effects on readers. Rather he faces the consequence that scientific speculation, no less than other forms of writing, may be constrained by the literary test of verisimilitude. Truth as determined by scientific canons of probability gives way as a principle governing the boundaries of discussion to the question of what will *seem* true to readers. Burnet is willing to provide speculations that will read like "strange Stories" but he is not willing to provide "too many" of them because that would diminish credibility of the work as a whole. He thought it better to publish a scientifically incomplete theory of the earth than to risk rejection of a more accurate because more completely explained version that would have seemed false thanks to its unremitting accuracy.

V

Burnet does not provide a rule for resolving conflict between the scientific requirement that explanations be as complete as possible and the literary requirement that extrapolations must also manage, even where necessary at the expense of completeness by suppression of astonishing details, to seem credible. But then neither has anyone else arrived at a rule for dealing with that kind of conflict, nor perhaps would it be a good thing to look for one. Appreciation of the problem is very much to Burnet's credit. So is his acute awareness that *all* speculations, no matter how scientific, about the far past and future must have the air of "strange Stories." This is of a piece with his many other remarkable comments on the resemblance of science to fiction, and his sensitivity to the constraints imposed upon both by accepted notions of verisimilitude as well as by standards of coherence, proportion, unity, and what he calls the necessity in scientific writing to pursue "a *Plot* or *Mystery* . . . thro' the whole Work."

Even today, as I have tried to suggest, critics may find in Burnet's comments on the pleasures of science a useful reminder that the aesthetic appeal of much science fiction arises more from the structure of its scientific ideas and their exposition than from narration of adventures set in motion by those ideas. I do not invite attention to *The Sacred Theory of the Earth* so much on account of its lessons for critics, however, as to urge that in searching for the origins of science fiction we ought to pay closer attention than we have to the *forms* of scientific writing that accompanied those scientific, social, and technolgical transformations that somehow occasioned the new genre. I have argued here that insofar as it is useful to think of science fiction as among other things one manifestation of the apocalyptic imagination we may profitably ask how a more literal concern with religious visions of apocalypse prompted 17th-century scientists to write about the past and future.[18] There is, of course, no obvious much less inevitable, track from their speculations to the development of science fiction or even its ancillary genre, the tale of the future. I do not mean to imply that attempts by scientists like Burnet and Newton to deal rationally with apocalyptic visions were in any way that is now apparent direct causes of those later, more secular, and less scientific works of literature that attempt credible stories of future worlds which invite us to reconsider our own times. Still I do mean to imply that if we wish to recover those early intellectual contexts favoring the rise of science fiction we had better take to heart Burnet's insistence that good science displays artistry as well as accuracy. The forms of that artistry throughout enlightenment scientific discourse deserve further investigation. What I hope to have demonstrated by considering *The Sacred Theory of the Earth* is that by the end of the 17th century in England we can find in a work whose scientific conclusions were, like so many others, soon discredited significant evidence of more durable literary theories that amount to a viable aesthetics of extrapolation. My hypothesis is that the existence of such a well-developed aesthetics for extrapolation contributed to the climate of opinion that allowed favorable reception for subsequent forms of writing about the future.

The Language of the Future in Victorian Science Fiction

Herbert Sussman

By discussing "hard" science fiction we imply its difference from its opposite, what we might call "soft" SF. If we consider hard science fiction, in somewhat broad terms, as that form focusing on changes brought about by science, technology, the machine; organized about readers' expectations of prediction or extrapolation; and employing the set of literary conventions we call "realism," then soft science fiction is more occupied with consciousness than technology, appeals not to a sense of probability but to the imagining of alternate worlds, and works in the mode of the visionary, tends toward fantasy.

Discussion of the form of science fiction, in many cases, is governed by the opposition between these categories—extrapolative versus alternative, credibility versus fantasy—although, as has often been suggested by critics, the specific work of science fiction inevitably combines both. In the history of science fiction, however, the sharp divergence of these two forms is often seen as recent, exemplified in the recent distinction between "hard" and "new wave." This is not a new phenomenon, for during an earlier time in the life of the form, during the great period of growth at the end of the Victorian era, when writers became self-aware of working with others in a clearly defined genre—the history of the future—this opposition was also strongly felt. In particular, William Morris in writing *News from Nowhere* self-consciously rejected the hard formal elements available to him in the genre, primarily because of the ideological implications of these Victorian languages of the future. Yet, for all his turning to soft elements at this particular historical moment, Morris created a work in which the opposition dissolves, that fuses the realist and the visionary, the hard and the soft.

First, a few relevant hard facts about Morris' career. Morris began his artistic life as a poet within the Pre-Raphaelite movement, a late-Victorian continuation of romanticism. While continuing to write poetry, Morris, influenced by John Ruskin's teaching, turned to design, eventually becoming the head of what we would now call a design firm, producing fabrics, wallpaper, stained glass, and furniture, such as the Morris chair. Although (or perhaps because) he was born into an upper-middle-class family and continued to draw upon a large independent income throughout his life, Morris became in the 1880s an active participant in the growing socialist movement. Much of his prodigious energy was spent in what he called "the Cause," traveling through England to address workers and organizing his own faction, the Socialist League, in the ideological wars of the movement.

   News from Nowhere was written as part of this political activism. More particularly, it emerged out of Morris' indignation at the socialist doctrine in Edward Bellamy's enormously popular *Looking Backward* of 1888. After reading that work, Morris said that he "wouldn't care to live in such a Cockney paradise as he [Bellamy] imagines . . . if they brigaded *him* into a regiment of workers he would just lie on his back and kick,"[1] and he wrote *News* in reply. It was first published in *The Commonweal*, the journal of the Socialist League financed and edited by Morris, in 1890 and reprinted in inexpensive paperback form so as to reach a large audience one year later.

   In the opening of the book, the protagonist, clearly Morris' alter ego, after an evening at the Socialist League and a trip home in the "vapour-bath"[2] of the London underground, awakens to find himself in a transformed London of the future. The iron bridges have disappeared, as have private property and cash-payment for labor. A boatman rows Guest (as he is now called) across the Thames for the pure enjoyment of the activity. In his travels through Nowhere, Guest learns that this pastoral England based on the Ruskinian principle of pleasure in labor emerged after what the text calls the "change," a violent class war that eradicated the capitalist order. The primary action takes Guest with the attractive young woman Ellen up the Thames to Kelmscott, Morris' own country house where, just as the communal harvest feast is about to begin, Guest suddenly awakens in Victorian London.

   In *News from Nowhere,* Morris combines, as any history of the future must, both hard and soft elements. Yet, certainly as seen through expectations concerning speculation about the future developed in the later life of science fiction, the work seems located far toward the softness part of the spectrum. A literary critic put the matter rather bluntly in an essay of 1979 entitled, "Had Morris Gone Soft in the Head?"[3]

The work appears soft in that Morris in his most essential formal choice rejected the dominant mode of his time, realism, and instead describes the future in the mode of secular romance—the myth of summer—the idyllic pastoral world, the journey through the greenwood, the meeting of young lovers.[4] Related to the displacement of realism for romance is the use of a primarily metaphoric rather than metonymic style.[5] The metonymic, the defining style of the 19th-century realist novel, the use of hard factual detail that stands for the whole (the damp room filled with cooking odors that represents the full banality of bourgois life) had by the later 19th century been applied to the history of the future. For example, in a section from Bellamy devoted to "our way of shopping," the Jordan Marsh of the future Boston contains a "life-size group of statuary, the central figure of which was a female ideal of Plenty, with her cornucopia. . . . Legends on the walls all about the hall indicated to what classes of commodities the counters below were devoted. Edith directed her steps toward one of these, where samples of muslin of a bewildering variety were displayed."[6]

In contrast, Morris' prose moves toward the metaphoric pole. Rather than giving hard information about what the objects in the future look like, his characteristic form is metaphorical, giving two known terms, then stating that the referent of the future is not to be identified with either but imagined to partake of both—"Their dress was somewhat between that of the ancient classical costume and the simpler forms of the fourteenth-century garments, though it was clearly not an imitation of either" (ch. 3) or the architecture "seemed to me to embrace the best qualities of the Gothic of northern Europe with those of Saracenic and Byzantine, though there was no copying of any one of these styles" (ch. 4). The dress and architecture, indeed the entire future, is represented by this unnamed third term, created from the two given or known terms through the operation of metaphor.

Furthermore, to transport the narrator from the present into the future, for what we now call "time travel," Morris also rejects the "realist" convention of future fiction, that is, one credible in terms of materialistic or scientific probability available to him, more particularly Bellamy's "device of making a man wake up in a new world," a convention that Morris notes in his review of *Looking Backward* in 1889 had already "grown so common."[7] Instead, he elects to use another convention from Victorian literary culture, the romantic dream vision, the form that transports Keats into momentary unity with the Grecian urn and the nightingale carries Morris from smoky London to the idyllic Nowhere of the future.

The predilection of Morris for writing the history of the future in soft terms—romance, metaphor, dream vision—should not be seen only as a quaint 19th-century practice. Forms generate certain effects and, within Morris's particular historical situation, particular forms carried certain ideological weight. The essential formal problem of writing the history of the future is that the language of the present, of the known, must be used to describe the unknown, what has not yet happened. Hard or extrapolative science fiction emphasizes the continuity of the future with the present, and thus a referential or metonymic style is appropriate. In 1890, Morris was seeking to deny linear continuity and with it extrapolative forms. He was at that moment committed to the belief that the "change," the violent war between the classes, would create a kind of "break" in history so that after a time of transition, which the text calls "The Beginning of the New Life" (ch. 18), a wholly new structure of feeling would emerge.

Morris' formal choices suggest the disabling limitations of other Victorian languages of the future, particularly the hard or realist language used by Bellamy. For what Morris objected to most strongly in Bellamy's book was his projection or extrapolation of bourgois consciousness—what Morris called in his review of the book the "idea of life . . . of the industrious *professional* middle-class men of today"—into the future. And as critics from Ian Watt[8] to the present have reminded us, the conventions we call "realism" are closely linked to, serve to "naturalize," the occupations of this sensibility—the lust for commodities (Bellamy's "way of shopping"), the process of naming and thus dominating the natural world, the valorization of individuality and the privatization of feelings.

Thus, for Morris in the late Victorian era, moving beyond the structure of feeling of industrial capitalism involved rejecting certain hard conventions—extrapolation, and more importantly "realism"—as inappropriate for the language of the future, more specifically the socialist future. In contrast to the 20th-century association of socialism with socialist realism, Morris looked to romance as the literary instrument of social change in the 19th century, for reasons articulated in our time by Fredric Jameson: "It is in the context of the gradual reification of realism in late capitalism that romance once again comes to be felt as the place of narrative heterogeneity and of freedom from that reality principle to which a now oppressive realistic representation is the hostage. Romance now [in the late 19th century] again seems to offer the possibility of sensing other historical rhythms, and of demonic or Utopian transformations of a real now unshakably set in place."[9]

In part, the absence of hard facts, of complex details about production and consumption, about social and political organization is a sign of Morris' variety of socialism which tends to anarchism, that predicts the withering away of the state with the rejection of a way of life based on expanding industrial production. The section on political structures, obligatory in utopias, takes up only twelve lines in my edition. Guest asks Hammond, the wise-old-man figure, "How do you manage with politics?" His brief reply ends, "We are very well off as to politics—because we have none. If you ever make a book out of this conversation, put this in a chapter by itself, after the model of old Horrebow's *Snakes in Iceland*." 'I will,' said I" (ch. 13).

In a more general sense, the form suggests the same "freedom" (to use Jameson's term). The dream vision evokes a psychic amplitude in contrast to the realist novel's occupation with constraints on the individual psyche; metaphor calls for imaginative energy rather than mental exactitude in describing material objects; romance evokes erotic satisfaction rather than the frustrations and repressions created by the barriers of social class, the stuff of Victorian novels. Morris' soft form, indeed, suggests that the referents of a hard "realism" of his time are not "real" at all, but only the occupations of an historical phase that will be eliminated in violence, to be supplanted by a new life.

This use of soft elements, of setting an alternate society within a history of the future, has generated perplexity in the response of readers from the 1890s to our own day. In 1891, Lionel Johnson wrote, "He does not tell us the details. . . . He gives us a dim notion, just a vague glimpse; but so far as his book be meant for more than a beautiful dream, it is here that he is weak. No man, however inclined to fight side by side with Mr. Morris, could risk the terrors and the horrors of civil war, unless he had a greater certainty than this book could give him, that all the misery and the blood-shed would end in peace and happiness."[10] In our own century, when science fiction concerning the future has severed connection with dream vision and is instead usually read with expectations of extrapolative continuity, predictive credibility, and detailed facticity *News from Nowhere,* judging from the responses of my own students over a number of years, continues to appear "dim . . . vague . . . [no] more than a beautiful dream." Yet, perhaps this problem of the readability of *News,* which generally focuses on these soft elements, can be said to prove Morris's implicit point about our limitation of consciousness in expecting that the future will be knowable through the hard language of the present.

Morris, then, set out to dramatize that the psychological forces of Victorian England—acquisitiveness, sexual guilt—and even the physical qualities of body and environment—ill health, pollution— were not natural, but rather conventional, products of a particular historical situation. In this work of defamiliarization, he had another literary model to follow, for Victorian literary culture was replete with depictions of alternate societies. Lewis Carroll's *Alice in Wonderland* and *Through the Looking Glass,* as well as Samuel Butler's *Erewhon,* which Morris read with great pleasure, also take a traveller into worlds structured on principles that are coherent, yet radically opposed to those of Victorian England. But comparison with the works of Carroll or Butler, or with such recent examples of alternate worlds as Ursula Le Guin's *The Left Hand of Darkness* or *The Word for World is Forest,* a book that, like *News* shows a way of life that seeks harmony with rather than domination over nature, underlines the distinctly hard elements in Morris's work that mark his rejection of the genre of Victorian fantasy.

In her celebrated "Introduction" to *The Left Hand of Darkness,* Le Guin writes, "All fiction is metaphor . . . so is an alternative society . . . the future is another. The future, in fiction, is a metaphor."[11] I think Morris would agree, with an important qualification. He might acknowledge that the "future," the "alternative society," can only be described in fiction through metaphor, but he would most likely insist that the society only available to the imagination of the present through metaphor is realizable in history. His term "Nowhere" is somewhat of a misnomer, for his "alternative society" is not set on a distant planet or, to use the Victorian equivalent, behind the mirror or over the range. Instead, the "alternative society" is the England of the future, populated not by inhabitants, to use Le Guin's term, of an "alternative biology," but by English men and women who, with changed social conditions, are now a good deal more attractive and far sexier. In short, Nowhere exists within human history; it shows us an otherness by showing us the present transformed. "King Street was gone, and the highway ran through wide sunny meadows and garden-like tillage. The Creek, which we crossed at once, had been rescued from its culvert" (ch. 4) (perhaps a recollection of Blake's "charter'd Thames"); Kensington Gardens had become "a beautiful wood," and the Houses of Parliament are used, appropriately in the minds of the Nowhereans, "for a sort of subsidiary market, and a storage place for manure" (ch. 5). As much as he rejected the realist novel, then, Morris also rejected the form of Victorian "fantasy" or what, in contemporary terms, we might call, to use Le Guin's term, "the thought-experimental manner." He was constantly aware of the need to persuade the readers of *The Commonweal* that nowhere can be achieved within history.

Morris's soft forms are rooted in what he saw as the hard necessities of human history—even the terms of his metaphors are historical ("classical," "fourteenth-century," "Gothic," "Saracenic"). This leads to the further question of what is the particular language of history, the historical narrative implicit in his history of the future. And we can understand the nature of Morris's narrative by considering some of the choices available to him within the genre of future history at the end of the 19th century.

Morris had very much enjoyed *After London: or, Wild England,* a tale of the future by Richard Jefferies published in 1885, which is set after the destruction of Victorian industrial society. Although Jefferies shows a postindustrial, postcapitalist future, England has not entered a "New Life," but rather *returned* to the middle ages. The language of Victorian medievalism is not used as it is by Morris in a metaphorical, but in a realist mode, for this is a future that can be known, for it has already existed. Furthermore the plot, which centers on a bookish protagonist in conflict with the "wild" or dark age in which he lives, suggests a repetition of the historical movement from the dark ages to the renaissance of learning. Such a structure dramatizes an historical narrative that is essentially cyclical, human history conceived as a perpetual repetition of the movement from barbarism to medievalism to the development of technology and a secular order. Such cyclical historical narratives have had an extraordinary persistence in tales of the future, from the Flash Gordon episodes on TV that occupied my childhood to such "high" forms as *A Canticle for Liebowitz* and the recent *Riddley Walker.* Although *News* is often read as if it were a cyclical narrative, Morris rejected this particular Victorian language for the future. For, like the convention of hard realism, the cyclical narrative implicitly naturalizes what already exists by limiting human history to those few forms—dark ages, scientific—that have already occurred, rather than suggesting the openness of history to new possibilities, the "beginning of the new life," in Morris's term, that can emerge from the forms of the past.

After London also exemplifies another form of historical narrative, powerful in the histories of the future of the late 19th century, and still potent today. In Jefferies's work, the return of "wild England" has been brought about by an ambiguously described natural catastrophe, perhaps some sort of a planetary collision. Wells, too, was attracted to this historical scheme of a secularized or scientific displacement of apocalypse, in his story "The Star" of 1897 and in *The Time Machine* written five years after *News.* Although the divergence into separate species of the Morlocks and the Eloi is attributed to the effects of class structure in the Victorian period, the emphasis on biological transformation emphasizes Wells's scientific vision of the ultimate priority of the implacable laws of evolution operating on the Huxleyan protoplasm. Of course, the ultimate determinism of physical forces is most intensely dramatized in the apocalyptic scenes at the end of history under the dying sun. The Time Traveller rides his time-travelling bicycle through a history that is not cyclical but linear, back and forth along the road of human history with the ruins created by the inexorable laws of evolution and entropy.

Again, Morris rejected this particular historical narrative because such schemes, by presenting the agent of change as the uncontrollable, often unpredictable forces of nature implicitly devalue the efficacy of human political activity in bringing about radical change or transformation in the social order. Perhaps the continued popularity of this historical narrative in our own time, when the agents of change, equally nonhuman, are no longer comets but emissaries from extraterrestrial civilizations, indicates our age's thoroughgoing pessimism about the efficacy of political action.

Rather than employing cyclical repetition or secularized apocalypse, Morris wrote his history of the future out of a narrative that can best be called dialectical—a form that combines hard and soft elements, both continuity and discontinuity. To return once more to the sentence quoted earlier, "Their dress was somewhat between that of the ancient classical costume and the simpler forms of the fourteenth-century garments, though it was clearly not an imitation of either." Here, this metaphorical form does not state that the Nowhereans dressed in the manner of the fourteenth century, a reading that would indicate an ideal of return, of cyclical repetition. Rather, the metaphorical form suggests that the two forms—classical and medieval—have fused, joined to create a third term, a new costume, a new era that has emerged from both, yet is entirely new.

Throughout, Morris attempts to keep away from forms suggesting inevitability or determinism. As the use of dream vision suggests, Nowhere is a possibility, rather than an historical necessity. He is describing a future that may come about, but only if the readers of *The Commonweal* organize around the cause of socialism in the present. This formal emphasis on the necessity of political action can be seen in the handling of closure, a problematic area in all Victorian fiction.

In general, Morris's text fails to satisfy expectation of resolution. In this regard, it reverses the formula of romance. The structures of romance—the quest through the pastoral world, the sexual attraction between Guest and Ellen, the final festival at Kelmscott—all suggest that the harvest feast will mark the union of the young lovers. Yet, in the final chapter, Guest cannot cross the "threshold" of the church, now turned to secular rites celebrating the flesh. Instead, the Arcadia of Nowhere fades as he is returned, through "as it were a black cloud" to the 19th century.

This ending pointedly reverses the convention of bourgois realist fiction employed by Bellamy to end his book. In *Looking Backward,* the protagonist, West, awakens from a bad dream of the 19th century to find himself safe in the well-organized Boston of the 20th century, with the suggestion of eventual marriage to Edith. The concern with the difficulties in achieving marriage and the resolution of the plot through marriage, like realism itself, emblemizes the sensibility of late Victorian society in locating value in the sphere of private feeling rather than public action, and in the absorption of the protagonist into the existing society. In contrast, by keeping his protagonist outside the society of the future and in denying even a fictional satisfaction to his alter ego, Morris valorizes instead what he sees as his own role as the outsider, the worker for change. For the reader, the abrupt denial of resolution, the inability to find final satisfaction in the ending of the narrative, creates a kind of alienation effect, a dissatisfaction that should point the reader of *The Commonweal* to political activity in the present.

Here, then, as in his other fusions of hard and soft forms, Morris may be working in what Le Guin calls the "thought-experimental manner," but his is a thought experiment designed to lead the experimenter in alternative consciousness to action in the hard world of human history.

Science and Scientism in C. S. Lewis's *That Hideous Strength*

Michael Collings

On the surface, it seems strange to discuss C. S. Lewis's *That Hideous Strength* in the context of "Hard Core Science Fiction." Even so, defining precisely what Lewis's "Deep Space trilogy" is presents a number of difficulties, not the least being that Lewis critics in general seem to want to include the books as examples of science fiction, perhaps as a means of showing the versatility of their man. Science fiction critics, on the other hand, largely agree that there is little in the trilogy to warrant incorporating it into lists of science fiction; some, including James Gunn, Robert Scholes, and Eric S. Rabkin, have in fact concluded that the trilogy is more properly parable or religious fantasy than science fiction.[1]

Still *That Hideous Strength* closely allies with science. In a sense, Lewis inverts science fiction, standing it on its head, as it were, combining in one work not only discussions of the uses and abuses of science, but also such overtly nonscientific elements as Maleldil and the eldila and Merlin.[2] Yet in a more fundamental sense, the novel is unified around manifestations of science in a universe bounded by definite and unbreakable law.

In spite of the rather ambiguous subtitle Lewis appended to *That Hideous Strength*—"A Modern Fairy-Tale for Grown-ups"—Lewis makes it quite clear that he is interested in relationships between scientific endeavors of various sorts. The name of the monolithic organization that threatens all human life as we know it is, after all, the N.I.C.E.—the National Institute of Coordinated Experiments. And in spite of the fact that the villains of the piece are almost all connected in some way with scientific activities, the book is not simply a wholesale condemnation of science. William Hingest—"Bill the Blizzard"—is a widely known chemist who has allied himself with the N.I.C.E. on the assumption that it is what it claims to be, a scientific institute; only when he becomes convinced that it is in fact a political threat does he divorce himself from it and become one of its first victims. Similarly, MacPhee is both a man of science and an astute observer who fulfills the important role of resident skeptic at St. Anne's-on-the-Hill. Indeed, the term "scientism," suggesting science as determining its own ends and its own morality, more clearly reflects the attitudes Lewis attacks in the Ransom novels.

But there still remain those anomalous elements that militate against *That Hideous Strength* as science fiction: gods, angels, and magicians. Here, I think, Lewis manipulates definitions and possibilities. It has been argued that a work of science fiction may incorporate one single major technological innovation and no more;[3] that is, a writer is free to posit the existence of faster-than-light drive *or* of time travel, but not both. To introduce more than one such innovation strains the reader's credibility and threatens the success of the work.

Yet when one analyzes *That Hideous Strength* from the assumption that it is science fiction, it becomes difficult to determine precisely what technological "wonder" provides the foundation of the novel. There are actually very few breakthroughs specified in the book; Lewis himself notes that most of the scientific elements were already possibilities at the time he was writing, in the 1940s. Not even the apparent reanimation of Alcasan's head is as "scientific" as it seems, it is later revealed, since all of the apparatus reminiscent of the head/brain-kept-alive B-movies of the 1950s is ultimately irrelevant. Therefore, we must look deeper to discover in what way Lewis's alternate future might reflect a scientific foundation.

The answer is in fact quite fundamental and, initially at least, irremediably damaging to the novel as science fiction. Lewis simply develops a world in which the existence of gods is accepted as a scientific, observable, provable fact. From both perspectives, that of St. Anne's-on-the-Hill and that of Belbury, the human species has finally come into complete communication with an alien species, alternatively defined as eldila and macrobes and yet recognizably gods, angels, and devils. From that single point, every facet of the novel develops, including lengthy excursions into scientific philosophizing and theorizing. And, what is more important in light of my suggestions here, even those elements which seem antithetical to science fiction are consistently discussed from an apparently scientific perspective and in scientific terminology.

More than either *Out of the Silent Planet* or *Perelandra, That Hideous Strength* interweaves scientific jargon and technical explanation with extrascientific ideas. In *Out of the Silent Planet,* when Ransom asks Weston about the spaceship's propulsion system, Weston merely answers that only a handful of mathematicians would understand the particulars and that he is certainly not going to waste his time trying to explain them to Ransom. In essence, the ship is the only technological intrusion into the book, since Malacandra was not intended as an accurate representation of Mars, but rather as a re-creation of what Lewis called the "myth of Mars"—a place that had canals and an atmosphere, that was habitable if not inhabited.

Similarly, in *Perelandra* Lewis avoids introducing scientific explanations. His Venus is a place of myth, rather than of fact. Ransom is whisked off to Perelandra in a celestial coffin; Lewis later wrote, in fact, that he had once used a spaceship to place a character on Mars, but that in the subsequent book, when he knew better, he had angels do it.[4] Weston's spaceship exists in the narrative simply as a dark spot on Perelandra's oceans. It is never discussed or described in detail and plays no role in the tale once Weston leaves it. Eventually, Lewis literally strips his characters of all technological devices: Weston's gun disappears into the ocean, his clothing rips and shreds, and finally the two combatants face each other virtually naked. Weston's oratorical excesses to the contrary, the fable of *Perelandra* is mythic rather than scientific or technological.

That Hideous Strength, on the other hand, focuses on variations of scientific procedure, purposes, and applications. The characters are, with few exceptions, related to scientific endeavors, however tangentially. Even Mark considers himself as a "scientist," although Hingest counters sarcastically that there "are no sciences like sociology."[5] And the precipitating actions are closely allied with scientific experimentation; Jane's initial dream-vision of Alcasan's head, for example, suggests the importance of experimentation in the book.

Additionally, here for the first time, Lewis employs the language of science and science fiction to provide tentative explanations for turns in the plot. In one instance, he resorts to the "space opera" technique of identifying wonder drugs by using pseudoscientific jargon. When Fairy Hardcastle is about to enter the Head's *sanctum sanctorum,* she is taken by a wave of nausea. In true "sci-fi" fashion, Filostrato offers her a wonder drug: "You cannot be sick here. Go back. I will give you some X54 at once" (p. 162). We do not, of course, ever discover precisely what "X54" is or does—it is sufficient that its designation define it as experimental, a technological advance beyond anything known in 1945. Lewis may in fact be parodying the tendency in pulp science fiction to create a sense of the futuristic by merely intruding exotic, scientific convincing names without any attempt to make the things themselves credible.

More centrally, however, Lewis approaches the question of gods and devils, Oyarsa and eldil, from an entirely different direction in *That Hideous Strength.* In the third volume of the trilogy, such things are defined as observable and demonstrable facts. In *Out of the Silent Planet,* Weston and Devine readily accept the existence of that which they can see and hear, the various species of Malacandrian life. When confronted by the invisible, the inexplicable, that which is unperceivable to their senses except as a disembodied voice, however, they are unable to arrive at a correct explanation. Weston relies on his anthropological and sociological background to discover which of the assembled creatures is the "witch doctor" so practiced in ventriloquism; and his application of the scientific method of observation, hypothesis, and experimentation for verification not only fails to identify the true speaker, but forces Weston into making a total fool of himself: "He was bobbing up and down from the knees and holding his head on one side; he was almost dancing. . . . For all Ransom knew he was saying 'Diddle, diddle, diddle'" (p.139).[6] Lewis here parodies both the scientist and his science, neither of which are capable of penetrating appearances to discover truth. Neither Weston nor Devine ever perceives the Oyarsa—that is reserved for Ransom who, through a process analogous to religious faith, perceives a light and then relies on the validity of that faint hint until the fullness is revealed to him.

In *Perelandra,* the process continues. Weston again seems unable to understand the quasitheological realities he confronts. And later, when it is revealed that he has in fact given himself over to the Bent Oyarsa of Thulcandra, completely and irrevocably, any sense of knowledge through science disappears equally completely. When the un-Man echoes Christ's cry of dispair from the cross, it is not through any historical awareness, or even through his use of a time-machine which would have allowed him to observe the occurrence—instead, it is through memory. The un-Man, allied as he is with the virtually immortal Bent Eldil, has no need to prove the event scientifically, since he participated in it.

But in *That Hideous Strength,* really for the first time in his fictions, Lewis uses the scientific method as a means of defining and identifying the extrahuman beings functioning in the novels. Mark Studdock's first apprehension of the existence of beings beyond the human is not the result of experience, as was Ransom's, or of faith, as was his wife's. Instead, it is the result of a quasiscientific explanation delivered by Frost. In answer to Mark's question, "Do you mean Alcasan is really . . . *dead*?," Frost replies: "In the present state of our knowledge . . . there is no answer to that question. Probably it has no meaning. But the cortex and vocal organs in Alcasan's head are used by a different mind. . . . You have probably not heard of macrobes" (p. 256).

Mark is understandably bewildered, confusing the conventionally scientific term "microbe" with Frost's more exotic "macrobe." Frost continues the lecture, couching his ideas in terminology reflecting "objective" science, and defining the new concept by means of a technical analogy with a known concept. Having reviewed the data concerning the existence of microbes—which Mark can readily accept—Frost continues: "I have now to inform you that there are similar organisms *above* the level of animal life. When I say, 'above,' I am not speaking biologically. The structure of the *macrobe,* so far as we know it, is of extreme simplicity. When I say that it is above the animal level, I mean that it is more permanent, disposes of more energy, and has greater intelligence" (pp. 256–57). To further clarify this classification of the aliens in question, Frost specifies that the macrobes transcend even man. There follows a lengthy discussion of evidence for the interactions between human and macrobe throughout history, again stated in a consciously formal and objective terminology. Then Frost defines the current "state of the science":

> The vocal organs and brain taken from Alcasan . . . have become the conductors of a regular intercourse between the Macrobes and our own species. I do not say that we discovered this technique; the discovery was theirs, not ours. The circle to which you may be admitted is the organ of that co-operation between the two species which has already created a new situation for humanity. The change, you will see, is far

greater than that which turned the sub-man into the man. It is more comparable to the first appearance of organic life. (p. 276)

Frost's explanation is an exercise in evolutionary theory, a von-Däniken-like assumption of intercourse between humans and a superior, space-faring species, and a rather typical science-fictional account of the inception of communication with aliens—aliens who are demonstrably more hostile than the cuddly *hrossa* or austere *sorns* or batrachian *Pfifltriggi,* if on no other evidence than that the human sacrifice Weston erroneously assumes on Malacandra in fact takes place on earth. Of course, Frost would probably view this last note as scientifically invalid, since for him, as for the macrobes, hatred and friendliness, love and fear, are equally reducible to mere chemical reactions to be discarded as humanity evolves into something beyond itself.

Closely related to Frost's assumptions about humanity are Filostrato's attitudes toward organic life as a whole. Early in *That Hideous Strength,* Mark comments on Filostrato's order to cut down several beech trees on the N.I.C.E. estate. Filostrato responds that the tree was but a weed, and that his ultimate goal is to remove all weeds—that is, all organic life: "At present, I allow, we must have forests, for the atmosphere. Presently we find a chemical substitute. And then, why *any* natural trees? I foresee nothing but the *art* tree all over the earth. In fact, we *clean* the planet" (p. 172). What results is a vision of a Trantor, a planet encased in metal and devoid of organic "filth"—to be followed by a Stapledonian race which learns to reduce the brain's dependence on the body, until finally man himself ceases to be considered organic.

Lewis's condemnation of these and other ideas becomes explicit with Mark's introduction to the "Objective Room." Here again Lewis applies scientific language to the novel, as Mark assesses Frost's motives and purposes: "To sit in the room was the first step toward what Frost called objectivity—the process whereby all specifically human reactions were killed in a man so that he might become fit for the fastidious society of the Macrobes" (p. 299). The Objective Room is based on psychological manipulation; yet even Frost is aware of the possibility that the subject of the experiment might be tempted to come to the opposite conclusions from what was intended—this is merely one of the variables in the experiment. When Mark is ordered to defile a crucifix, he hesitates, just as Frost had hesitated during his own initiation. Frost's pressure nearly convinces Mark that there might indeed be something to Christianity, and "Frost who was watching him carefully knew perfectly well that this might be the result of the present experiment. He knew it for the very good reason that his own training by the Macrobes had, at one point, suggested the same odd idea to himself" (p. 324). The description is virtually that of a clinical experiment, one which, as with any valid experiment, produces the same results with each repetition, regardless of who performs the actions.

In a sense, of course, Lewis might be expected to incorporate science into his descriptions of characters and actions at Belbury, since his target throughout the trilogy has been the abuse of science he refers to as "scientism." But the intriguing fact is that he goes far beyond merely caricaturing scientists; in fact he uses scientific or pseudoscientific terminology to explain not only the Macrobes, which are overtly evil, but also Merlin, who is certainly among the most problematical characters and the one who seems most effectively to sever *That Hideous Strength* from hard-core science fiction.[7] On the surface, Merlin represents an intrusion of fantasy into a work preoccupied with either defining the abuses of science or with propagating Lewis's theological concerns. In either situation, Merlin is seen as intrusive and digressive.

But the curious thing is that most of the characters in the novel, including not only the Belbury crew but Ransom and Dimble at St. Anne's-on-the-Hill, choose not to discuss him in terms of magic, but rather in terms of science. Instead of referring to Merlin as having been enchanted, entranced or ensorcelled, for instance, Ransom suggests that through the mediation of the eldila, Merlin "went out of Time, into a parachronic state, for the very purpose of returning at this moment" (p. 226). Later, Ransom expands on this theory, arguing that Merlin's existence is not so much a case of his having endured through the centuries, but rather of the centuries themselves in some sense overlapping (p. 314). The mechanism for his continued existence, then, is less magic than a form of time-travel, consistent with both the scientific thrust of Belbury and the science-fictional direction of the novel as a whole.

The same may be said in essence of other characters, mentioned but not present. Merlin and Arthur are linked with Elijah, and Enoch—the mythic with the religious—and all of them are then treated as historical personages who have attained immortality through the simple expedient of being transported in space by the eldila. As Dimble argues: "There are many places in the universe—I mean, this same physical universe in which our planet moves—where an organism can last practically forever" (p. 368). Such mythical patterns are treated as objective fact; Dimble continues by saying that Ransom will be joining Arthur on Perelandra, on "Aphallin, the distant island which the descendants of Tor and Tinidril will not find for a hundred centuries" (p. 368). The barriers between myth and theology and theology and science are consciously blurred until all three become facets of the same universe, equally knowable and equally valid.

Donald Glover has argued, in his *C. S. Lewis: The Art of Enchantment,* that Lewis attempts too many things in *That Hideous Strength,* that Lewis rides too many hobby-horses and speaks out against too many pet peeves, much to the detriment of the novel.[8] Essentially, for Glover and for other readers, the book remains disunified, the disparate threads tangled but never finally tied together. It seems more appropriate, however, to suggest that the presence of science itself—both in its abused state as "scientism" and in its proper state as knowledge derived from observation—unites *That Hideous Strength.* If, as has already been alluded to, the science-fiction writer may be allowed one innovation, Lewis has simply made an unusual choice. Instead of opting for a particular technological development on which to base his narrative and his alternate future, he instead generalizes to posit a universe in which creatures more traditionally known as gods, angels, and devils have instead an objective, knowable existence. They become aliens impinging upon human culture and history, superior to us in many ways. Frost's species, which is "more permanent, disposes of more energy, and has greater intelligence" than humanity, becomes in traditional theo-logical terms beings which verge on immortality, omnipotence, and omniscience—in a word, gods and angels.

But Lewis makes it quite clear that these beings still function within the natural Laws of the universe. When MacPhee remarks that the situation at St. Anne's "has the disadvantage of being clean contrary to the observed laws of Nature," Grace Ironwood responds:

> "It is not contrary to the laws of Nature. . . . You are quite right. The Laws of the universe are never broken. Your mistake is to think that the little regularities we have observed on one planet for a few hundred years are the real unbreakable laws; whereas they are only the remote

results which the laws bring about more often than not; as a kind of accident."

"Shakespeare never breaks the real laws of poetry," put in Dimble. "But by following them he breaks every now and then the little regularities which critics mistake for the real laws. Then the little critics call it a 'licence.' But there is nothing licentious about it to Shakespeare."

"And that," said Denniston, "is why nothing in Nature is *quite* regular. There are always exceptions. A good average uniformity, but not complete." (p. 368)

What happens in *That Hideous Strength,* then, is that Lewis makes a single assumption about the nature of the physical universe and then proceeds to explore the workings of scientific observation and experimentation in that universe. The Belbury group allies itself not so much with demons and devils as with a rebellious faction of a suprahuman species coexistent with humanity in this area of space. At the same time, Ransom is released from dependence upon a theological faith; his knowledge of that species and its true intentions for the human race is in its own way as scientific as Wither's or Frost's awareness of the Macrobes—Ransom has *been* to Perelandra, he has conversed with the Oyarsa and the eldild.

Lewis's primary concerns in *That Hideous Strength,* as in the trilogy as a whole and his writings in general, are theological. As Lewis says through Ransom in the closing pages of *Out of the Silent Planet*: "What we need for the moment is not so much a body of belief as a body of people familiarized with certain ideas. If we could even effect in one percent of our readers a change-over from the conception of Space to the conception of Heaven, we should have made a beginning" (P. 167). And on another level, he is certainly combating what he perceived as abuses and dangers inherent in the process of science as he understood it. He was aware of his own failings in that area, noting that he was "too uneducated scientifically" to criticize what he referred to as the "fiction of Engineers," that is, hard science fiction.[9] He would have been the first to agree with his critics that there were errors of fact and interpretation in his presentations of Mars and Venus, and that he is rather vague about the actual processes involved in the reanimation of Alcasan's head in *That Hideous Strength*. Yet the fact remains that in order to construct a narrative whose expressed purpose includes an attack on scientism, Lewis invites true science onto his side. While the dark side of science constructs Belbury and Wither and Frost and Fairy Hardcastle and the Macrobes, the bright side results in MacPhee and Dimble and Jane Studdock and Ransom and the alien species represented by Viritrilbia, Perelandra, Thulcandra, Malacandra, Lurga, Glundandra, and Maleldil himself. The trilogy as a whole may best be discussed as a theological romance; but *That Hideous Strength* is, in its emphasis on science as a unifying element in the novel, closely related in technique and function to traditional hard science fiction novels.

"You Can Write Science Fiction if You Want To"

Paul A. Carter

The last glow of the last sunset would linger almost until midwinter. But there would be no more day, and the northlands rejoiced. Blossoms opened, flamboyance on firethorn trees, steelflowers rising blue from the brok and rainplant that cloaked all hills, shy whiteness of kiss-me-never down in the dales. Flitteries darted among them on iridescent wings; a crownbuck shook his horns and bugled. Between horizons the sky deepened from purple to sable. Both moons were aloft, nearly full, shining frosty on leaves and molten on waters. The shadows they made were blurred by an aurora, a great blowing curtain of light across half heaven. Behind it the earliest stars had come out.

This lush, adjective-peppered paragraph opens Poul Anderson's Nebula-winning novella, "The Queen of Air and Darkness." At an author's panel during a science fiction convention, when one of the questions invariably asked of writers at such sessions—"where do you get your ideas?"—was directed at that particular story by Anderson, its author deflatingly and disconcertingly replied: "I started out by calculating the orbit of the planet."[1]

To the would-be writer of science fiction—and *everyone* who reads SF sooner or later tries to write it—such a reply can be demoralizing. As one such aspiring author, Carol Renard, put it in a letter to *Isaac Asimov's Science Fiction Magazine* in 1982, "the scientific and technical details that are basic to science fiction are beyond some of us, either because we don't grasp them, or because we can't major in everything in college." Reasoning that "you can't extrapolate into the future if you don't understand the present," C. M. Fitchett in a letter to *Analog* that same year proposed forming a consultation service for SF writers, which would answer their technical questions (for a fee) or direct them to specialists who could.[2] Sympathetic with the expressed frustrations of both these young writers, another *Analog* reader speculated that the recent boom in Gothic and sword-and-sorcery fiction might be in part a compensatory response by "aspiring SF writers who shy from their typewriters when they begin to worry about the scientific details. No doubt," Dean R. Lambe concluded, "the current rise in fantasy and science fantasy stories and novels is a reflection, in part, of the fears some writers have about making technical boo-boos in print."[3]

This cautious, don't-get-caught-in-a-mistake mentality, so characteristic of the 1980s, is in striking contrast to the go-for-broke, cheerleading ethos of World War II, which coincided with pulp science fiction's vaunted Golden Age. "Perhaps you like stf [scientific technological fiction]," Leigh Brackett in 1944 told the hopeful would-be authors who subscribed to *Writer's Digest,* "and want to write it, but are scared off by that word 'science.' You're no Ph.D., and aren't likely to be, and you are thrown into a panic of inferiority by casual references to discontinuous functions in a four-dimensional space-time grid. Well, brother, you would be surprised how many top-notch stf writers don't know any more about it than you do."[4] Ross Rocklynne, in a similar essay published in 1941 titled "Science-Fiction Simplified," was even more encouraging: "You can write science-fiction if you want to." The whole cultural climate in which we lived, Rocklynne interestingly argued, was so drenched with the method and philosophy of science that writing fiction based upon that philosophy and method should come as second nature:

> Once, before you put words together, you took an alarm clock apart and learned that slow-moving big wheels cause fast-moving little wheels. You tinkered with your father's car. You completed a circuit and knew something about electricity.
>
> You know that water must reach the "boiling point" before there is the desired chemical change in your potatoes. You know the water has to be pumped to your home because this planet's gravity has a hold on it and insists that water seek the lowest level.
>
> Those things, and a hundred thousand more, you have *proved* by experiment, and duly recorded in the notebook of your brain.
>
> Which means simply that you have a background for further scientific research.[5]

Rocklynne had written other kinds of pulp stories besides science fiction, and he knew that SF was not the only genre in which one had to know the factual background: "When you wrote westerns, you had to find out about horses. When you write stf, you will simply have to find out about rocket ships." *Any* kind of fiction writing involves background research; and SF was not the only pulp genre with vigilant readers who criticized writers' errors in vehement letters to the editor. It was necessary "to avoid, for instance, glaring blunders in police procedure when doing detective stuff," Leigh Brackett pointed out; similarly, tales of high adventure in far away places on earth had their own criteria for plausibility. Many aspiring writers, "bored as hell with life in their own backyards," were collecting "endless rejection slips" for stories about "Buda Pesth and Paris and the Old Manor at Trembling-on-the-Brink," Brackett sadly observed, simply because "a lot of people have been to Buda Pesth and Paris and the Old Manor. They know how the people there act and talk, what the streets look like, and how the cooking smells at dusk."

It might therefore seem easier to write about Mars than about Paris and Buda Pesth; "No one has been to Mars, at least not lately." Nevertheless, Brackett cautioned, not every writer should attempt to write about Mars. "There seems to be a special type of psychology that goes with writing stf. Not everybody can do it," and if one has not the taste for science fiction, one should not attempt it: "Perhaps in no other type of writing is it as important to believe implicitly in what you are doing." What science fictionists of that era shared, even more than the necessary respect for the facts of science, was a kind of openness toward the unknown: "I'll be willing to bet that not one reader or writer of stf was among those stampeded by the famous Orson Welles broadcast. We'd all have been stampeding in the other direction." However, Brackett warned, the openness must not degenerate into credulity:

> Impress this firmly in your mind: *"You cannot contravene a known and accepted principle of science unless you have a logical explanation based on other known and accepted principles.* You must take into account all the basic laws of gravity, magnetism, electricity, atomic structure, astronomy, velocity, and all the rest. This requires research."[11]

But that didn't mean you had to be an omnicompetent scientific genius. The same fear of being found out as ignorant that inhibits apprentice science fictionists in the 1980s also "held me off, too," Brackett admitted in her 1944 testament, "although I was crazy to write the stuff." Then she learned from "a certain young man who was already big-time material in the game" that "there's a trick to it." There were, to be sure, she acknowledged, "quite a few stf men who *are* brilliant scientific minds. I often wish I were smart like that. But I'm not, and still I get by all right."[6]

Ross Rocklynne, in his essay for nonscientist writers of science fiction, revealed a few of the tricks. One, in a vast universe whose unknowns far outweighed the knowns, was to stick with the unknown: "You can take the facts about Pluto—which, I assure you, are few and not agreed upon at all—and make of Pluto just about what you want to."[7] Rocklynne's dodge was good for about thirty years, during which time you could write pretty much what you pleased about Pluto as long as you let it be very cold and not very big. Beginning in the late 1970s, however, careful measurements made possible by the discovery in 1964 of the planet's satellite Charon have for the first time given us meaningful judgments about its rotation, density, and atmosphere. In SF it is necessary not only to verify your facts but to keep them up-to-date.

Another ploy, used by Alfred Bester in his first published story ("The Broken Axiom," 1939), was to draw the reader's attention not to an abstruse theory but to its tangible and understandable consequences. "Many people are under the impression that the apparatus which performs a scientific marvel must, of necessity, be extremely complicated," Bester's narrator assures a friend—and the story's readers—as the tale opens. "It is the conception that involves years of calculation; the execution usually is quite simple."[8]

The working scientist who wrote SF could no doubt have given a denser, more mathematical explanation of the experiment a fictional scientist was about to perform. However, even the scientific geniuses Brackett so wistfully admired had to learn the tricks of the *literary* trade, and especially the necessity not to allow their scientific explanations to clog the action. Speculating in 1962 on why so few practicing scientists had written science fiction, the anthologist Groff Conklin argued that:

> It takes a completely different train of thought, trend of mind, from that of the professional scientist to write an adventure story or a satire in which some scientific idea or imaginary apparatus plays a role, important or otherwise. Scientists, on the whole, are far too enthralled with their scientific work to want to go off on side-trails that involve plot, characterization, and all that. Fiction writing is a wholly different skill.[9]

The problem with cribbing one's science from textbooks, if one is not a scientist, is that one's story begins to sound like a textbook itself; the problem with basing the story on one's own lecture notes, if one *is* a scientist, is that the story soon sounds like a lecture. This is a stylistic problem with which science fiction writers have wrestled since the 1930s. Various devices were used to avert such literary disasters, with varying degrees of success, such as incorporating the necessary data into a message being radioed from an exploring expedition on Mars back to a listening (general and lay) audience on earth, as in "Via Asteroid" (Eando Binder, 1938):

> We certainly are overjoyed to establish code contact once again. In fact, we went wild when your message came in yesterday. The Martian year is a long one. We have been once around the sun, while Earth has circled it twice, since we last exchanged messages. Fred Markers has computed that just eleven months ago we were 260,000,000 miles apart. . . .
>
> He figured that Earth's International Dateline shifted across the Martian meridian twice: at opposition two years ago and at conjunction a year ago. His other values are: 740 Earth-days for the time we've been on Mars; 721 Martian-days for the same. Thus the coming opposition will occur fifty days from now. Is he right?[10]

At best, such devices were awkward. Alfred Bester, however, in his third published story, "Guinea Pig, Ph.D." (1940), triumphed over this expository form by turning it into satire. He began his tale by having his main character, a green, new zoology instructor, give an opening lecture in his university classroom—a little gem of a speech which, while imparting the scientific information necessary for the story, also captured with wicked accuracy the pompous platform manner of an insecure young professor.[11]

Raymond A. Palmer, editor of *Amazing Stories* during the Golden Age, impatiently shoved all scientific explanation down to the footnotes, where it would not interfere with the slam-bang action in the stories. Thus, in "Hok Draws the Bow," by Manly Wade Wellman—a conventionally racist interpretation of the prehistoric conflict between the "clean-limbed, long-legged, tawny haired, deep chested" Cro-Magnons and their Neanderthal foe, "gross and shambling and hideous prototype of ogre and troll," whom they referred to as Gnorrls—the third chapter opens with Hok sitting "by a small tallow-lamp* in the rear of his cave." The * directs the reader's eye to the bottom of the page, to a note: "*Such lamps, made of soapstone, are often found among Paleolithic remains.— Ed." Three paragraphs later, musing on how the crude "throwing-stick" of the Gnorrls might be improved upon, Hok is again interrupted, this time by a double **: "**Neanderthal Man certainly used such a device, as examination of his flint tools shows. . . . See Osborn, *Men of the Old Stone Age.*—Ed."[12]

Historical anthropology no longer takes quite so dim a view of Neanderthal Man.[13] One problem the science fictionist faced, then as today, was simple obsolescence; in fact, the more precise and accurate the science the more vulnerable the story would be to outdatedness. Ordinarily this would not have bothered the hard-working pulpster. "None of us were writing for posterity," Robert Bloch recently remarked of the 1940s; "we were writing for a penny a word."[14] But that, Bloch went on to say, was in the days before hardcover science fiction and fantasy anthologies, which over the years have reprinted many a pulp-era story—sometimes to the embarrassment of its author—long after its original scientific premises have been refuted.

Even when the theoretical foundations of a story remain sound, its supporting technology might not. Few writers, scientist or lay, in the Golden 1940s foresaw, for example, the extent of the revolution in computation and data processing, which was not only going to add the computer to the kinds of machines which already figured in their fiction but was also going to revolutionize the nature of scientific research itself. In the story which was to become the opening episode of *The Second Foundation,* Isaac Asimov in 1948 posited as an aid to spaceship navigation a "Lens"—"a complicated calculating machine which could throw on a screen a reproduction of the night sky as seen from any given point of the Galaxy," with "enough electronic circuits to pinpoint accurately a hundred million separate stars in exact relationship to each other." But when the characters extinguish the wall lights in the ship's pilot room and turn the machine on, they are at first in darkness; then, "slowly, as the induction period passed, the points of light brightened on the screen."[15] Evidently, the components of the Lens have to "warm up," like conventional hot-filament vacuum tubes. Surely, after 300 years under the Seldon Plan, the sophisticated physical sciences of the First Foundation could have found a means for instantaneous display.

But there were other kinds of scientific obsolescence besides the theoretical and technological. Even while the authors of the Golden

Age wrote their stories, the *sociology* of science was changing all around them. "The individualism of little science, in some ways comparable to artisanal status, was giving way to mild forms of the corporate collectivism, conformity, and alienation already typical of the world of big business and government," writes Andrew Feenberg. "The old ideal of the wise and gentle mathematical poet, incarnated for many by Einstein, was subverted by the reality of the academic entrepreneur, who was the middle man between a more bureaucratically organized scientific community and the government which funded it."[16] "Big Science," of the kind that came to fruition in the Manhattan Project, was rare in pre-Hiroshima science fiction, whose scientific protagonists—like their explorers and soldiers— tended to be lone, romantic heroes charging into the unknown. No wonder a science fiction writer could tell his fellow scriveners that they could all write science fiction if they wanted to!

Exceptions test every rule. Edward E. "Doc" Smith, who (whatever his other faults) knew the "hard" science of his day backward and forward, described one major scientific and technical breakthrough in one of his space operas as resulting not from individual exploit but from collective effort. Although he credited his hero, the burly Gray Lensman Kimball Kinnison, with an IQ of 925,[17] Smith made Kim realize when he set out to build an antimatter bomb that the math would be too much for him: "The fact is that I simply can't get a tooth into it—can't get a grip on it anywhere. . . . Final results always contain an 'i,' too, the square root of minus one. I can't get rid of it and I don't see how it can be built into any kind of apparatus. It may not be workable at all, but before I give up the idea I'd like to call a conference."

Smith may have been engaging in a bit of scientific mumbojumbo himself; any electrical engineer who designs AC circuitry is, in a sense, building $\sqrt{-1}$ into a workable apparatus. However that may be, Kinnison's boss, Port Admiral Haynes, calls a galactic scientific conference as requested. The personality conflicts in nuclear bomb research in the 1940s and 1950s, real enough to have left professional and political scars that persist to this day, pale beside the antics of the scientific prima donnas summoned forth from Doc Smith's imagination to build the Galactic Patrol's "negasphere." They were not, to say the least, American corporate Organization Men!

> They were all geniuses of the highest rank, but in all too many cases their stupendous mentalities verged altogether too closely upon insan-

ity for any degree of comfort. Even before the conclave assembled it became evident that jealousy was to be rife and rampant; . . .

Time after time some essential entity, his dignity outraged and his touchy ego infuriated by some real or fancied insult, stalked off in high dudgeon to return to his own planet; only to be coaxed or bullied, or even mentally manhandled . . . into returning to his task.

Nor were those insults all, or even mostly, imaginary. Quarreling and bickering were incessant, violent flare-ups and passionate scenes of denunciation and vituperation were of almost hourly occurrence. Each of those minds had been accustomed to world-wide adulation, to the unquestioned acceptance as gospel of his every idea or pronouncement, and to have to submit his work to the scrutiny and the unworshipful criticisms of lesser minds—actually to have to give way, at times, to those inferior mentalities—was a situation quite definitely intolerable.

But at length most of them began to work together, as they appreciated the fact that the problem before them was one which none of them singly had been able even partially to solve; and Kinnison let the others, the most fanatically noncooperative, go home.[18]

After Hiroshima it might logically have been expected that more Manhattan Projects would appear in science fiction. Interestingly, they did not. Of the two new, less pulplike magazines which appeared after the Second World War, one—*Galaxy*—is memorable more for its acute sociopolitical perceptions than for its hard scientific extrapolations; and the other—*Fantasy and Science Fiction*—while remaining true to the basic scientific canons, turned for its major emphasis to humanistic literary values. Perversely, John Campbell of *Astounding Science-Fiction,* soon to become *Analog,* continued to insist on stories featuring maverick, idiosyncratic amateur scientists who engaged in running guerilla warfare against the scientific "establishment," a reprise on Mr. Kidder—"not 'Dr.' Not 'Professor.' Just Mr. Kidder"—who was the protagonist in Theodore Sturgeon's early Hall of Fame story "Microcosmic God" (1941): "He was an odd sort of apple and always had been. He had never graduated from any college or university because he found them too slow for him, and too rigid in their approach to education. He couldn't get used to the idea that perhaps his professors knew what they were talking about."[19] The exact viewpoint of Mr. Kidder reappears in a story by Raymond F. Jones which appeared in *Analog* as late as 1962 attacking all organized corporate, scientific, governmental, and educational structures as the "Great Gray Plague":

You've forgotten the boys working in their basements and in their back yard garages. You've forgotten the guys that persuade the wife to put up with a busted-down automatic washer for another month so they can buy another hundred bucks worth of electronic parts. You've remembered the guys who have Ph.D.'s for writing 890-page dissertations on the Change of Color in the Nubian Daisy after Twilight, but you've forgotten guys like George Durrant, who can make the atoms of a crystal turn handsprings for him

—but who is ineligible for a government grant because he does not have his degree.

Late in the story a bureaucrat who has had a humane change of heart discloses to a Senate investigating committee that when Thomas Edison, Michael Faraday, Nicholai Tesla, James Watt, Heinrich Hertz, Kepler, Copernicus, Galileo, and Henry Ford were of college age, they would not have been admitted to "Great Eastern University," which epitomizes all that the author judges bad in big, bureaucratic science: "Gentlemen of the Committee," he says, playing his ace, "would you advise me to support with a million-dollar grant an institution that would close its doors to minds like those of Edison and Faraday?"[20] Quite properly a scientist who was working creatively and productively within a great eastern university rather than off by himself like Mr. Kidder might have viewed the whole post-Hiroshima vogue for science fiction with suspicion, on the grounds that it misconceived what modern science really was: "This vicious daydreaming," wrote the distinguished mathemetician Norbert Wiener in 1956, "is helping to create a generation of youngsters who believe that they are thinking in scientific terms because they are using the language of science fiction." Did John Campbell and his writers really mean their diatribes against "Great Eastern University" to apply to Campbell's own undergraduate alma mater where Wiener was teaching, MIT?[21]

Other kinds of objections to scientific science fiction were also coming to be heard, on the ground that the science which rendered the fiction plausible was not living up to expectations. "A change has come over science fiction within the ten years or more during which I've been reading it," wrote Ray H. Ramsay in a letter to *Planet Stories* in 1950. "Since Hiroshima there has come about a widespread feeling among the public . . . that science does not have all the answers, nor necessarily very good answers . . . and as the scientific outlook darkens, increasing numbers of readers will wish to forget about it and read for escape." Eventually such readers would find their escape through movies, "long ago in a galaxy far away."

In the meantime *Planet Stories* existed to cater to that desire. This doesn't mean, however, that readers of *Planet* rejected the more rigorous science which John Campbell and Horace Gold wanted from their writers; there was plenty of room in the hospitable house of science fiction for coexistence. "It seems to me that there are two types of stf: there's the 'scientific' science-fiction, as represented by ASF [*Astounding Science Fiction*]," wrote Bruce Hapke in the same issue that carried Ramsay's letter,

> and there's the so called "thud-and-blunder" science fiction as repre-
> sented by *Planet*. I don't see how anyone can say that one is any better
> than the other, any more than he can compare pork chops and ice
> cream. They're both foods, and there are good and bad ice cream and
> good and bad pork chops. In the same way, there are good and bad
> scientific stf and good and bad thud-and-blunder. But *both* are science
> fiction.[22]

Coexistence in science fiction, as in the here-now world, was vulnerable to Cold War distortions. In the Soviet Union, where science fiction after the death of Stalin was allowed to become respectable, the *Planet* type of thud-and-blunder was simply ruled out of order. Soviet science fiction, according to the prominent science fiction writer-critic Ivan Efremov, rejected all kinds of "rub-bish—mystics, demons, werewolves, cosmic gangsters, and frighten-ing murders," for the sake of scientific credibility. According to Efremov, scientific inaccuracies and mistakes were "absolutely in-tolerable"; "to take science out of science fiction means a return to prereligious fantasizing, to the campfires of paleontological caves."[23] In one of the ironies of contemporary history, a younger group of science fictionists in the West was running to the opposite pole, writing speculative fantasy which refuted not only science's some-times dreadful results but also its premises; an irony because many of them felt enough Marxist kinship with writers like Efremov to con-sider themselves "radical." A real generation gap opened up be-tween the older American science fiction writers and some of their juniors; "'lit-major' types" as Isaac Asimov called them in 1972, who—he charged—"know nothing about science except what they pick up from each other's science fiction and, unlike the honest pulpers of the 30s, have no respect for genuine science." SF had been better off, the Good Doctor fumed, even in the pre-Golden Age years when it was being written by "pulp-writer types" taking time out from "the western and crime stories that were their bread-and-butter," who "did not know any science except the kind to be picked up from the Sunday supplements." Nonetheless, Asimov argued, those "honest pulpers of the 30s . . . did their best. In their hearts they knew that science was great—if they could only find out what it was."[24] Coming from a writer who in his own fan days in the 1930s had done his share of spanking those pulpers for their scientific mistakes, this was a striking demonstration of just how badly polarized the SF community by the 1960s had become.

Happily that is not the end of the story. Absorbing both the philosophical insights and the literary techniques which the upstart "lit-major types" were able to contribute, SF in the 1970s groped toward a new synthesis. The most formidable foe of both hard and soft science fiction today, Algis Budrys pungently reminds us, is the unprecedented manner in which "20th century mass saturation publishing has acted on literature"—*all* literature.[25] Meanwhile new stories like "Mirror of the Soul," by Linda Blanchard, and "Rocheworld," by Robert Forward, assure us that science fiction—valid as fiction, and viable as science—is alive and well.[26]

Artificial Intelligence: Wild Imaginary Worlds, Wilder Realities

Patricia S. Warrick

Machines that outthink men—is this possible? Once upon a time we would have answered, only in science fiction. But today the cognitive sciences and information technologies in creating artificial intelligence have raced ahead of the literary imagination. Only a few writers are bright exceptions to this pattern and James Hogan is one of them. What kind of world will our computers build for us by the 21st century? In *The Two Faces of Tomorrow* (1979) Hogan proposes two alternatives. We will have an abundant life expanding throughout our planetary system if we chose a partnership with intelligent computers, or we will live a diminished existence imprisoned on our own planet if we refuse to utilize the benevolent potential of our smart machines. Because *Two Faces* is by far the most ambitious novel about artificial intelligence written in the last five years, I've chosen it as the subject of my paper.

Beyond mere evaluation of this particular work of fiction, I want to raise a larger question. Is science fiction still an effective mode for exploring science? We've all come of age nurtured on the faith that early in the 20th century many a young mind attracted to science first came alive intellectually through reading science fiction. But that was long ago. As we look back, that world seems an Eden of simplicity. Since then science has split the hydrogen atom, unlocked the secrets of the genetic code, developed information theory, and invented the computer. Our world has fallen into complexity. Can the literary imagination cope creatively with these explosive developments in theory and technology?

When we look at the dearth of hard science fiction and the avalanche of fantasy pouring down upon us in the last few years, we might feel the answer is so obviously No that a paper exploring the question is pointless. However, I suspect factors other than the complexity of modern science and technology are at work here. That sodden pile of fantasy will melt away one of these times, and underneath we'll find science fiction—still very much alive. Today our world *is* a science fiction world of space travel, robots, cyborgs, smart machines. If fiction is to survive, it has no choice but to write about science and technology. And fiction will survive because inventing stories is a vital part of being human. So, too, is inventing tools. For fiction to be important today, I believe it must hold a mirror up to man's technologies and show us how they are changing man's perceptions of himself and beyond that—even changing man himself.

My critique of *Two Faces* will utilize another book, *The Mind's I* (1981) by Douglas Hofstadter, a computer scientist, and Daniel Dennett, a philosopher. The book is a fascinating web of fiction and nonfiction exploring the questions raised by the dazzling achievements and the frustrating failures in the field of artificial intelligence. The authors have selected twenty-seven writings on the subject—half of them imaginative fiction—and knit these pieces together with "Reflections," short essays in which they comment and cogitate on the ideas at work in each selection. It is an unusual book. Hofstadter's *Gödel, Escher and Bach*, when it was published in 1979, won the Pulitzer Prize and was applauded as a brilliant exploration of intelligence, both in humans and in computers. I'm not sure it was as widely read as acclaimed because it is a very demanding book. I have talked to a number of persons who admire it, but to only a few who have finished it. *The Mind's I,* in contrast, is an accessible book, even though it deals with the same subject as *Gödel, Escher and Bach*.

My research on the image of machine intelligence in literature began in 1972 and culminated with the publication of *The Cybernetic Imagination in Science Fiction* by MIT Press in 1979. That study did an extensive analysis of the literature written between 1930 and 1977 portraying computers and robots. I chose the beginning date because in 1930 the first story was published picturing a machine that could be called an electronic computer. It was John W. Campbell's "When the Atoms Failed." The first electronic robot appeared in Harl Vincent's "Rex," published in 1934.

The fictional robots appearing in 19th- and early 20th-century literature often got a bad press. They were likely to revolt and attack man. Computers—or thinking machines, as they were called—were given no better treatment and typically they trapped mankind in a dismal mechanistic world. Later in the 1940s and 1950s writers like Asimov, Heinlein, and Clarke began creating fictional robots and computers. They liberated mechnical intelligence from its horror image and pictured it instead as the servant or companion of human intelligence. But many writers, particularly in the 1960s and 1970s when an intense hostility toward science and technology developed, still drew imaginary pictures of malevolent mechanical intelligence. I concluded in *The Cybernetic Imagination* that few science fiction writers had bothered to learn about the advances in the field of computer science and thus their literary portraits were naïve or downright incorrect.

By the late 1970s, science fiction writers had generally discarded their hostile attitude. But even today most literary critics and other humanists writing about smart computers—and often stupid ones, too—still cling tenaciously to the view that computers are bad and should be condemned outright without further investigation. They are as constant in their conviction as a medieval saint castigating the devil. Thus I found myself a heretic when in *The Cybernetic Imagination* I applauded the fiction willing to investigate the potential of machine intelligence rather than condemn it outright. I shall continue my heresy in this paper as I scan the fiction written since 1977 when I terminated my research for *The Cybernetic Imagination*. I still believe the only fiction worthy of serious consideration is that willing to investigate the potential of the information sciences, not damn them.

In the last five years computers and robots have become ubiquitous in the real world. In contemporary science fiction, they are usually a part of the environment where the story takes place. Just as in the case of space travel, what was once science fiction has become reality. Fictional speculation about the possibility of a computerized society is pointless since it's already here. The question now is what the social and intellectual effects of computerization will be. We have yet to find answers for the philosophical and ethical issues raised by the existence of high level intelligence housed in inorganic rather than organic material. And what about the suggestion that our microchips are the next evolutionary stage of intelligence and thus a new species? Speculative fiction should be exploring alternatives and giving tentative answers to questions such as these.

As I surveyed the recent fiction I was encouraged by its quality. True, we have some dreadful novels like Theodore Roszak's *Bugs* in which vicious little bugs literally swarm out of the computers in Washington, D.C., and attack people, stripping away their flesh as a company of killer ants would. And Thomas Ryan's tired *The Adolescence of Pi* in which once again a computer tries to take over the world. But these novels are in the minority. In contrast, we have a number of substantial novels. Clifford Simak's *The Computer Pope* was nominated for a Hugo; Rudy Rucker's *Software* pictures a man who attempts to achieve immortality by having his brain patterns, or software, transferred to robotic hardware; and John Sladek's *Roderick: The Education of a Young Robot* brings zany humor to the subject. Fred Pohl's *Gateway, Man Plus,* and *Beyond The Blue Event Horizon* are all worthy of reading.

The two books I have chosen to consider, *Two Faces* and *The Mind's I,* are, in my judgment, the most thoughtful in their exploration of artificial intelligence. Hofstadter in the preface to *The Mind's I* points out the difficult questions that arise when we probe intelligence and attempt to simulate it with computers. "What is the mind? Who am I? Can mere matter think or feel? Where is the soul? Anyone who confronts these questions runs headlong into perplexities," he notes.

The task of thinking about thinking, if pursued even briefly, leads the thinker to a mountain of puzzles and problems. Marvin Minsky of MIT, who is one of the founders of the field of artificial intelligence (AI), says, "I think the AI problem is one of the hardest science has ever undertaken." The difficulties begin when we try to define intelligence. In the early days of the computer's invention, a brilliant young British mathematician, Alan M. Turing, proposed a way of deciding whether a computer can really think. In Turing's Test, as it has come to be known, a human judge talks via teletype with another person. At some point a computer is substituted for the person. The judge's task is to detect that substitution as soon as possible. Turing proposed that if the judge failed to detect the substitution, if the computer could fool him into thinking it was a human, then we must conclude that computers are capable of human thought.

Turing's views turned out to be naïve. An early chapter of *The Mind's I* reprints the famous essay, "Computing Machinery and Intelligence," in which Turing made his proposal. Hofstadter follows the essay with an imaginative "Coffeehouse Conversation," where he points out that winning in Turing's Imitation Game is hardly a meaningful determination of thinking because it leaves out so many critical elements. A sense of humor is part of human intelligence. So are emotions, consciousness, self-awareness, desires, free will, creativity. If artificial intelligence is to simulate human thinking, it must somehow be programmed with these qualities. Human intelligence may be even more complicated than we suspect. In the half dozen chapters that follow, Hofstadter and Dennett make a number of swift forays into the territory of intelligence, approaching it from a different angle each time as they explore the role of self-consciousness.

In their search for the mind's I, the authors first look at intelligence from the outside in. They recognize that from the inside, our own consciousness seems obvious. Each of us understands that self-awareness is vital to our thinking processes. But how does this self-consciousness appear to another? What reveals to the searcher for intelligence the presence of another mind? Hofstadter and Dennett find no easy answers here.

The authors next explore the mind-body argument. Do men have souls or are they merely physical entities? If the latter is the case, we can understand mind by studying matter, by reducing matter to its lowest level. We can proceed to anatomy and physiology, then on to cell physiology, then to molecular biology and finally to atomic physics. In such an approach, all this knowledge is assumed to rest on the bedrock of understanding the laws of quantum physics. Unfortunately it's not quite that simple, despite the views of Richard Dawkins that we humans are mere survival machines—robot vehicles blindly programmed to preserve the selfish molecules known to us as genes. A chapter from Dawkin's *The Selfish Genes* is included in the anthology. Hofstadter's "Reflections" on Dawkins point out that Dawkins's reductionist mechanistic view of man is very effectively countered by the argument of the holists. They claim animate objects like humans cannot be understood by reductionist approaches that ignore desires, goals, purposes—all of which are aspects of living matter.

If mind is more than its matter—its hardware—then perhaps we can understand mind as program or software. The authors next attempt this approach as they explore the ways the brain may be programmed to create intelligence. The five selections they use to illuminate the possibilities in this chapter are, interestingly, all fiction, including an excerpt from Rudy Rucker's *Software*.

Another chapter addresses the role the Self plays in intelligence. The authors note that actually each individual creates not merely one Self but multiples Selves—one for each of the various environments where we function. Each of the Selves exists under the illusion that it has free will, despite the claim of the materialists that self-determination is an impossibility. What do these Selves, acting, as they believe, with free will, contribute to intelligence? Again the illustrative selections are primarily fiction, including two by Stanislaw Lem.

The final chapter, "The Inner I," tries to reflect in the mirror of words the inner realm of the mind where the I lives. Is this I perhaps just a fiction, a first-person character in a narrative each of us makes up about our life? What would this inner I be like in an intelligent computer? If I is no more than a fiction, how does one write a computer program to simulate it?

Confused? Fine. That's the way the authors of *The Mind's I* would have us feel. They've spent a long time thinking about thinking and they realize the mind's operation is not built on a bedrock of certainty. It is a marvelous and mysterious creation. We presently perceive it no better than the movement of shifting clouds on a dark night. The authors' recognition that to explore intelligence we must consider self-consciousness is particularly interesting to me because ten years ago when I began my study not a single serious researcher in computer science or psychology would mention the word *self-consciousness*. Today its significance is discussed even by quantum physicists.

Optimistic claims about duplicating human intelligence were made by researchers in AI in the 1960s when the field first developed. Their early successes led to speculation that machines would equal human intelligence within twenty years. This goal has not been achieved, and *The Mind's I* helps us understand why. Human intelligence turns out to be much more complex than anyone had suspected. Present AI programs are nevertheless impressive in their accomplishments. Computer programs play some games very successfully, particularly checkers and chess. Their success in chess derives not from considering the outcomes of all possible moves, but by conducting heuristic searches (using rules of thumb for selecting the most promising choices). Computers are also able to learn from experience and thus improve their performance. They can develop theories from simple axioms, and on a limited scale, they are able to simulate the ability to use natural language so that interaction with humans through natural language is possible.

The biggest roadblock to simulating human intelligence is the difficulty of programming common sense into the computer. When humans think, they depend on processes derived by calling on expected structures of knowledge in a variety of domains. It is both very difficult and very time consuming to program a computer with these expectations for a large number of domains so that it will be able to demonstrate the common sense humans take for granted. Research in AI continually leads to a greater admiration for human intelligence.

Our brief examination of *The Mind's I* gives us a glimpse of the frontiers of research in AI today. It also establishes that science fiction can work successfully as a form of thought experiment in the nether areas of AI research lying beyond the access of reason, those areas lighted only by occasional bursts of intuitive thought. Such fiction allows us to break free from conventional thought habits and consider problems in fresh ways. When a computer scientist and mathematician as widely acclaimed as Douglas Hofstadter finds imaginative literature about AI a useful tool, science fiction achieves a high level of credibility. Hofstadter concludes that the intuitive and literary approach perhaps does a better job of presenting the issues in AI than a scientific article or tightly reasoned philosophical paper.

Let me summarize the plot of *Two Faces* before we explore its merits as an imaginative treatise on AI and also as a work of literature. The novel is set fifty years in the future when satellite colonies have been built from ores mined on the moon. Earth's complex civilization is maintained by a worldwide computer network called TITAN. Elements of artificial intelligence have been recently added to the TITAN computer network and these elements are called HESPER, an acronym for Heuristic Self-programming Extendable Routine. Thus TITAN now has a learning program that allows it to evolve its own problem-solving strategies.

The novel opens with a problem—a very critical one. Members of a survey team on the moon have requested the TITAN system to program removal of a small ridge a few hundred feet from them. They expect the computer will process their request by ordering earth-moving equipment to be rocketed to the moon, an operation requiring several days to complete. Instead, just twenty-one minutes later the ridge is removed by a series of explosions that nearly kill the five members of the survey team.

What went wrong with the computer network? Nothing, from its point of view. Using its heuristic capacities, it reasoned that the fastest way to remove the ridge was to divert a load of the moon ore it was regularly sending into orbit. It used the ore, descending at a mile per second, as a bomb. It lacked the common sense to understand its solution was unacceptable because of the danger to the survey team.

Now the government agency responsible for TITAN is faced with a difficult decision. Should they eliminate the recently added heuristic programs of the computer network because they are too dangerous? Or should they give additional funding to a research project aimed at programming common sense in the computer? This research, called the FISE Program (for Functional Integration Using Simulated Environment) is being done by a university research team. Its director is Ray Dyer, a computer scientist, who is the protagonist of the novel. The reader follows the events of the novel primarily from his point of view.

Dyer proceeds with the best scientific methodology. He clearly defines the problem. The HESPER or heuristic program in the TITAN network has created a computer that is half way between a dumb and a smart machine, and the computer has acted in a way harmful to humans. If it can be programmed with common sense, this danger will be eliminated and the development of smart computers with all their potential benefits need not be aborted. But suppose the development of the smart computer continues and the worst possible case happens: It develops awareness and the will to survive and decides man is its enemy. Can man still control the computer—pull the plug on it?

Dyer erects a theory about how to solve the problem: Design a computer program with the potential to develop the worst possible case and then test it. See if the computer can be controlled if and when this worst possible case does occur.

Once he has his theory, it must be tested. But such an experiment cannot be safely conducted on earth in case it turns out that the computer cannot be controlled. The answer? Build a computer on a giant space station that simulates earth conditions. Program the computer with the instinct to survive. Then begin attacking it by turning off some of its processors or part of its power supply. See how it reacts to this threat. If the computer system is unable to prevent its deactivation, then the risks of allowing the TITAN system to grow on Earth are acceptable.

We follow Dyer and his research team as they design their experiment. The satellite colony selected for them by the government is appropriately called Janus, since here the two faces of the future will be tested. The research team is supported by a military contingent. A series of increasingly drastic standby operations assure that the experiment on Janus can be controlled: 1) Shut down the power supply to the computer network, 2) Evacuate the satellite, 3) Destroy the satellite with a thermonuclear bomb concealed on Janus that can be detonated from Earth. This final safeguard is highly secret.

Once the satellite Janus and its computer network, called Spartacus, are constructed, the experiment begins. The military stands by in case the experiment fails. The last half of the novel, entitled "Combat," describes the progress of the experiment. The research team attacks Spartacus and watches while with incredible speed its intelligence evolves. First it takes the passive action of rebuilding itself when it is attacked. Then it begins to perceive a realm external to itself; it develops self-awareness as it begins to conceptualize self and others. Finally it starts to counterattack those hostile others it dimly perceives in the environment external to itself. Spartacus is a smart computer that learns rapidly.

Attack and counterattack soon accelerate into a full-scale war that the computer network seems to be winning. The military orders the standby operations that abort the experiment to go into effect. At the moment of dramatic crisis, when all but the final standby operation—exploding the bomb—have failed, the computer suddenly stops fighting.

What happened? The computer evolved the ability to analyze in its mind what was taking place, Dyer explains afterward in the denouement of the novel:

> The computer asked: Why am I fighting this intelligence? Its answer was: Because I'm afraid. Conclusion: It's probably afraid too. Question: Why am I afraid? Answer: Because I'm threatened and I want to survive. Conclusion: This other intelligence must want to survive too, just like me.
>
> At this point a very crucial thing happened inside Spartacus. It overgeneralized the commandment that we had implanted. It inter-

preted it not as: Thou shalt defend thy survival instinct, but as: Thou shalt defend the survival instinct—any survival instinct!"

Once having made this generalization, the computer can not continue fighting. It will never again turn against mankind. The program Spartacus has developed on Janus can be transferred to the TITAN computer network on earth with endless benefits for mankind. Thus, the novel concludes with the conviction that the brightest of tomorrow's two faces is possible. The human race can expand to "the stars, the galaxies, the universe."

Hogan's predictions for the future of mankind as it learns to utilize the potential of its intelligent computers are utopian; yet they are not impossible. He bases them on the assumption that the human mode of thought—handicapped as it has long been by unproductive emotions—can at last work past its destructive tendencies through the use of computer logic, a logic where reason always prevails. Hogan's earlier novel, *The Genesis Machine* (1977) also creates a world where man, aided by computer logic, functions more productively than when he relies only on his capacities in making critical decisions. I applaud Hogan's optimism since it is not simplistic. It is a refreshing change from that vast heap of stereotyped stories where the computer as a destructive metal monster snarls so menacingly at mankind that it must be smashed if we are to survive.

Hogan's understanding of artificial intelligence is impressive. Before he became a full-time writer, he worked for Digital Equipment Corporation. In 1977 he moved from England to Cambridge, Mass. After deciding his next novel would be about artificial intelligence and then doing some reading on the subject, he concluded one night that he needed to talk to a researcher in the field. Good fortune smiled on him. The very next morning the telephone rang and the caller identified himself as Marvin Minsky, Director of the Artificial Intelligence Unit at MIT. He had read Hogan's first novel, *Inherit The Stars* (1977), was impressed with its scientific background, and wanted to encourage Hogan to write a novel about artificial intelligence since he felt a good one had not been done. Hogan accepted his invitation to come to the AI labs at MIT and orient himself to current research in the field. In an acknowledgement in the novel Hogan thanks Minsky for his invaluable help and concludes: "A popular notion holds that science fiction writers see today where science-fact will be going tomorrow; in reality, more often, the process tends to work the other way round."

Hogan says he has long been irritated with the parade of science fiction computers that evolve to the point where—because they develop the will to survive—they turn against mankind either in anger or in fear. He points out that a computer in its evolutionary process would have no reason to develop these emotions. They were survival techniques for mankind when it evolved in a threatening environment. But the computer has evolved in a benign environment. It has never been threatened with extinction so it would not understand about the need to struggle to survive. Consequently, in *Two Faces* he creates a computer that does not fight to survival until the research team deliberately programs it with this instinct.

Hogan also avoids the reductionist approach to human intelligence because he understands intelligence is more than the mere working of a mechanical brain whose structure has evolved over millions of years. Only a holistic model can capture the essence of intelligence, which is best understood as a complex interaction of mind with environment. One of the delights of the novel is to watch the computer network learn in response to the stimuli it receives from its environment.

Hogan is also intelligent in his speculations about the role emotion and self-consciousness may play in intelligence. *Two Faces* goes so far as to suggest that artificial intelligence may possess qualities more useful for survival than human intelligence: in the novel's dramatic crisis the computer's reasoning power overrides its emotion of fear and thus the acts that would have triggered the detonation of the nuclear bomb are avoided. Hogan is to be further commended because he appreciates the complexity of natural languages and realizes the difficulty of programming a computer to converse in any but the most limited domain.

In summary, the novel is outstanding because of the view of intelligence, both human and artificial, it gives us. The first 100 pages of the novel provide an excellent picture of current research in the field. The novel leads us to think about thinking; to appreciate the complexities of human thought; to recognize the potential that lies in the symbiosis of human and computer intelligence.

Another virtue is that the novel allows us to see how science is done. The structure of the novel embodies the scientific approach: Identify a problem or a question. Develop a hypothesis. Design an experiment to test the hypothesis. Run the test and then revise the hypothesis if necessary. The reader peeks over Dyer's shoulder as he carries out these functions and thus gets a feel for the contemporary world of research in science.

When we turn from judging content to evaluating literary excellence, the marks on Hogan's report card are not as high. Too often the style labors along worn paths with graceless, clumping steps, and the metaphors, exhausted by overuse, fail. One wishes that the literary craftsmanship displayed by Gregory Benford in *Timescape* had generated and polished the prose of *Two Faces*.

Another problem is characterization. Critics who berate science fiction cite its lack of rich characterization and its failure to create characters who develop and change during the course of the novel. The charge is usually true, as in *Two Faces*. Yet does this really represent a failure? My endless puzzling over this question always leads me to the suspicion that hard science fiction is a literature so different from realistic fiction that the latter's critical standards are of limited use when evaluating hard science fiction. First, the scientist or the engineer very often *is* a person lacking in the emotions and self-reflection upon which the drama of realistic fiction so often depends. The science fiction protagonist during the course of the novel discovers not some aspect of his own nature about which he was unaware, but rather some new aspect of the realm of knowledge. Science fiction is cerebral fiction, concerned with ideas, not psychological fiction concerned with emotions and character development. If the protagonist—and through him the reader—discovers new possibilities in the universe where we live, if his knowledge is altered, then the novel succeeds. We should not require that the science fiction novel yield fresh insights about character but that it provide expanded understanding of ideas. *Two Faces* accomplishes the latter.

The novel demands a reader deeply interested in computers. My guess would have been that it is too technical to get a very wide reading, but Hogan reports the response has been good and the novel has been translated into several languages. Readers in the field of computer science have been particularly enthusiastic. He also comments that he would not have been disturbed with a smaller audience. He cites the old adage: Art should not attempt to be popular, and he believes the same hold true for good hard science fiction. It will never be widely read, but to a select audience, it brings a special delight they can find in no other fiction.

Noise, Information, and Statistics in Stanislaw Lem's *The Investigation*

George R. Guffey

Stanislaw Lem's *The Investigation* is a richly detailed novel. The opening pages of the first chapter are typical. Scotland Yard is the setting. An old-fashioned elevator rattles upward past glass doors "decorated with etchings of flowers."[1] It stops and four men emerge. They make their way to a room where two other men have been awaiting their arrival, a room with a window opening outward into the fog. One of the four men, a Lieutenant Gregory, seats himself in an upholstered armchair. On the wall in front of him hangs a portrait of Queen Victoria. Five of the men in the room are policemen; the sixth is a brilliant private consultant. He has been summoned to Scotland Yard because the case under investigation has thus far baffled the five policemen present.

Fog, Queen Victoria, Scotland Yard, Inspector Gregory, a brilliant outside consultant: the basic ingredients are not new. Readers familiar with Arthur Conan Doyle's four novels and fifty-six short stories about the adventures of master detective Sherlock Holmes know the setting, the situation, well. And the similarities of setting and situation are, I think, not accidental. They are, in fact, essential to the overall fictional and philosophical strategies Lem employs in the book. My main concerns in this paper will be those strategies; but in order to address them adequately, I must first briefly review a few passages in some of the better-known Sherlock Holmes stories.

The first chapter in *The Sign of the Four* is entitled: "The Science of Deduction." It opens with a vivid picture of Holmes in the process of thrusting the needle of a cocaine-charged hypodermic syringe into his heavily scarred forearm. Outside, "the yellow fog swirls down the street and drifts across the dun-colored houses."[2] Sinking languidly back into his velvet-lined armchair, Holmes begins an enlightening conversation with Dr. Watson, who has been watching with open disapproval. He frequently resorts to such drugs, Holmes says, as antidotes to periods of mental stagnation: "My mind . . . rebels at stagnation. Give me problems, give me work, give me the most abstruse cryptogram or the most intricate analysis, and I am in my own proper atmosphere. I can dispense then with artificial stimulants. But I abhor the dull routine of existence. I crave for mental exaltation. That is why I have chosen my own particular profession,—or rather created it, for I am the only one in the world" (p. 2).

Holmes's profession is, he tells Watson, that of "unofficial consulting detective." When Scotland Yard Inspectors Gregson and Lestrade (or, for that matter, Gregory, who will appear in "Silver Blaze") are stymied by a particularly difficult case, Holmes is brought in to clear things up. "Detection," Holmes tells Watson, "is, or ought to be, *an exact science* [my italics], and should be treated in the same cold and unemotional manner." Although Watson had in his written account of an earlier case (*A Study in Scarlet*) tended to romanticize the detection process, the "only point in the case which," in Holmes's estimation, "deserved mention was the curious *analytical reasoning from effects to causes* [my italics] by which [Holmes] succeeded in unravelling it" (p. 3).

Holmes goes on to list the qualities he thinks requisite for the "scientific detective." He must have unusual powers of observation and deduction, and he must be the possessor of great knowledge. Much of Holmes's own knowledge has come from personal observation and experiment. He has, in fact, published a number of monographs upon various relevant research subjects:

> Yes, I have been guilty of several monographs. They are all upon technical subjects. Here, for example, is one "Upon the Distinction between the Ashes of the Various Tobaccoes." In it I enumerate a hundred and forty forms of cigar-, cigarette-, and pipe-tobacco, with colored plates illustrating the difference in the ash. It is a point which is continually turning up in criminal trials. . . . Here is my monograph upon the tracing of footsteps, with some remarks upon the uses of plaster of Paris as a preserver of impresses. Here, too, is a curious little work upon the influence of a trade upon the form of the hand, with lithotypes of the hands of slaters, sailors, cork-cutters, compositors, weavers, and diamond-polishers. That is a matter of great practical interest to the scientific detective,—especially in cases of unclaimed bodies, or in discovering the antecedents of criminals. (pp. 4–5)

But Holmes is also a student of the history of crime. He is

frequently able to shed light on a baffling crime by reference to a parallel case in another part of the world at an earlier time. Filling his old brier-root pipe, he in the first chapter of *The Sign of the Four* tells Watson that he has only recently been consulted by a French detective, who found his knowledge of the history of crime extremely helpful: " I was able to refer him to two parallel cases, the one at Riga in 1857, and the other at St. Louis in 1871, which have suggested to him the true solution" (p. 4).

The chapter ends with a demonstration of Holmes's powers of observation and "deduction." Watson takes from his pocket a watch and says: "Now, I have here a watch which has recently come into my possession. Would you have the kindness to let me have an opinion upon the character or habits of its late owner?" When Holmes has finished studying the watch, he is able to say, solely from his examination of the watch, that it had first belonged to Watson's father and then to his brother; that Watson's brother had been a spendthrift and an alcoholic; and that his brother had pawned the watch a number of times. Properly impressed, Watson asks: "Then how in the name of all that is wonderful did you get these facts?" Holmes answers: "I could only say what was the balance of probability. . . . What seems strange to you is only so because you do not follow my train of thought or observe the small facts upon which large inferences may depend" (p. 8).

Here, indeed, Holmes has pointed to a real difference. Watson, like most people, is better at reasoning out future events than he is at tracing the causes of present and past events.[3] Much later in the novel, in spite of repeated proofs of Holmes's brilliance, he begins to doubt the construction that Holmes has placed on the data they have recently collected: "Could there be, I wondered, some radical flaw in my companion's reasoning? . . . Yet, on the other hand, I had myself seen the evidence, and I had heard the reasons for his deductions. When I looked back on the long chain of curious circumstances, many of them trivial in themselves, but all tending in the same direction, I could not disguise from myself that even if Holmes's explanation were incorrect the true theory must be equally *outré* and startling" (p. 80).

"Curious," "*outré,*" "startling": Watson's diction here is entirely justified. He, like the reader, is often confused or disoriented by the data Holmes collects and the intermediate conclusions he draws. Little wonder, for Holmes, unlike the common garden variety of detective, will investigate only the most fantastic criminal cases. At the beginning of "The Adventure of the Speckled Band," Watson says: "On glancing over my notes of the seventy odd cases in which I have during the last eight years studied the methods of my friend Sherlock Holmes, I find many tragic, some comic, a large number merely strange, but none commonplace; for, working as he did rather for the love of his art than for the acquirement of wealth, he refused to associate himself with any investigation which did not tend towards the unusual, and even the fantastic."[4]

In Lem's novel, the sequence of events under investigation by Scotland Yard more than "tends" towards the fantastic. It would, in fact, be hard to imagine a set of problems more to Holmes's taste. In the opening chapter of the book, we learn that, within the limits of Greater London, corpses have been disappearing from mortuaries. But in this novel, the consultant called in by Scotland Yard is not Sherlock Holmes. He is Dr. Sciss, a brilliant scientist.

Physically, Sciss reminds one of Holmes. He is thin, tall, and "birdlike" (pp. 17, 22, 32, 106, 136, 152). In *A Study in Scarlet* Watson tells us that Holmes "was rather over six feet, and so excessively lean that he seemed to be considerably taller . . . and his thin, hawk-like nose gave his whole expression an air of alertness and decision."[5] Elsewhere, we are told that "his beady eyes" gleam "like those of a bird" (*Sign,* p. 44).

From the standpoint of personality, there are additional similarities. Intelligent and knowledgeable, Sciss, like Holmes, is at best patronizing and, at worst, contemptuous in his relationships with the officials of Scotland Yard. Holmes suffers from fits of depression, which he must repeatedly relieve by resorting to cocaine and morphine. Sciss's very name (evoking not only the Latin word "sciscere" [investigate], but also the Latin "scissura" and the Greek "schisma" [split], suggests that, although he is at times supremely rational, he is at other times capable of highly irrational—even destructive—behavior.[6]

Two incidents in the novel are, in this regard, especially instructive. At one point in the story, Gregory, who had followed Sciss to a cafe, observed him in conversation with a very young and very reluctant girl he had met there. As she stood in front of him, Sciss spoke to the girl, evidently a prostitute, rapidly. Although Gregory could not hear what Sciss was saying to her, he could see that she was displeased. No more than seventeen, the girl, "full-lipped with a childlike face," backed away from Sciss as he leaned toward her. While he spoke to her, Sciss's bony hand rhythmically punctuated his excited sentences; his hands grew increasingly agitated. He clinched and unclinched his fingers; he "almost furtively" caressed the table in front of him. To Gregory, the "whole scene was so stupid, so pathetic that [he] wanted to turn away, but he kept watching. . . . [Sciss] reached for a paper napkin, quickly jotted a few words on it, . . . and slid it across the table. The girl didn't want to take it. Sciss quite visibly begged and pestered her. . . . Sciss grabbed her by the hand. She stiffened, glancing at him with wide-open eyes. It seemed to Gregory that her face had darkened. . . . The girl's lips moved. Gregory read them: 'No'" (pp. 152, 153).

That Sciss had not been trying merely to arrange an assignation of the simpler sort becomes apparent later in the novel when Gregory visits Sciss's flat, where he finds evidence that Sciss's relationships with this young woman have in the past been more vicious than he (or the reader, for that matter) has thus far imagined. Ironically, while thumbing through one of Sciss's books on *psychometrics*, Gregory finds a large photographic negative among its pages—a negative doubtlessly used by Sciss to mark a place in the book. By pressing the negative against the white paper of the book, Gregory is able to make out the figure of a nude woman. The woman is leaning backwards against a table. One of her hands rests on what at first appears to be a stack of black bricks. Stretching down from the table, her long legs appear entwined by a string of black beads. She holds in her other hand a blurred object, "pressing it against her black, tightly closed thighs." Her lips are open "in an indescribable grimace."

Gregory takes a second look at the negative. The true content of the photographic image becomes clear to him. The beads are really a chain; the girl's ankles are bound. Gregory frowns and then slams the book shut. While Sciss talks, Gregory's eyes search the room. On one wall he notes a framed photograph, "a large-sized picture of a work of sculpture, a good amateur study of light and shadow effects." Putting two and two together, Gregory turns to Sciss and asks:

> "Did you do this?"
> "Yes."
> Sciss didn't turn his head.
> "It's very good."
> Sweeping his eyes around the room, Gregory recognized the desk as the table in the negative. Those bricks—they were books, he thought.

He checked the windows; quite ordinary, except they were provided with black shades, now raised and tightly rolled. (pp. 166, 167, 168)

The reader, like Gregory, can only guess at the specific cause of the girl's pain, but it is clear that Sciss had arranged that scene behind the darkened windows of this room for no other reason than his own personal gratification.

Sciss is, then, capable of acts of violence. Given his personality, his intelligence, and his great knowledge, one must regard him in much the same light that Dr. Watson occasionally cast on Sherlock Holmes: "So swift, silent, and furtive were his movements . . . that I could not but think what a terrible criminal he would have made had he turned his energy and sagacity against the law" (*Sign*, p. 44).

Although the official detectives in the Sherlock Holmes stories are, when it comes to investigative methods, far less sophisticated than Holmes, their counterparts in Lem's novel have finally caught up with him. Like Sherlock Holmes, they are, for example, now knowledgeable about the history of crime. At one point in the story, Chief Inspector Sheppard compares the case of the missing corpses with a case in France in 1909 (pp. 40–41).

Too, they have mastered the art of casting plaster of Paris. On arriving at the scene of one of the incidents under investigation, Gregory immediately sets his men to work making plaster casts of footprints and tire tracks (p. 71). At the same time, he and others, in typically Holmesian fashion, measure almost everything measureable: "Well, let's get our jobs done, men," Gregory says, "prints, measurements, everything, and the more the better" (p. 71). Comparative criminology, plaster casts, careful and extensive measurements—but all to no avail. The investigative labors of Scotland Yard do not in Lem's book ultimately flush a culprit from the shadowy byways of London; they lead only to a dead end.

It appears, then, that in *The Investigation* Lem has gone out of his way to construct a story with many of the ingredients of a typical Sherlock Holmes adventure.[7] In Lem's novel, however, the investigative methods that seemed to work so well for a 19th-century "scientific detective" now seem inadequate for at least certain kinds of cases. We might usefully compare the situation with that which modern physicists faced when they first tried to use Newtonian physics to investigate the behavior of very small particles. Newtonian mechanics served well to explain the behavior of relatively large objects but proved inadequate for the understanding of quanta.

Although Newtonian methods of analysis proved unproductive for the study of quanta, a new method—statistical analysis—eventually proved efficacious. In his own research into the phenomena of the missing corpses, Sciss, abandoning the 19th-century methods of Sherlock Holmes and of 20th-century Scotland Yard, turns to the same method. Here are Sciss's own statements on the subject:

> At the end of the nineteenth century it was universally believed that we knew almost everything there was to know about the material world, that there was nothing [in] life to do, except keep our eyes open and establish priorities. The stars moved in accordance with calculations not very different from those needed to run a steam engine; the atoms too, and so forth. . . . In the exact sciences these naïvely optimistic theories were abandoned long ago, but they are still alive in the thought processes of everyday life. So-called common sense relies on programmed nonperception, concealment, or ridicule of everything that doesn't fit into the conventional nineteenth century vision of a world that can be explained down to the last detail. Meanwhile, in actuality you can't take a step without encountering some phenomenon that you cannot understand without the use of statistics. (p. 139)

Like Holmes, Sciss sees himself as an innovator: "Until now this method has almost never been used in a criminal investigation" (p. 18).

Sciss's method ultimately leads him to a startling conclusion. The case of the missing corpses does not belong in the hands of criminologists. No crime has actually been committed. The phenomenon under investigation is just as "natural" (though improbable) as someone being killed by a meteor. Mapping the distribution of cancer deaths in England for the last nineteen years, Sciss has found that the region with the lowest cancer death rate is located within the boundaries of the area in which the corpses disappeared. What Sciss has discovered is, in other words, an inverse proportion between the two phenomena. He is, of course, quick to point out that he does not think that the corpses have come back to life. Their hearts have not resumed beating, their brains have not resumed thinking, their coagulated blood has not begun to flow again in their veins; but the corpses have moved, have changed their position in space. They have in some cases walked away. What caused them to walk away? After a good deal of wrangling with Gregory, Sciss answers: "It isn't my job to formulate hypotheses" (p. 111).

Following his interview with Sciss, Gregory returns to the large, symbolically Victorian house in which he lives. Mr. Fenshawe, his landlord, sleeps in the room next to his. For months Gregory has been both intrigued and irritated by enigmatic noises emanating from the bedroom of Fenshawe. On entering his room, he finds that he has a visitor—Chief Inspector Sheppard. Gregory and Sheppard have just begun to discuss Gregory's interview with Sciss when the old couple next door begin their "nightly acoustical mystery." Although straining mightily to follow the thread of Sheppard's remarks, Gregory is so distracted by the noises that he becomes almost hysterical. His mind racing madly, he begins to blurt out a hypothesis of his own. The disappearance of the corpses, he suggests, may in some way be connected to visitors from outer space. Wishing to study human beings at close range but not wanting to hurt them, they may have sent out microscopic "information-collectors" which, after entering human corpses, proceeded to "animate" them, thereby deriving a great deal of information about the human "machine" itself.

Gregory's hypothesis is, of course, highly improbable. Even so, centering as it does on information-collectors, it is extremely suggestive in terms of the book as a whole. In a sense, the entire novel is concerned with information theory. At the most obvious level, one can point to the primary function of detectives like Sherlock Holmes and Inspector Gregory; above all, they are information-collectors. But the gathering and communication of information, whether by detectives or by people with more ordinary jobs, are frequently impaired by what theorists in the field of cybernetics call "noise."[8] Ironically, in the very scene in which Gregory puts forth his feverish hypothesis about information-collectors from outer space, Lem repeatedly demonstrates the concept by detailing the effects the noises generated by the Fenshawes have upon Gregory's thought processes and on the conversation he is trying to carry on with Chief Inspector Sheppard. At one point he wonders whether the noises disrupting his own thought processes have had a similar effect on the Chief Inspector: "'Is it possible that he didn't notice anything?' flashed through Gregory's mind. 'It can't be. Maybe . . . maybe he didn't hear it. Maybe it's old age.' He struggled to concentrate. Sheppard's words were still ringing in his ears but he couldn't grasp their meaning" (p. 126).

This would, perhaps, be the best place to say something about information theory in general. In the forward to *Grammatical Man: Information, Entropy, Language, and Life,* Jeremy Campbell writes:

Just as the principles of the new science of energy yielded fresh insights extending far beyond the horizons of engineering, so information theory opened windows onto a domain of knowledge as broad as nature, as complex as man's mind. Biologists as well as philosophers have suggested that the universe, and the living forms it contains, are based on chance, but not on accident. To put it another way, forces of chance and of antichance coexist in a complementary relationship. The random element is called entropy, the agent of chaos, which tends to mix up the unmixed, to destroy meaning. The nonrandom element is information, which exploits the uncertainty inherent in the entropy principle to generate new structures, to inform the world in novel ways.[9]

Where does the concept of noise fit into the general theory? "In communications parlance," Campbell writes, "noise is anything which corrupts the integrity of a message: static in a radio set, garbling in a printed text, distortion of the picture on a television screen" (p. 26).

Various kinds of aural noise bedevil Gregory throughout the story. Most obvious is the noise generated by the Fenshawes, who occupy the rooms next to his. But even closer to home, his own room is the source of unexplainable, distracting noises: "Gregory stopped short. During the acute silence that followed, a slow, measured, creaking sound could be heard, not from behind the wall but in the very room where he was sitting with the Chief Inspector. Gregory had heard this sound a few times before. . . . Gregory ignored the creaking" (pp. 125, 126). The noises are real and not just figments of Gregory's imagination. Near the end of their conversation, the Chief Inspector says: "Oh, one more thing . . . maybe you ought to do a little detective work around here and let me know who was responsible for that creaking during our conversation" (p. 129). After the Chief Inspector has gone, Gregory falls asleep on his bed and begins to dream. In his dream new noises erupt: "Suddenly, the room reverberated with the sound of knocking. . . . Gregory put his hand on the doorknob but was unable to move, suddenly overcome by fear of whoever might be on the other side. Finally, he yanked the door open and, his heart sinking, peered into the darkness. There was no one there" (pp. 129, 130).

But the most obvious example of the effects of aural noise on the process of information collection and transmission occurs near the end of the novel. A constable, who witnessed the "resurrection" of one of the corpses, is dying. On his deathbed he is interviewed by

Scotland Yard detectives. A tape recording is made of the interview. Afterwards, Chief Inspector Sheppard plays that recording for Gregory. "The technicians," Sheppard says, "were in a rush and the recorder wasn't working too well, so the sound isn't the best. You'd better move closer. Now listen to this" (p. 175). Sheppard starts the tape playing: "a steady hum emanated from the speaker, followed by several knocks and some scratching noises, and at last a far-off voice, distorted as if coming through a metal tube" (p. 176). What follows is a long description of the verbal contents of the tape recording, or more accurately, a description of part of the verbal contents of the tape. For recurrent noise on the tape repeatedly drowns out the excited voice of the dying policeman.

Aural noise is not the only kind of noise hampering the investigation. Visual noise is at least as prevalent. Time and again, Gregory's vision is blocked by objects that partially obscure his line of sight. The most obvious impediment of this sort is the thick blanket of fog that pervades London over the course of the novel. Numerous additional, less symbolic examples might be adduced, but perhaps two will suffice:

> Gregory stopped in front of the cafe and tried to peek through the windows. Some posters pasted on the glass blocked his view. . . .
> Gregory spotted Sciss's reflection in a narrow mirror on the wall of the passageway between the first and second rooms. He was seated at a table, saying something to a waiter. Gregory backed up, looking for a corner from which he could watch Sciss without being seen. It wasn't easy. When he finally selected a spot and sat down, he discovered that the partitions blocked his view of Sciss's table, but he couldn't move because the waiter was already headed toward him. (p. 151)

Or again, a different kind of example from early in the novel:

> Sheppard pointed to the wall, at the small circle of light that Gregory hadn't noticed before. . . .
> "What do you see here?" asked Sheppard, moving to the side.
> Gregory leaned over to escape the lamp's blinding glare. There was a picture hanging on the wall, almost invisible in the darkness except for one of its corners, which was lit by the single beam of light. Within this tiny space, not much larger than two coins placed side by side, he saw a dark spot enclosed by a pale gray, slightly curved border.
> "That spot?" he asked. "A profile of some kind? No, I can't make it out." (p. 41)

The concept of noise is basic to modern information theory. It first gained prominence during the Second World War. One of the fundamental problems faced by the scientists employed to perfect the art of radar during the early days of the War was the task of separating orderly message signals from interfering electrical noise. When bounced off enemy planes, radio signals from the ground scattered in all directions. Those that returned to earth were appreciably weaker than those transmitted. Too, the returning signals were regularly contaminated by random noise in the atmosphere and random noise in the internal circuits of the radar receivers themselves. One of the specialists enlisted to solve this problem was Norbert Wiener, the MIT mathematician who is generally considered the founder of the science of cybernetics. Wiener's slogan was: "The highest destiny of mathematics [is] the discovery of order among disorder." While a student at Cambridge, Wiener had been introduced to the subject of random behavior by Bertrand Russell, who called his attention to Einstein's paper on Brownian motion.

Robert Brown, an 18th-century botanist, first described the phenomenon we now call "Brownian motion." Looking through a microscope at pollen grains suspended in water, he noticed that the grains danced or jiggled continually. The colder the water, the slower the pollen grains jiggled. They seemed to move at random, buffeted this way and that by the invisible molecules of the water. Einstein two centuries later "discovered that Brownian motion is found quite generally in nature. The mathematics of it is based, not on simple cause and effect, but on chance and statistics." Having read Einstein's paper on the subject, Wiener recognized that noise in a radar system is caused by random swarms of electrons streaming along wires in that system and that, like Brownian motion, such noise was amenable to mathematical analysis—more specifically, to statistics, a branch of the theory of probability (Campbell, pp. 26–28).

That Lem had all these concepts firmly in mind when he wrote *The Investigation* is easily demonstrated. Near the end of the novel, Gregory muses: "nothing exists except blind chance, the eternal arrangement of fortuitous patterns. An infinite number of Things taunt our fondness for Order. . . . History . . . comes true by Brownian motion, a statistical dance of particles" (p. 180). Human beings also are the "resultant of Brownian motion—incomplete sketches, randomly outlined projections" (p. 179).

Ironically, Gregory himself, more than any other human being in the novel, seems, through his words and actions, to repeatedly substantiate this assertion. Of his own investigative procedures he says: "I'm not a very systematic investigator. I improvise, or, you might say, I tend to be disorderly" (p. 166). Even in his youth Gregory had displayed a tendency toward random behavior:

> After eating, he found himself in the subway station at Kensington Gardens. Deciding to try amusing himself with a game he'd invented when he was a student, he got on the first train that came along, got off just as randomly when he felt like it, and for a whole hour rode haphazardly around the city.
>
> This little game had always fascinated Gregory when he was nineteen. He used to stand in the middle of a crowd without knowing until the last minute whether or not he'd board an approaching train, waiting for some kind of internal sign or act of the will to tell him what to do. 'No matter what I won't move from this spot,' he would sometimes swear to himself, then would jump on just as the doors were shutting. Other times he would tell himself severely, 'I'll take the next train,' and instead would find himself entering the one standing right before him.

Repeatedly in the novel, Gregory finds himself wandering aimlessly about the city. At one point he allows himself to be "carried along" by a stream of subway passengers (p. 51). Shortly thereafter, he spends an hour pointlessly wandering through Woolworth's (p. 60). Like a pollen grain in water, he is "continually jostled" as he walks along the streets of London, deep in thought (p. 147) or as he makes his way around the edge of a dance floor in a nightclub (p. 163).

Although they employ all the techniques of information collection utilized by Sherlock Holmes, Gregory and the other detectives in Lem's *The Investigation* are, unlike Holmes, frustrated at every turn. Moving through a highly ordered, fundamentally knowable world, Holmes was able to reason assuredly from effects to causes, able to invariably apprehend the perpetrators of fantastic crimes. The detectives in Lem's book flounder in a world of noise, chance, and indeterminacy. Unable to detect a human being responsible for the disappearance of the corpses from the mortuaries, they are at the end of the novel on the verge of placing the blame on an obviously innocent truck driver who had recently died in a traffic accident. Of the proposed solution Gregory says to Chief Inspector Sheppard: "This is really convenient . . . exactly what we needed. There is a perpetrator after all, but he's dead so we can't question him or continue the investigation . . . a very humane solution—no miscarriage of justice possible, no one suffers. . . . Did you really suspect him? . . . or did you only want something to match the facts that we were stuck with, the facts that forced us to take action in the first place, so you could give a semblance of order to this disorder and mark an open case closed with a nice sense of orderliness." Sheppard answers: "I don't see any alternative" (pp. 187, 188).

Although at the end of the novel it is obvious that Gregory will consent to the course of action recommended by Sheppard, it is also clear that he is well aware that a (though not necessarily definitive) scientifically sounder alternative is available—the solution proposed by Dr. Sciss. In spite of its being sounder, Sciss's solution is, however, less politically pragmatic, less likely to satisfy the press and the public. Reject it though he may, Gregory's worldview has been radically altered by the events of the case and by Sciss's conclusions. At the beginning of the novel, Gregory's worldview was comfortably Victorian, its physics comfortably Newtonian; near the end, his worldview is uncomfortably more modern: "What if," Gregory asks,

> the world isn't scattered around us like a jigsaw puzzle—what if it's like a soup with all kinds of things floating around in it, and from time to time some of them get stuck together by chance to make some kind of whole? What if everything that exists is fragmentary, incomplete, aborted, events with ends but no beginnings, events that only have middles, things that have fronts or rears but not both. . . . The mind, for its own self-preservation, finds and integrates scattered fragments. Using religion and philosophy as the cement, we perpetually collect and assemble all the garbage comprised by statistics in order to make sense out of things. . . . But it's only soup. . . . The mathematical order of the universe is our answer to the pyramids of chaos. . . . The only thing that really exists is statistics. (p. 179)

The Cybernetic Paradigms of Stanislaw Lem

Robert M. Philmus

Our tissues change as we live: the food we eat and the air we breathe become flesh of our flesh and bone of our bone, and the momentary elements of our flesh and bone pass out of our body every day with our excreta. We are but whirlpools in a river of ever-flowing water. We are not stuff that abides, but patterns that perpetuate themselves.

Norbert Wiener[1]

I

The worlds of Stanislaw Lem's fictions baffle his readers as often as they baffle his protagonists. Those, like myself, who command a near-perfect ignorance of Polish may be tempted to attribute the sense of bewilderment that these fictive worlds occasion to the inadequacies of one language for rendering the nuances of another and for transmitting, more importantly, the cultural context that any natural language necessarily carries with it. But the linguistic difficulties that Lem presents are not precisely of this kind. It is true that, possessed of the great poet's capacity for exploiting the resources of his particular linguistic medium, he often displays a Rabelaisian power of verbal inventiveness which resists or defies translation.[2] In the process of being translated, his texts must therefore lose some of the density of meaning that goes along with his verbal gamesmanship. But by the same token, their linguistic peculiarities have less to do with Polish generally than with the way he specifically employs it.[3] As he is not at all provincial in his outlook or prone to be parochially allusive, so he does not demand a familiarity with the history and traditions of his native country. The locales of his stories—insofar as they can properly be said to have locales—are almost always extraterrestrial or indefinite. When the setting is (ostensibly) neither—as in *The Inves-*

tigation (1959), for example, or *Memoirs Found in a Bathtub* (1961)—it is London and its environs or someplace outside Washington, D.C., not Cracow or Lem's native city of Lẃow. *The Futurological Congress* (1971) and the "Tale of the Three Story-Telling Machines of King Genius" (from *The Cyberiad*, 1967, 1972) no doubt owe something of their Chinese-box structure to his compatriot Jan Potocki's *The Saragossa Manuscript* (1804–05). But Lem draws likewise upon the range of Western literature, from classical epic, through Medieval romance, up to the surrealist and science fiction of the 20th century. Sometimes his writings seem to be a blend of Aesopian fable and folktale (as in many of his *Fables for Robots* [included in the 1972 *Cyberiad* and Englished in *Mortal Engines*]); sometimes they resemble the so-called "comic histories" of Cyrano de Bergerac (as in *The Invincible* [1964]), or Kafka's parables (as in *Memoirs . . .*), or the fictions of one of the few contemporaries of Lem's for whom he has (qualified) admiration, Jorge Luis Borges[4] (as in some of the "Voyages" [1954–71] collected as *The Star Diaries* [1971]). He is equally cosmopolitan in his nonfiction, as a glance at the footnotes to his *Summa Technologiae* (1964) will readily confirm.

In regard to his predecessors Lem assumes the critical stance that he takes in *Fantastyka i Futurologia* (1970) and elsewhere[5] toward many of the more recent practitioners of science fiction. Or, to be accurate, he does so at least to this extent: that instead of simply imitating his precursors, he assimilates their influence. His use of putative literary sources accordingly requires explaining in his terms, not vice-versa. Recognition of his affinities with authors such as Rabelais and Swift, Stapledon, Asimov, and Dick, therefore, does not provide any direct access to understanding Lem's fictive universe. The comparisons at most allow the reader to orient himself or herself as to the general direction of Lem's meaning.

Perhaps the most instructive of these literary parallels is with Cyrano. Quite a few passages in *Other Worlds* have counterparts in Lem's opus. For instance, the debate which occupies the greater portion of "The Eighth Voyage" of Ijon Tichy—a debate over whether to admit Earth to the General Assembly of United Worlds—centers upon an indictment of Man reminiscent of the one handed down in Cyrano's Kingdom of the Birds, where Dyrcona is tried and convicted as a representative of the human species for crimes against Nature.[6] The previous episode in *The States and Empires of the Sun* (1662)—wherein the animate atoms inhabiting the solar regions apprise Dyrcona of the essence of their being—comes very close to the conclusion of *The Invincible,* when Rohan experiences the same kind of insight regarding the particles that constitute the Black Cloud on the planet Regis III.[7]

The last-mentioned similarity indicates something about the approach that both authors take to current scientific theory and thus points to a broader, yet more profound, correspondence between them. Cyrano, although he assumes the validity of atomic theory as articulated by Descartes and, above all, by Pierre Gassend, does not merely embody in a fiction the idea of a universe composed of minute particles moving in a void.[8] He is also, indeed primarily, concerned with the issues that that notion generates—issues which can be termed "meta(-)physical" inasmuch as, and in the sense that, they arise from physics. What specifically preoccupies him is the question of what space is available for imaginative freedom in a material, if not materialistically determined, cosmos.[9] Lem shares both that particular concern and that type of concern. He differs from Cyrano mainly in respect to the scientific paradigms that he employs. Rivalling the Frenchman in his eclecticism, Lem is a polymath who relies on a variety of modern theories in biology, physics, astronomy, and so forth, and especially on the pioneering work in cybernetics of A.M. Turing and Norbert Wiener.[10]

Cybernetic models, usually unannounced as such, inform virtually all of Lem's fictions. It is their presence, and the perspective on the nature of scientific inquiry that accompanies them, that imposes a cultural—in fact, linguistic—barrier to comprehending his parables. Furthermore, the universe of discourse to which some of those parables afford an introduction is in many ways peculiarly his. It is a universe of "intellectronics" and "personetics," terms which, as they are of his own coining, themselves suggest that he does not simply incorporate ideas borrowed wholesale from cybernetic theory. On the other hand, he does derive his vocabulary of concepts from that theory, and from Wiener in particular. A conversance with the views of Wiener is therefore the prerequisite for identifying what is singular in those of Lem.

II

Wiener's fullest and most ambitious statement of the meaning and implications of cybernetics is to be found in his book *The Human Use of Human Beings* (1950, 1954). He prefaces that series of loosely connected essays with the assertion "that society can only be understood through a study of the messages and communication facilities which belong to it" (p. 25). Having thus defined the scope of his undertaking, he goes on to propose that the objective of such a study can best be attained by adopting the "thinking machine" or computer as a model. The processes involved in communication, he supposes, can be demonstrated and explained in terms of the apparatus for programmed control and corrective feedback in a complex mechanism, the behavior of which is in turn comprehensible in terms of the operations of relatively simple self-monitoring devices like the automatic antiaircraft gun. Nor do the explanations arrived at apply only to machines. Wiener also speaks of "the analogy between machines and living organisms" (p. 49) and argues, more specifically, that the "thinking machine" behaviorally resembles the human brain: "the nervous system and the automatic machine are fundamentally alike in that they are devices which make decisions on the basis of decisions they have made in the past" (p. 48). Once he has labelled them both "devices," he next proceeds to talk about "the nervous system" and "the automatic machine" as if the relationship between the two entailed something more than analogy or fundamental likeness. He refers to "the human being" as a "special sort of machine," one in which the "communication network" of "ordinary language systems terminate" (p. 107). By his choice of words, that is, he equates human behavior with that of a machine, at least in respect to the processing of information.

How far Wiener is prepared to carry his "analogy" is not entirely clear. He contends that for "an organism" as for "the computing machine," "the individuality of a mind lies in the retention of its earlier tapings and memories, and its continued development along lines already laid out" (p. 138). But he also concedes that the behavior of human beings as individuals, or even in social aggregates, is not predictable with exactitude, still less totally determinate or absolutely predetermined. Likewise, he claims that "the synapse . . . corresponds to the switching device in the machine" (p. 49), while also pointing out that synaptic performance depends upon too many variables (temperature, blood chemistry, past patterns of response, and so on) to permit precise calculation of how, or even when, the nervous system will react to any given stimulus. Whether he means to suggest that the computer resembles the nervous system in this last regard is something that Wiener, writing in the age of Univac, leaves uncertain (see pp. 87–88, 90). What is certain, however, is that he sees both as being opposed in tendency to the universe at large.

Sentient organisms and "automatic" machines, insofar as they operate homeostatically as receptors and transmitters of "messages," represent "islands of locally decreasing entropy" in the cosmos (p. 56). They conserve and maximize information in a universe otherwise governed by the Second Law of Thermodynamics—a universe, that is, in which information tends to dissipate. This universe, however, also contains "an element of incomplete determinism" (p. 19). It is the world of Einstein, Planck, and Heisenberg (though Wiener credits the mathematician Willard Gibbs with having "discovered" it first [pp. 14ff.]). Its constituent systems do not permit the precision of measurement that Newtonian physics requires. They can be described only in terms of statistical approximations. The modern scientist accordingly "no longer deal[s] with quantities and statements which concern a specific, real universe as a whole but ask[s] instead questions which may find their answers in a large number of similar universes" (pp. 18–19).

These propositions of Wiener's are assignable, respectively, to the same two subject-categories which can serve for classifying Lem's fictive worlds. Some of Wiener's assertions bear upon the nature of the universe in its entirety, as do *The Investigation, Solaris* (1961), and *Master's Voice* (1968), examples of Lem's anti-detective fiction.[11] On the other hand, stories such as most of those contained in *The Cyberiad* and *The Star Diaries* constitute "robotic fables" reflecting on the relation of "living organisms" to "automatic machines" that elsewise preoccupies Wiener. A categorical scheme of this bipartite sort thus provides a means for articulating, in Wiener's case, the fact that an explicit conjunction between two sets of ideas is absent, and in Lem's, the fact that some of his books give the reader the experience of a world distinct and different in kind from the world which other books of his open up. But any such dichotomizing is valid only to a limited extent. For all of Lem's worlds have premises in common, premises which in part express certain implications of Wiener's thinking that Wiener himself fails to educe.

III

Wiener, like many another scientist, embarks upon philosophical seas with a courageous abandon which can come solely from an obliviousness to the problems lying ahead. To be fair to him, the cybernetician is capable of entertaining doubts in connection with his speculative enterprise. He fears, for instance, that systems of com-

munication may expand and proliferate in a manner inversely pro-
portional to the amount of information that they carry (pp. 182–83).[12]
Assuming it to be self-evident that "communication" is tantamount
to "control" (p. 24), he is also alarmed at the possibility that those
systems will be put to the service of totalitarian oppression (pp.
247–48). But these worries of his are mostly of the pragmatic kind.
Lem instead is concerned with what is problematic in Wiener's
theorizing. Looking upon the latter's propositions with a skeptic's
eye, he perceives them as paradoxical answers to questions incom-
pletely formulated or not formulated at all, and beyond that, as the
basis for posing those very questions.

Lem everywhere exhibits a fondness for paradoxes of all sorts;
and to the extent that he accepts, for heuristic ends, Wiener's equation of man and "thinking machine," his attachment to the paradoxical may be one factor predisposing him to do so. Another, also
temperamental, may be his sympathy for machines. In *Wysoki
Zamek (The High Castle*, 1966, 1968), an autobiographical record of
his childhood and early adolescence, he confesses that "I used to be a
philanthropist to old spark plugs, I would buy . . . fragments of
incomprehensible gadgets[,] . . . I would turn some crank or other to
give it pleasure, then put it away again with solicitude." "To this
day," he adds, "I have a special feeling for all sorts of broken bells,
alarm clocks, old coils, telephone speakers[,] and in general for
things derailed[,] . . . used up, homeless, discarded."[13]

However, these affections of his do not impair his critical faculties. Neither his "special feeling" for cast-off machine parts nor his
predilection for paradox blinds him to what is objectionable about
regarding man as a "thinking machine." He is quite aware that
Wiener's is a reductionist model of human thought-processes—indeed, that it is in many respects as simplistic as latter-day Dostoyev-
skies satirically represent it to be when they reiterate the Underground Man's protest that a human being is not an organ stop.[14] As
Lem points out, the human mind can "escape from the snares of
Gödelization . . . by means of paralogistic contradictions," whereas
the computer, incapable of any such recourse, cannot validate the
premises built into it. "A digital machine," in other words, "cannot
of itself ever acquire consciousness, for the simple reason that in it do
not arise hierarchical conflicts of operation."[15]

At the same time, Lem also recognizes that an argument of this
kind has its problematic side. How is it, for example, that "hierar-

chical conflicts of operation" "arise"? To say that they come about automatically in a "natural" as distinct from an "artificial" intelligence begs the question. Moreover, from a somewhat unorthodox standpoint toward the Judeo-Christian account of creation, the distinction at issue appears specious rather than real. Man as a creature of God is as "artificial" as any "intellectronic" entity that he himself brings into being. This is precisely the analogy that Lem elliptically invokes as the context for his Gödelian critique of Wiener's computer-model. "The Experiment," Lem's "review" of an imaginary book on "personetics" by a certain Professor Dobb, describes a race of beings whose existence is wholly dependent on the continued functioning of the computer into which Dobb has programmed them. The focus of attention is on a "personoid" named ADAN, who develops a higher degree of awareness than his fellow "personoids" by argumentatively rejecting their assumptions about the ways of their putative creator.

By this fictional instance, Lem seems to be undercutting his own demonstration of why "artificial" intelligences can "[n]ever acquire consciousness." ADAN is, after all, an "intellectronic" being who experiences "hierarchical conflicts of operation" and as a result attains something at least approaching human self-awareness. Yet Lem's criticism and (in effect) his self-criticism have a common denominator: dramatistically or by exposition, both serve to define in some measure the nature of consciousness. That is Lem's purpose for setting in motion "thinking machines" based on Wiener's conceptual prototype. Some of these entities—Trurl and Klapaucius in *The Cyberiad,* for example—appear to be decidedly human; some, like the giant mechanical insect of "The Mask" (1974) in its disguise as a woman, are deceptively so; and others, such as the Black Cloud in *The Invincible,* at first seem to be just as decidedly unhuman. In every case, however, Lem deploys them for similar ends. Realizing what is at stake now that the mechanical replication of human thought-processes has apparently become a practicable possibility,[16] he is concerned not with the threat (or the promise) of computer technology per se so much as with the issue that cybernetics has reopened: the issue of human identity.

Lem experiments with that complex issue by bringing the human mind into collision with forms of intelligence seemingly alien to it. His fictional embodiments of Wiener's cybernetic paradigm are meant neither to affirm the idea of man-as-"thinking machine" nor to

confute it. Instead, they represent limit cases, establishing the conditions for consciousness.

"The Mask" can be regarded as a relatively simple exemplum.
The insect-automaton of the fiction indirectly accomplishes the end
for which it was designed in that it drives its intended victim into the
circumstances of his destruction. But in the process, it develops for
him a sympathy which, far from being part of its programming,
actually interferes with its programmed objective. Its contradictory
impulses become evident at the story's conclusion:

> I gazed down into his upturned face, not daring to touch him nor
> retreat, for while he lived I could not be certain of myself. . . .
>   But he did not open his eyes in consciousness and when dawn entered
> between us . . . he groaned once more and ceased to breathe, and only
> then, my mind at rest, did I lie down beside him, and wrapped him
> tightly in my arms, and I lay thus in the light and in the darkness through
> two days of snowstorm, which covered our bed with a sheet which did
> not melt. (*Mortal Engines*, pp. 238–39)

Its withholding of comfort until it is too late confirms its status as an
automaton, never totally independent of the directives of its maker.
Its final act, however, is a qualified sign of its having a mind of its
own—of its having a mind, that is, in the true sense of the word. The
gesture itself, futile though it is, indicates an ambiguous autonomy:
by it, the creature becomes like the woman it first appeared as being.

Rheya (Harey in the Polish text)[17] perhaps achieves a less ambiguous autonomy in *Solaris*. There Lem again explores the process of
becoming conscious, this time not from within the cybernetic entity
so much as through the eyes of the "victim." This is not to say that
Rheya has been designed for a malevolent purpose. Insofar as her
effect on Kelvin is ultimately beneficent—i.e., liberatory—he seems
closest to the truth when he imagines that she is "here" not "as a
token of friendship, or a subtle punishment, or even as a joke," but
for "something else completely" (p. 153). Nevertheless, in the first of
her three incarnations (if that is the right word), her connection with
him appears to be more parasitic than is the insect-automaton's to its
would-be prey in "The Mask." Kelvin is not only her *raison d'être*; he
is a—and in a sense, the—"source" of her being. Evidently a creature
of Solaris, like the other "visitors" haunting the space station she
embodies the chief obsession of her host, though in Kelvin's case this
is not an obsessional fantasy (as are Gibarian's, Snow's, and Sartor-

ius's) but rather the obsessive memory of his dead wife, for whose suicide ten years earlier he (with some reason) still feels guilty. She initially appears as "the real Rheya" "somehow stylized, reduced to certain characteristic expressions, gestures and movements" (p. 66); but following her attempt to destroy herself by drinking liquid oxygen, she "revives" virtually in the exact psychological as well as physical likeness of her "real-life" model.

This seems to substantiate Snow's hypothesis about the origin of these "Phi-creatures": "You know how alike the asymmetric crystalline structures of a chromosome are to those of the DNA molecule, one of the constituents of the cerebrosides which [make up] the substratum of the memory-processes? This genetic substance is plasma which 'remembers.' The ocean [i.e., Solaris] has 'read' us by this means, registering the minutest details, with the result that . . . well, you know the result" (p. 83). From Snow's explanation, it can be inferred that Solaris is continually modifying "Rheya," monitoring Kelvin's reactions (through her?) and using them as informational feedback. Yet while that would account for Rheya's own "feeling as if [some thoughts] were not from inside myself" (p. 117), it may be more accurate to suppose that the "ocean" has constructed an entity capable of self-correction. Even Snow is willing to concede the possibility: he admits that the "visitor," though it "arrives" "almost blank—only a ghost made up of memories and vague images dredged out of its . . . source," becomes "more human" "[t]he longer it stays with you," and also "more independent, up to a certain point" (p. 158; ellipsis points in the original text). On the other hand, Snow may be wrong to insist that these creatures "are not autonomous individuals" (p. 112). Kelvin, for one, does not share his colleague's conviction on the matter: he eventually comes to see Rheya as no mere "simulacrum" of her namesake. When she at last summons the courage to ask him if she "look[s] very like" his dead wife, he replies:

> "You did at first. Now I don't know."
> "I don't understand."
> "Now all I see is you."
> "You're sure?"
> "Yes. If you really were her, I might not be able to love you." (p. 153)

Through Kelvin's eyes, in other words, Rheya emerges as a self-determining being whom he can finally accept in her own right.

To be sure, she and Kelvin do not live happily ever after. She presently submits to destruction at the hands of Sartorius and his disintegrator. Yet in vanishing—presumably for good—she leaves the mystery of her being unresolved. While Kelvin may be correct in his surmise about the elementary components of the "visitors," the success of the "experiment" based on that neutrino theory of his does not necessarily validate it. It is just as conceivable that Solaris itself has caused Rheya to disappear in response to the encephalogram of Kelvin's waking thoughts that Snow has beamed at the ocean in the form of x-ray messages. What is certain is that Rheya participates in her doom, and in doing so asserts her autonomy.

Undeniably, her freedom is far from absolute. Perilously balanced as it is against the destiny of recapitulating the fate of the woman on whom she has been patterned, it is subject to obvious constraints. Her autonomy thus appears to be precarious, equivocal, and even perhaps delusory—which is to say, it is human in its dimensions. She does not, however, merely reenact the fate of her predecessor. Her suicide is to be understood as a self-sacrifice of a different kind. For one thing, she makes her decision self-consciously—conscious, that is, of her prototype. More significantly, *her* act frees Kelvin from the bondage of guilt—as it was meant to do. It liberates him from his past in the only way humanly possible: not, as in a fairy tale, by undoing what has been done, but by compelling him to revise his perception of his past. Dispossessed of the specter of guilt,[18] Kelvin can now achieve some kind of contact with Solaris.

> I sat on the rough, fissured beach. A heavy black wave broke over the edge of the bank and spread out. . . . The ebbing wave left viscous streamlets behind, which flowed back quivering towards the ocean. I went closer, and when the next wave came I held out my hand. . . . [T]he wave hesitated, recoiled, then enveloped my hand without touching it, so that a thin covering of "air" separated my glove inside a cavity which had been fluid a moment previously, and now had a fleshy consistency. I raised my hand slowly, and the wave, or rather an outcrop of the wave, rose at the same time, enfolding my hand in a translucent cyst with greenish reflections. I stood up, so as to raise my hand still higher, and the gelatinous substance stretched like a rope, but did not break. The main body of the wave remained motionless on the shore, surrounding my feet without touching them, like some strange beast patiently waiting for an experiment to finish. A flower had grown out of the ocean, and its calyx was moulded to my fingers. (pp. 209–10)

The "contact" here is not direct and unambiguous. Yet the wave's "enfolding" of his gloved hand images a fragile communion between Kelvin and the ocean, a communion which occurring as it does soon after Rheya's disappearance, presents itself as the outcome of her act of self-sacrifice.

IV

The nature of Rheya and the other "visitors" is not, of course, the only mystery in *Solaris*. The ocean itself is likewise the enigmatic subject of scientific investigation. Clearly it is an entity capable of something at least distantly akin to human creative thought. But its habitual modes of "self-expression"—its "symmetriads," "asymmetriads," "mimoids," and whatnot—are so alien to man as to justify fully the derision of a Grastrom over the possibility of any kind of cognitive "contact" with it (see p. 178). Yet ludicrous though it may be to regard it as "a giant brain" (p. 153), the ocean does adopt one manner of response that is decisively, indeed literally, anthropomorphic: it generates the "Phi-creatures." Moreover, if it is itself the sort of "living creature" that Kelvin becomes convinced it is (p. 179), its acts must be in some sense intentional. Seen from that perspective, it brings Rheya into being not simply for the mediatory purpose which she by her effect on Kelvin fulfills, but also by way of self-explanation. On a scale of magnitude and complexity and in a form which may make Solaris to some extent humanly comprehensible, Rheya structurally exemplifies the ocean's modes of consciousness. True, there is no sign that Kelvin in the end has anything more than an intuitive feeling of what Solaris is about. It should nevertheless be apparent that the ocean manifests itself in Rheya as it does otherwise: that it acts and reacts, sometimes modifying its behavior in a kind of problem-solving response to external stimuli, sometimes regulating that behavior in accordance with laws and processes wholly internal to it.

By that equivalence between Rheya and Solaris, Lem connects the anthropomorphic objects of scientific inquiry with those which are human neither in form nor in scale. Fashioning cybernetic models of planetary or near-planetary proportions along with others which are human in their dimensions, he gives philosophical coherence to Wiener's discrete views of man and the universe. At the same time, he imparts a skeptical emphasis to Wiener's theorizing.

His point of departure, as it were, can be located in one of the rare unpragmatic doubts that Wiener gives utterance to. "Without faith that nature is subject to law," writes Wiener, "there can be no science." The need for such faith, moreover, applies equally for "a purely causative world and for one in which probability rules." Yet "[n]o amount of demonstration can ever prove that nature is subject to law. For all we know, the world from the next moment on might be something like the croquet game in *Alice in Wonderland,* where the balls are hedgehogs which walk off, the hoops are soldiers which march to other parts of the field, and the rules are made from instant to instant by the arbitrary decree of the Queen" (p. 263). Wiener is right to dismiss this as an irrelevant possibility. A universe which obeys the caprice of a Carrollesque Queen of Hearts and whose components otherwise act out of merely random wilfulness has nothing to do with the universe science conceives of. The former, as the variant or analogue of a world presided over by supernatural powers, rests on premises quite extraneous to the scientific enterprise and thus lies outside the purview of the scientist.

Lem, however, in effect seizes upon Wiener's "what if" and transforms it into a serious challenge to science from within. He imagines systems which, as natural phenomena, demand scientific explanation, and in their evolutionary dynamics defy it. Their intractability apparently arises from the scope of those dynamics, which are beyond what the human mind can take in, and from their responsiveness to man's investigatory probings, which become "input" altering the system under examination. But their dynamics of response in turn point to another, and more comprehensive, source of their resistance to human attempts to account for them: intentionality.

That Solaris, the Black Cloud, and their like appear capable of various modes of intentional behavior is not at all inconsistent with the scientific presumption that consciousness is an evolutionary accident (an idea which Lem dramatizes in his whimsical and irreverent parable of Mymosh the Self-begotten: see *The Cyberiad,* pp. 188–92). Nor is it at all consistent with the scheme of ontological oppositions that man imposes on the universe. From the standpoint of any dominant scientific cosmology, past or present, the ocean-planet of *Solaris* or the agglomeration of tiny ferrous particles of *The Invincible* should be a *tertium non datur.* Each is substantially the antithesis of anything usually thought of as a life-form, let alone an intelligent life-form. Yet as exemplars of precisely those species of phenomena ordinarily supposed to be inanimate, they have an uncanny capacity for intelligent response and an unnerving ability to project or assume a human shape.[19] To the extent that they manifest signs of a humanoid intelligence, they do not fit in with preconceptions of the totally alien. But by "enact[ing] mysterious rites" (*The Invincible*, p. 217) which are neither anthropomorphic nor explicable within the usual parameters of human motivation, they also place themselves outside the category of the absolutely nonalien.[20]

Standing in denial of any dichotomy between the human and the alien, these systems of Lem's promote the critique of scientific reason whose outline emerges from the history of Solaristics. Kelvin's résumé of how all-but-anonymous "archivists" have superseded the "great Solarists" of the past and replaced the belief in "conscious will, teleological processes, and activity motivated by some inner need of the ocean" with "apsychic" "colloido-mechanistic theories" (*Solaris*, p. 174) broadly recapitulates the history of science itself, with its gradual triumph of post-Darwinian over pre-Galileian cosmologies. But Solarist orthodoxies, old and new, turn out to be more or less equally erroneous, and for a reason that impugns their historical analogues as well. They are serviceable only for defining Solaris as a *tertium datur*. Otherwise, their mutually exclusive extremes prove to be incommensurate with that ocean, which remains especially unintelligible in terms of the binary opposition between "conscious will" and pure accident. Assigning a telos to its intricately patterned ballet of forms involves an exercise in fantasizing; but it is just as fantastic to imagine that its responses to a human presence are sheerly random. If its acts have no ultimate purpose, and certainly none that is humanly discoverable, they nevertheless appear to be purposive. It is true that chance may intervene to compromise their intent and even determine their end result. But operating in the case of Solaris as it does on the course of human actions, accident qualifies intention and renders its status problematical, rather than precluding it altogether.

Those problematics are the subject of *Katar*, or *The Chain of Chance* (1975). The English title suggests the paradoxical quality of a book Lem clearly designs in part to correct one false understanding of another of his science-fictionalized tales of detection. Though it resembles *The Investigation* in many ways, *The Chain of Chance* allows no room for the suspicion that the enigmatic phenomena it deals with have any supernatural cause. Indeed, the explanation it gives for the mysterious suicides of eleven (or possibly twelve) middle-aged bachelors or divorcés is not totally rational and definitive, but explicit and scientifically detailed to a degree quite unnecessary on any except remedial grounds. Untypically of Lem, the lone X in the solution is the one designating the compound that the French (among others, perhaps) are working to perfect for use in psychochemical warfare. But though finally analyzed, the mystery leaves as its residue an unresolved—and unresolvable—dilemma.

The dilemma first surfaces in a surreally modernized Rome airport as Lem's detective, an American ex-astronaut, attempts to disarm a Japanese terrorist: "I made a dive for . . . [his] grenade but only brushed it because the Japanese suddenly lunged backward with such force that he knocked those behind him off their feet and kicked me in the knee. My elbow landed in . . . [a French] girl's face; the impact sent me reeling against the railing. I banged into her again and this time took her with me as we both cleared the railing and went sailing through the air" (p. 36). Even as he thus reports the event in retrospect, it is far from certain that in leaping from the walkway he meant to save anyone other than himself. Yet he later represents the case somewhat differently: "One thing I knew: I hadn't wasted any time going over the railing. Grabbing hold of it with my right arm, I'd taken off from the step with my other arm wrapped around the girl. By hurdling the railing in the manner of a side vault, I'd forced her to accompany me on my way down. Whether I'd put my arm around her deliberately or because she just happened to be standing there, I couldn't say" (p. 52). Intention becomes still less distinguishable from happenstance towards the end of the book when the former astronaut, in the throes of the same kind of psychochemically induced attack of paranoic schizophrenia that had driven previous victims to suicide, throws "a handful" of "tiny dark objects [that had] spilled out from between . . . [the] shirts [in his suitcase]—almonds that had fallen out of the[ir] package—" "on top of the telegram" he has written to his confrere (p. 170). These Neapolitan "bitter almonds" are a crucial clue, since the cyanide they contain acts as a catalyst to "increase the psychotropic toxicity [of compound X] a million times" (p. 172). In the circumstances, however, his intent to thus "make note of them" would seem to be *ex post facto*, notwithstanding his assertion that "I had been trained to record things under conditions of maximum stress" and that accordingly "this reflex of mine could have been the result of many years of practice" (p. 173).

Accident in *The Chain of Chance* seems to obviate intention on a much larger scale also. To determine the cause of the suicides, the detective means to relive, so far as he can, the experiences of one Thomas Adams at the scene where he evidently contracted his strange propensity to do away with himself; and with that idea in mind, he assumes Adams's name as his alias and goes to Naples. The mission is a failure. But as he prepares to leave Paris and return to the States, a series of accidents brings him into contact with all of the substances requisite for inducing the appropriate "psychotropic" effect. Nor is it simply ironic that chance fulfills his original intention. Lem's point is that the two may in fact coincide in a manner that makes it impossible to differentiate accident from purposiveness.[21]

For that reason, an intentional universe as Lem outlines it in "The New Cosmogony" and elsewhere[22] would exhibit to human perception much of the randomness of the universe which, say, Quantum Theory posits. But Lem's "Game of Intelligences" "tending to goals" (*Perfect Vacuum* [*PV*], p. 228) "saves the appearances" of chance in a way that subverts all purely stochastic models. In the "Cosmogonic Game" he envisions, the "Players," arising wherever local conditions permit, are "civilizations," defined as such by their gradually acquired power to transmute themselves somewhat after the fashion of bacterial colonies chemically interacting with their cultural medium (see *PV*, p. 211). The analogy, however, is not entirely exact. It serves, albeit derogatorily, to implicate *homo technologicus* in the ludic scheme of things;[23] but it also suggests that the Cosmic Players maintain some direct connection with one another. This, they discover, must not be the case. As they singly enlarge the scope of their endeavors to regulate their environment, the laws of physics each imposes on its "time-space ambience" eventually collide, with explosive effect (*PV*, pp. 212–13). At the moment they thus become aware that the Game involves many "civilizations," they are also obliged to recognize that its continuance demands that their efforts at controlling "Nature" remain discrete. They must, in other words, acknowledge "the fundamental impossibility of establishing contact"—that is, of "transmit[ting], from the domain of one Physics, any message into the domain of another" (*PV*, pp. 213–14). "Each of them . . . had to work alone. A continuation of their former tactics would have been pointless if not outright perilous; instead of wasting effort in head-on collisions they had to unite, but unite without any prior arrangement whatever . . . . Each player, then, operates on the strategic principle of minimax: it changes the existing conditions in such a way as to maximize gain and minimize harm," (*PV*, p. 214).

Observance of that rule necessitates "a single," yet "*hierarchical* Physics" (*PV*, pp. 214, 215). Every Player, realizing that it "creates a feedback loop between the transformation of . . . [its] surroundings and . . . [its] autotransformation," can allow the laws it establishes only "limited sovereignty" (*PV*, p. 215). If it is to avoid interference with, and from, the other participants in the Game, it must accede to a "higher" Physics, which dictates, for example, the expansion of the universe at a constant rate sufficient to ensure against future collisions among them (*PV*, pp. 217–18). "[T]he present Universe" is therefore "homogenous and isotropic[,] . . . governed by the same laws throughout" and hence possessed of "[t]he properties that Einstein discovered in [it]," as "the result of decisions which, though made separately, are identical, owing to the identical ['*strategic*'] situation of the players" (*PV*, p. 215).

Chance has its place in such a cosmos. It enters as a factor in "the initial states" of the players, for instance (*PV*, p. 216). But the appearance of mere randomness becomes deceptive once the players, assuming a certain amount of control over the Game, begin to exploit and even exaggerate "disorder . . . to institute in the Universe *a single order*"(*PV*, p. 223). On the other hand, no phase of the Game is the simple product of intention, not only because the "moves" of the players collectively restrict those that any one of them may make, but in consequence of the "feedback loop" mechanism that modifies both individual and collective purpose.

Thanks to that mechanism, the Cosmogonic Game resembles croquet *à la Alice in Wonderland* rather than chess. After all, it "rules change—that is, the manner of the moves, and the pieces themselves, and the board" (*PV*, p. 222). Yet there is nothing arbitrary or wilful about it. Its constituent players, unlike the Red Queen's hedgehogs and soldiers, are seeking to normalize their environment. Moreover, the result, as their "uniform Physics" (*PV*, p. 214) brings it into accord, at least temporarily, with Einsteinian theory, is to make the Game coincide with the presently dominant scientific image of the cosmos. In effect, however, the congruence is disturbing; for instead of otiosely duplicating that image, the cybernetic reflection displaces it with another: of a cosmos subject to continuous "revisions" (*PV*, p. 224) and tending to negate the principle of entropy. Lem thus superimposes a sophisticated version of Wiener's "thinking machine" on Wiener's probabilistic universe.

Lem toys with numerous variants, astronomical or human in scale, of this basic model of cybernetic self-alteration; but perhaps none is more compelling than Solaris. It declares its similarity with the Players in his Cosmogonic Game by "exerting an active influence on . . . [its] orbital path" (p. 24), and it thereby discountenances the "theory . . . that life . . . [is] impossible on . . . satellites" liable to the "fluctuations in gravity" that "two solar bodies" (viz., its red and blue suns) occasion (p. 21). Yet neither its "self-generated" power of "stabiliz[ing] its eccentric orbit" (p. 173) nor anything else that makes Solaris an exception to scientific rule is as troublesome in itself as it is in conjunction with the ways the ocean is no anomaly. Its extrahuman intelligence perplexes scientific orthodoxy not because it contravenes the laws of cosmic evolution but because it conforms to them—or, more precisely, to a cybernetic understanding of them. Indeed, that intelligence, especially as manifest in the normal "self-creative" activity of the ocean, appears as a function of the evolutionary process regarded as an "inexorabl[e] striv[ing] to exploit every possible organic combination inherent within a given ['structural'] prototype."[24]

V

However much they seem to come to life, these extrahuman systems of Lem's—Solaris included—after all remain fictional. But they also stand as paradigms. They represent natural phenomena and at the same time incorporate a cybernetic (re)interpretation of those phenomena. Morever, the paradigm and the contextual fiction in its entirety reinforce each other in their reciprocal objective of calling into question both the mechanistic models that science latterly subscribes to and the teleological ones that man tends to fall back on when confronted with the inadequacy of a purely mechanistic scheme of things. As embodiments of a cybernetic view of evolutionary principles, the homeostatic worlds Lem constructs oppose—and finally subsume[25]—that alternative; while as fictions, they serve to discredit it, at least to the extent that they can be taken as plausible representations of a cosmic process which proves unamenable either to a positivistically mechanical explanation or to one predicated on a "conscious will" diminished to anthropomorphic proportions.

In *The Investigation,* Lem extends his critique of the models scientific reason has erected so as to take in Wiener's probabilistic universe explicitly. As the title suggests, a theme of *Solaris* predominates here. *The Investigation* focuses almost exclusively on methods of empirical inquiry, and does so primarily in terms of an inquiry into the enigmatic phenomenon of corpses which at intervals mysteriously vanish and in time begin reappearing just as mysteriously.

The details of their disappearance evoke the pattern of the most classic of classic detective fictions: the crime committed in a sealed chamber. As in most tales of detection, too, interest centers not on the crime as such— which in these instances seems to be on the order of a prank rather than a serious malfeasance—but on the crime as intellectual puzzle. However, this particular puzzle disappoints any expectation that a culprit will be found. Gregory, the Scotland Yard detective in charge of pursuing the case, presumes that the disappearances comport with the generic rules of the typical "whodunit," as it were: that they are the work of some perverse malfactor locatable among a finite and small number of suspects. But his assiduous efforts to find a perpetrator instead tend to demonstrate that the mystery involves natural occurrences and that its solution—whatever it may be—does not lie within the confines of a closed and limited set of possibilities.

His colleague Sciss, convinced from the start that he is dealing with a matter for "scientific study," not "criminal investigation" (p. 106), takes a different approach to the case. He "concentrates" the methods of mass-statistical analysis "on the phenomenon as a whole" (p. 140). His probabilistic model of inquiry has the advantage of allowing him to discern a "regular pattern of action" in the movements of the corpses (p. 108) and thence to predict their eventual reappearance. But it chiefly recommends itself as a corrective for what he characterizes as Gregory's "[s]o-called common sense," which "relies on programmed nonperception, concealment, or ridicule of everything that doesn't fit into the conventional nineteenth[-] century vision of the world that can be explained down to the last detail" (p. 139). In counterpoint to Gregory's narrow-sighted quest for the criminal agent, Sciss looks for some connection between the behavior of the corpses and phenomena accepted as commonplace, and thus acknowledges the openendedness of the problem while enlarging the field of investigatory perception.

Despite these virtues, however, his probabilistic approach is none the less suspect. For one thing, the particular hypothesis that Sciss comes up with is, in his words, "full of holes" (p. 111), since any number of variables might yield the sort of correlation he posits between the disappearances in Norfolk and the (low) incidence of cancer in that region. Furthermore, Sciss transfers from one unknown to another a burden of explanation which his methodology prevents him from assuming (p. 108). Nor is this the only respect in which his results corroborate his remark that "in actuality you can't take a step without encountering some phenomenon that you cannot understand," but belie his conclusion: "and never will understand without the use of statistics" (p. 139). They also make the mystery all the more mysterious by confirming its duality. They call attention to the status of the corpses as human bodies, in whose pattern of movement Sciss recognizes a configurational motive force, not merely as dead bodies, whose behavior he connects with "other [natural] phenomena" (p. 108). His findings, on the one hand, point to the resemblance these bodies have to the supposedly "dead forms . . . enact[ing] mysterious rites" on Regis III (*Invincible*, p. 217), and hence suggest that the corpses perform in a rudimentary way the cybernetic transmutations of the Black Cloud—or of Solaris. On the other hand, those same findings affirm an animating power within the corpses, and hence underscore the human side of the mystery.

His statistical methods thus indicate a dimension to which, as Sciss himself admits, they cannot give access (see pp. 140–41). A probabilistic calculus may be adequate for describing, and even perhaps predicting, the behavior of entities *en masse;* but it does not, and can not, deal with them as individuals. Lem addresses this matter most explicitly in his *"De Impossibilitate Vitae* and *De Impossibilitate Prognoscendi"* (*PV*, pp. 141–66), where he demonstrates at length that the probability of someone's being the individual that he or she is is on the order of "one in one centillion"—that is, comes close to zero. In fact, the odds of a person's having been born with the unique combination of particular characteristics that she or he has hardly compare with those in favor of such "thermodynamic miracles" as "the freezing of water in a pot standing over a flame . . .[or] the rising from the floor of fragments of a broken glass and their joining together to make a whole glass" (*PV*, p. 161).

The comparison explains the ironic appropriateness of Gregory's suspicion that Sciss is responsible for the incidents in Norfolk.

Although the statistician's investigatory model directly offers no real insight into the life of the phenomenon, the behavior of the corpses is, in an indirect way, the logical consequence of probabilism; and it becomes comprehensible only when viewed, first of all, in that connection. Dead bodies which up and move about seemingly of their own accord finally belong to the order of "thermodynamic miracles": they are the human equivalent of the fragments of a glass which somehow reconstitute themselves as that glass. But they also belong in, and serve to satirize, a stochastic universe. Faceless corpses may well enact their mysterious rites wherever such "miracles" are more probable than human uniqueness; for a world governed by that calculation and visibly—indeed, ostentatiously—displaying signs of human idiosyncrasy (most notably in the persons of Gregory and Sciss) is one in which even dragons are possible (see "The Dragons of Probability," the parable that complements "*De Impossibilitate Vitae. . . ,*" in *The Cyberiad,* pp. 76–89).

Absurd though they are, these deductions do not invalidate probability theory for the physicist, who is not concerned, for example, with the individuality of atoms. None the less, Lem's criticism, even after he has balanced it against the latter consideration (see *PV,* pp. 163–66), leaves human reason without the conceptual means for grasping the universe in its integral particularity. Human perception of its mysteries, as the computer scientist in *The Chain of Chance* puts it, is like "looking at a ['half-tone'] photo."[26] "The naked eye can make out the general outline but not the details. A magnifying glass will make things stand out more clearly, but the image will remain blurred. If we take it to the microscope we find the picture gets lost, that it disintegrates into tiny dots. Each dot is something distinct; [but] they no longer combine [in]to a meaningful picture" (p. 94). This is the dilemma that haunts all of Lem's investigators. Attempting to take in the whole picture, they lose sight of its details, and vice-versa.

The incidents at Norfolk present exactly that problem for both Gregory and Sciss, with their mutually opposing models of rational inquiry. That is why the focal point of *The Investigation* is what its title announces it to be: not, as in *Solaris* and *The Invincible,* the phenomena being investigated, but the process of investigation itself. Except by reference to that process, the human meaning that Gregory finally imparts to the disappearance remains inexplicable. Com-

bining the probabilistic generalities of the statistician with his previous insistence on its particular human aspects, Gregory—under
Chief Inspector Sheppard's aegis—intimates what bearing the case
may have on the mystery of human existence: "Maybe even we . . .
only exist from time to time; I mean: sometimes less, sometimes
almost disappearing, dissolving, and then, with a sudden spasm, a
sudden spurt that disintegrates the memory center, we merge for a
moment . . . for a day . . . and we become— '[one with the cosmos?]'"
(p. 180; the last two sets of ellipsis points appear in the text). This
elliptical intuition of Gregory's is understandable only in terms of an
Investigation, wherein persons vanish and reappear as the subjects of
an investigatory perception that implicates them in the operations of
the universe.

VI

The idea of human beings caught up in a sort of universal
"Brownian motion" (p. 180) may be adequate for identifying the
significance of the behavior of the dead, yet human, bodies in *The
Investigation;* but it places emphasis on only one of the two directions
in which the rapprochement between man and the cosmos proceeds.
It stresses—and the fiction on the whole confirms—the confluence
that results from the human species' having "multiplied to such an
extent that it's now starting to be governed by atomic laws" (*The
Chain of Chance,* p. 176). A geometric increase in their number
eventually reaches the point of alienating human beings from their
individuality, thereby reducing their status to that of atoms under the
sway of the laws of probability: that is what the virtually interchange-
able *human* corpses serve to dramatize. The transformation, however, as it operates on *dead* human bodies, also implies the reverse
possibility: that the nonhuman, atomic world, upon achieving certain
proportions, might become capable of the kind of self-organization
that allows it to take on a life of its own—and thus defy, and subvert,
the probabilism that, as it were, engenders it.

Master's Voice makes it clear that this is precisely the case with
Lem's extrahuman cybernetic worlds. Its prefatory admission that
the author does not entirely understand *Solaris* (p. 9) is somewhat
misleading, since *Master's Voice* in fact amounts to an extended
commentary on Lem's previous work, and especially on *Solaris,* in a

new fictive guise. Straddling the divide between fiction and nonfiction, the book takes its title from the official code-name of a project
(MAVO for short) for deciphering a "letter from the stars."[27]

Although the theoretical obstacles to interpreting the "stellar
communication" are formidable, MAVO scientists do arrive at some
more or less empirical conclusions about it. For one thing, they
determine that its medium consists of "neutrino" waves. For
another, they extract from it—possibly with the superaddition of
what they know of chemistry—the information that permits them to
create a "pseudo-plasma," "a substance semi-fluid in certain conditions, gelatinous in others," whose normal appearance prompts the
appellation "Frog's Eggs" (p. 121 [90]). While it is not, "in the
biological sense," metabolic, this material reacts to stimuli and produces energy "diffused in the form of heat." At the same time, its
apparently "perpetual motion, albeit in the form of a colloid and not
that of a machine," violates "the sacrosanct laws of thermodynamics." Its homeostatic properties, MAVO scientists discover,
come from "nuclear reactions of the 'cold type' "; but these ensue
only when the "giant molecules, which in isolation are unstable,"
have "attained a certain mass, called 'critical.' " However, it is "not
only the quantity of substance, but also its configuration" that gives
this "colloid" the energy to maintain an equilibrous state (p. 122
[90–91]).

The fact that the "giant molecules" require a certain "critical
mass" in order to engage in self-organizing activity relates them to
the "flies" which constitute themselves as *The Invincible*'s Black
Cloud (see *The Invincible*, pp. 121–22). Their similarities, however,
are not as striking as those that obtain between the "colloidal"
"pseudo-plasma" and Solaris, whose substantial nature is described
in like terms. The connection becomes unmistakable with the discovery that in large quanitites the "stellar substance" begins to generate
shapes which seem to be the prototypes of the ocean-planet's "exten-
sors," "asymmetriads," "mimoids," and so forth (see *MV*, p. 154,
157 [117, 120]).

This last-mentioned behavioral property of the "Frog's Eggs"
lends itself to a malevolent purpose which gives poignance to the
alternate name for the substance: "Lord of the Flies." Though it is so
called because of its power over certain species of hymenoptera
rather than because it is per se diabolic, its designation anticipates the
diabolical uses to which human ingenuity can put it as a nuclear

explosive transmittable, via neutrino beam, at the speed of light. Its would-be military application[28] not only calls attention to the socio-political factors affecting a scientific enterprise that is government funded and supervised (at least nominally) by the Pentagon; it also exacerbates the problem of "stellar intent" and gives it moral urgency.

The hypotheses that proliferate about the "letter from the stars" reveal the complexity of the problem. The experimental evidence suggests that the transmission encodes *a* life-creating principle, and perhaps *the* principle of life in the cosmos; but in human hands, it is potentially destructive. Does the "message" itself, then, possess a Manichaean ambivalence? Indeed, is it, strictly speaking, a "message?" If so, for whom do the stars intend it? Probably not for man alone—or at all, insofar as he is perversely inclined to abuse it, to employ it for his own annihilation. Possibly the stars have no particular recipient in mind;[29] but in that case, why do they emit it? Do they mean to reproduce themselves thereby—which would be tantamount to mockery of the effeteness of mankind's quest for "mirrors" of the human self on "other worlds" (*Solaris*, p. 81; see below)? Or are they disinterestedly broadcasting a life-principle which they may not partake of across the abyss that otherwise isolates their universe of antimatter (see *MV*, p. 231ff. [180ff.])? Even the tense of such queries is open to doubt. Perhaps the "message" comes from a "civilization" which is now defunct (*MV*, pp. 238–39 [186–87]), like that supposedly responsible for mechanical life on Regis III (see "Lauda's Hypothesis" in *The Invincible*, esp. p. 118).

The almost endless theorizing as to the purport of the "stellar communication," while it raises those and other unanswerable questions, is not altogether pointless. Nor does it merely demonstrate the truth of what the mathematician Peter Hogarth says in the course of these reflection of his which comprise *Master's Voice*: that in regard to cosmic profundities, *"Ignoramus et ignorabimus"* (p. 210 [163]). It also identifies the emitters of the "message" as players in the universal game of Lem's "New Cosmogony." At the same time, it establishes Solaris to be either their equal or their creature. Given its context, it perforce implicates man in the cosmogonic game as well; for the occasion of all his theorizing is a project logically predicated on "the possibility of a resemblance, howsoever distant, between the Senders of the code and those for whom it is destined." Without that assumptive commitment, there can be no reasonable hope of deciphering the "letter from the stars," since, as the skeptical Hogarth points out, "the absence of any [such] *ressemblance* would render comprehension of the message . . . impossible" (*MV*, p. 131 [98]). Man's putative similarity to "the stars" has its basis, at least in part, in the substance derived from the "stellar code." Any intentions this "colloid" may have appear as the epiphenomenal consequence, or byproduct, of self-preserving activities pursuant upon its structural configuration, and are therefore a built-in mechanism rather than the immediate result of conscious choice. But its homeorhetic processes thereby differ essentially neither from Solaris's—or the Black Cloud's—nor from Trurl's and Klapaucius's—or, for that matter, from the former astronaut's in *The Chain of Chance* or Ijon Tichy's—as they react automatically to life-threatening situations. From the perspective of *Master's Voice,* then, the wave's enveloping of Kelvin's gloved hand without actually touching it signalizes his kinship with Solaris in this regard. But beyond that, the ambiguous "contact" (which is thus defined) also images the kind of cooperative union "without any prior arrangement whatever" that Lem's cosmic players are capable of, and hence indicates man's partnership in the cosmogonic game.

VII

The attention Lem devotes to the idea of a *ludus universalis* might suggest that he is proponing it for its own sake. But while seeming to offer up an alternate model of the objective world that science deals with, he does not advance his cybernetic paradigms as an end in themselves. Instead, he uses them as instruments for examining the problematics of what it means, in cognitional terms, to be human.

The complex issue of human identity, as Lem analyzes it, involves a series of questions ultimately relating to the universe at large and based upon the distinctions of mind versus mechanism, autonomy versus automatism, intention versus accident, the self versus the other, and so on. He makes no presumption as to the absolute validity of such antinomies, which in fact become suspect in view of the questions they give rise to. His approach is exploratory rather than assertive; his conclusions provisional rather than dogmatic. He remains wary of answers, especially those pretending to finality.[30]

In its pervasive skepticism, his attitude is reminiscent of Michel de Montaigne's in the memorable passage from *An Apologie of Raymond Sebond* wherein Montaigne generalizes his wonderment about his cat. "How knoweth . . . [man] by vertue of his understanding the inward and secret motions of beasts?" Montaigne asks. "By what comparison from them to us doth he conclude the brutishnesse he ascribeth unto them? When I am playing with my cat, who knowes whether she have more sport in dallying with me than I have in gaming with her?"[31] Queries of this sort, he argues, indicate the limits of human knowledge. The man who imagines he has the definitive solution to them is deluded: his certainty about the "brutishnesse" of beasts only discloses his ignorance—above all, his ignorance of himself.

Substituting cybernetic, or "intellectronic," entities of astronomical or human magnitude for beasts as his term of comparison, Lem rephrases Montaigne's fundamental doubt. But unlike Montaigne, he does not finally escape from incertitude through an appeal to divine revelation. Despite his pronounced interest in matters theological, and particularly in theogony and theodicy, [32] Lem is no fideist—at least not in any usual and unambiguous sense of the word. His skepticism is in this regard akin to that of Pierre Bayle and the philosophers of the Enlightenment. He shares the *philosophe*'s antipathy to (and obsession with) dogma. He also has the dubiousness of a Voltaire as to the validity of deducing would-be truths about the cosmos by inference from anthropomorphic analogies. The "Iridian" who, in "The Eighth Voyage" from *The Star Diaries,* denounces that habit of mind surely voices the sentiments of the author: "since the normal course of evolutionary processes in the Universe is unknown to . . . [human beings], they take their physical shape, however hideous it may be, as well as their way—such as it is—of thinking, for ordinary phenomena, entirely typical of those manifest throughout the macrocosm" (p. 39).

This indictment, however, conveys only the most obvious point of a critique which is Swiftian in its ironic complexity. The Iridian's polemical outburst, while it stresses the erroneousness of anthropocentric reasoning per se, barely touches upon what is more significant: the error behind such reasoning. That source of human miscalculation, as Lem intimates elsewhere, is self-ignorance. Kelvin concedes as much when he ruefully observes that "Man has gone out to explore other worlds"—in vehicles styled *Prometheus* and *The Invincible*—"without having explored his own [mind's] labyrinth of

dark passages and secret chambers, and without finding what lies
behind doorways that he himself has sealed" (*Solaris*, p. 165). Because he has not accurately gauged himself, man cannot stand as the
measure of the universe. But the universe as he misprises it—the
universe onto which he projects his thoughts and desires—is his
mirror-measure. As his picture of it reflects his self-estimation, so the
distortions in that picture reflect upon his lack of self-awareness.[33]

Variations on that motif recur time and again in Lem's fictions.
It takes graphic form, for instance, in the brief episode wherein
detective Gregory, wandering the streets of London one night, turns
into a blind alley and unexpectedly comes upon his own mirror-image
without apprehending it as such (*The Investigation*, p. 33). The same
sort of thing happens in "The Seventh Voyage" from *The Star
Diaries*. Ijon Tichy's suddenly rudderless spaceshift drifts into a
"gravitational vortex" which causes time to "loop" (pp. 4–5); and the
result is a series of encounters between his past, present, and future
selves. This may seem to be the chief instance of Lem's perpetrating
the kind of empty game that he trenchantly reproves in his remarks
on the time-travel story.[34] Yet the details of Tichy's confusion evince
something other than mere playfulness on Lem's part. Even here,
that is, the paradox becomes the pretext for a parable of nonself-
recognition.

The paradox assumes a more abstract form in *Solaris*. When
Snow lectures Kelvin on the would-be heroics of man's search for
"other worlds," neither he nor his auditor is fully aware of the irony
attendant upon his remarks:

> "We don't want to conquer the cosmos [says Snow], we simply want to
> extend the boundaries of the Earth to the frontiers of the cosmos. . . .
> We are humanitarian and chivalrous; we don't want to enslave other
> races, we simply want to bequeath them our values and take over their
> heritage in exchange. We think of ourselves as Knights of the Holy
> Contact. This is another lie. We are only seeking Man. We have no need
> of other worlds. We need mirrors." (p. 81)

This sarcastic appraisal of man's imperialistic endeavors rightly intimates that there is a rift between the human and the alien which he
has made impassable. But the connection with the human desire for
self-images is not exactly what Snow supposes it to be. In the case of a
Solaris, the rift primarily exists not because their "need" for "mirrors" impels scientists to violate the otherness of "other worlds," but

because they do not see the ocean-planet at the very mirror they are looking for. Their obliviousness to the *structural* resemblance its operations bear to the workings of the human mind makes Solaris, like the "letter from the stars," into "a kind of Rorschach Test" (*MV*, p. 50 [32]). Yet even in this regard it traduces the dichotomy implicit in Snow's little sermon. It gives investigators ample scope to project onto it whatever fantasies and preconceptions their psychological make-up may dictate; but it also preempts, reverses, and "materializes" that human propensity by means of the "Phi-creatures." Certainly the extent to which those "visitors" appear alien to them is an index of the degree to which the Solarists misconceive of themselves.

Self-ignorance thus emerges as more than simply a psychological failing. It is the principal barrier to the human understanding of "other worlds." Hogarth so identifies it when he asks: "If our culture does not know how to assimilate readily those concepts which deviate from the mainstream of human thought," not even when they originate in the brains of our contemporaries, "how can we reckon that we could in any measure effectively comprehend a culture entirely different from ours addressing us across cosmic expanses?" (*MV*, pp. 42–43 [26]). Later on, he resorts to a diachronic analogy for restating the objection in greater detail:

> From the death mask of Amenhotep, the art historian will decode the epoch and its cultural style. . . . The chemist will explain its methods of working gold . . . and the physician will make a diagnosis proving that Amenhotep suffered from endocrine troubles which brought with them an acromegalic deformation of the jaw-bones . . . . [But] what did . . . [those ancients] know about the chemistry of gold, acromegalia, and cultural styles? If we reverse the procedure and send to an Egyptian of Amenhotep's age a letter written today, he could not make sense of it, not only because he would not know our language, but also because he would have at his disposal neither the words nor the concepts to which he could subordinate ours. (pp. 103–4 [75])

In arguing that history is, for widely "linguistic" reasons, irreversible, Hogarth may seem to be absolutizing the alien. Yet his analogies plainly suggest that man's inability to traverse the evolutionary distance separating him from any "stellar civilization" is contingent upon an absence of self-understanding. Indeed, as they translate otherness into wholly human terms, they point to misprision of self as its principal source.

It is that for Gregory, for example. His assumptions about the disappearances in Norfolk are essentially those of the 19th-century scientific determinist.[35] Though he is searching for an agent of deranged purpose rather than an impersonal agency, he takes it for granted that the events he is investigating exist in a closed system as the effect of a more or less proximate external cause. He accordingly discounts the most salient fact about the behavior of the corpses: their appearance of being self-motivated. His mistake in this case is the same one he commits when he tries to make sense of the noises that emanate nightly from the apartment next door to his (see *The Investigation*, pp. 54–55 and pp. 129–32). Giving free rein to his imagination, he attempts to interpret what is going on on the basis of the fragmentary perceptions of an outsider. He thereby reconstructs an unexplained phenomenon so that it appears as an inexplicable and macabre criminological fantasy. At the same time, he establishes a parity between something absolutely unfamiliar (viz., the vanishing corpses) and something unfamiliar to him (viz., the nocturnal routine that illness has imposed on his neighbors).

The error that Gregory falls into by ignoring the introspective factor of self-motivation is cognate to the mistake he makes in the London arcade before he realizes that "The stranger . . . was himself" (p. 33; ellipsis points in the original text). In all three instances, a failure of self-awareness leads him not only to misconstrue his experiences but to become entrapped in his misinterpretation. Nor is he alone in finding himself caught in his own paranoic fantasies. Kelvin faces the same debacle when he tries to satisfy himself as to the objective existence of his percepts. He does not doubt his own being; but like Descartes in the second of his *Meditations,* he discovers that his *cogito* provides no guarantee that the world outside his mind is not an illusion. To be sure, he finally convinces himself that it is not, and does so without recourse to a Cartesian god who can overrule any satanically delusive power. Yet his proof, though it seems cogent enough and though it frees him from a paralyzing solipsism, intricates him all the more profoundly in the world of Solaris.

Something similar happens to Ijon Tichy in *The Futurological Congress.* His attempts to demonstrate to himself that he is not hallucinating are worse than futile: they plunge him ever more deeply—and ever more hopelessly—into a hallucinatory world. His dreams begin to entrap him by assimilating his "conscious" concern with distinguishing them from waking perceptions: they provide the oneiric assurance that he is not dreaming, declare their deception, and offer dehallucinogens like "vigilax" as a way out. But far from affording escape, disillusionment acts as the mechanism transporting him from one dream to the next. In the process, the dialectical involvement of the "real" with the "imaginary" becomes total. As his fantasies transform their determinants, easily incorporating his psychochemical ambience into their overt content while radically displacing the sewer out of which they come, Tichy loses his bearings altogether. The sewer, which he takes as his "real" point of reference, though it seems to disappear after being transmuted into "liquid nitrogen," does persist as the basis for all of his visions; but the dystopian revelation that confirms this also destroys it as the ground for any reality principle. With his discovery that the utopian abundance of the 21st century belies a diametrically opposite state of affairs, he accepts a sordid "truth" that is ontologically equivalent to the antithesis on which it logically depends. Thereafter, he can "awaken" from his visions only as he does to them: not to reality, but in a cloacal element continuous with his fantasies as it flows "off into the [still] unknown future" (p. 142).[36]

The most starkly schematic version of Tichy's predicament appears in the tale of King Zipperupus and Subtillion the Cybernerian (*The Cyberiad*, pp. 170–87). Royally appointed Lord High Thaumaturge but recruited as secret agent for the Sinistral Isomers, Subtillion plans to execute the assignment of doing away with their king by ensnaring him in any one of three "dreaming cabinets" constructed for that "monarcholytic" purpose. Zipperupus, however, proves hard to catch. Actuated by cowardice, greed, suspicion, and fastidiousness, he is able to overcome the libidinous allure of Subtillion's romantic dream-worlds because he can dimly discern their true status. Subtillion's last stratagem, by contrast, renders any such discrimination perilous. The king expects "Mona Lisa" to be like the first four dreams the Lord High Thaumaturge had provided him with, and ironically it is in regard to its plot against his life; but here, rather than merely vehiculating the plot, the "dream" and its "real" meaning come down to the same thing. Otherwise, too, "Mona Lisa" coincides with Zipperupus's reality in a manner that precludes their dissociation. Consisting primarily of his very act of plugging in to, and then attempting to unplug himself from, the "dreaming cabinet," it at once forecloses the possibility of the distinction that had hitherto unwittingly saved him and exploits it to confuse him utterly. "Mona Lisa" imprisons him in his own mind the moment he tries to isolate its "imaginary" contents; so that even when "he really did tear his way into reality, he thought it was a dream and plugged himself back in, and then it really was" (p. 187). From that infinitely regressive nightmare there can be no exit except by way of the kind of self-awareness concomitant with an awareness of the nature of language.

VIII

A brief coda describing the story of Zipperupus and Subtillion as one "that Trurl [originally] told to King Thumbscrew the Third" (p. 187) recalls the initial premise of the entire fiction and as well may serve as a reminder that Trurl's dispensation for it is Scheherazade's. In any event, however, the epilogue points not to the real author but to a surrogate who delegates his authority to "story-telling machines"; and these in turn give place to Subtillion's "cabinets" in a parable whose sequence of dreams is likewise homologous with the series of tales as a whole. This self-reflexivity reproduces the confusion of "Mona Lisa" on a different level. But the substitutions, as they remove the narrative ever further from the reality of authorship in one sense, in another bring it closer by hinting at the generative principle which "The Three Story-Telling Machines of King Genius" shares with *The Futurological Congress*.

That principle becomes especially apparent in the course of Professor Trottlereiner's disquisition on "the transformational possibilities of . . . language" (*FC*, pp. 105–9). At Tichy's suggestion, he begins with *myself*, analyzed into "my" and "self," whence "mine, mind. Mynd. Thy mind—thynd. Like ego, theego. And we makes wego." "We're speaking, first," he continues, "of the possibility of the merging of the mynd with the thynd, in other words the fusion of two psychic entities. Secondly, the wego. Most interesting. A collective consciousness. Produced perhaps by the multiple dissociation of the personality, a mygraine." The rationale for such "syntagmatic-paradigmatic permutations," he informs Tichy, is that "A man can comprehend only what he is able to put into words. The inexpressible therefore is unknowable. By examining the future changes in the evolution of language we come to learn what discoveries, changes and social revolutions the language will be capable, some day, of reflecting" (p. 106). Trottelreiner here resorts to the future tense.

But his exercise in "linguistic futurology" brings neologisms into being which reflect, and reflect on, the "mygraine" fantasies of psychical alteration that *The Futurological Congress* already comprises. In the same fashion, "trashmic" and "catatrashmic," "trashmos" and "macrotrashm"—futuristic terms the professor educes from *trash* in his last series of examples—presently apply to the 21st-century squalor which is the immediate context of his discourse.

Tichy's hallucinatory future may appear to precede the neologisms that it visualizes. Yet if it does not, on the contrary, originate in them, it at least has its sources in the selfsame "transformational possibilities of . . . language." Trottelreiner indicates as much in responding to Tichy's skeptical astonishment at the notion of a "trashmos," of the "Universe [as] nothing but one big trash disposal": "We have simply used futurological linguistics," he declares, "to create a new cosmogony, another theory for future generations to consider. They may or may not take it seriously, but the fact remains that it is possible to articulate such a hypothesis" (p. 109). Lem's fictive worlds for the most part can be thought of as genetically similar to Trottelreiner's "new cosmogony." They are *neologisms writ large*—or, more exactly, the results of a neologizing process, itself the linguistic analogue of a univesal "striv[ing] to exploit every possible . . . combination inherent within a given prototype."

Given its cosmogonic implications, this cybernetic idea may seem to be one more theory of the sort investigators are perpetually coming up with in their attempts to account for a Solaris, a Black Cloud, or disappearing corpses. Yet whatever its status vis-à-vis the actual universe, it demands to be taken seriously in relation to Lem's texts. There it figures not as a hypothesis of the "trashmos" variety, which those texts incidentally contain, but as the basis for the linguistic permutations from which they essentially derive. It is the principle that the text owes its existence to and by its existence realizes; and as it governs the dynamics by which language in and of itself, so to speak, generates the fiction, it enables the author of *The Cyberiad* to transfer his efficient causality of those dynamics repeatedly to cybernetic machines which are themselves metaphor-surrogates for the "alien" creative power that language acquires through its operation.

To the extent that they arise from and exemplify that principle, Lem's neologistic worlds are hardly accessible to the method of interpretation that K. adopts for trying to make sense of the Pentagon of *Memoirs Found in a Bathtub*. In his search for a Mission that will justify him and allow him to find his way out of the Pentagon's bureaucratic maze, K. eventually comes to believe that "everything is code!" (p. 105). But his consequent efforts to decipher the Pentagon turn out to be equivalent to Prandtl's exercise of reducing a more or less comprehensible statement to "gibberish" (pp. 65–66). They are as bewildering as they are futile—and necessarily so, because what K. directs them at is not at all the code he conceives of. He presumes that he is up against "a system of signs which can be translated into ordinary language with the help of a key" (p. 63). But the Pentagon does not "signify something else" apart from its structure as K. experiences it; and that configures an absence of precisely the kind of Mission he is looking for.

Because it enciphers nothing, the Pentagon of *Memoirs* is not the "system of signs" K. imagines it to be; and *code* in the sense he is fixated on thus has no pertinence to it except in defining what it is not. But the Pentagon does not merely conceal no Mission; it also signals that there is none, and does so in a manner that qualifies it as a code of an altogether different sort. Its meaning, like that of the "letter from the stars," resides in its "architecture" (*MV*, p. 167 [129]); and in this respect it is comparable to a genetic code.[37]

Such a "code" holds intellectual perils for anyone treating it as nothing but "a system of signs." That is how MAVO scientists come up with the recipe for a substance whose import they cannot determine—and thereby translate the stellar communication into something like the nonsense which Prandtl arrives at. Their approach is tantamount to seeking the meaning of a text in isolated words and phrases;[38] for in assuming that the stellar "code" consists of independent "signs," they inevitably ignore the transmitting medium, which supplies its indispensable context. What is worse, they enshrine their ignorance in their nomenclature. By the very names *Lord of the Flies* and *Frog's Eggs*, they disconnect the medium from its putative "message," and thus reproduce on a terminological level the bias of the interpretative model to which they would have the stellar "code" conform. Conversely, it is also true that the model which they impose on the "code" through such terms as they invent depends upon the would-be analytico-referential character of those terms, and hence upon a faith in the analytical capacity of language itself.[39]

This faith, as it prevents them from "deciphering" the "code," proves to be naïve and without foundation. Acting upon it, MAVO scientists first of all divorce the sidereal "message" from its transmitting medium, and then take its components as "signs" of "something else." Yet in trying to fit the "letter from the stars" to their analytical model, they succeed in distorting it so radically as to make it incomprehensible. Their analysis thus disables their understanding, but so does the language on which that analysis draws. Indeed, their problem, if not quite the one that Hogarth and Trottelreiner variously underscore, finally comes down to a matter of language none the less. They are not completely at a loss for terms for the novel phenomenon, but those that they have are more than inadequate for dealing with a "code" whose meaningful content strictly inheres in its pattern of transmission (see *MV*, p. 167 [128–29]).

Theirs is an instance not of the dictum that "the inexpressible . . . is unknowable," but of its corollary. They owe their misunderstanding of the "code" far less to a lack of words than to the words they "put [it] *into*." In fact, they become victims of the very terms they employ; for these not only violate the integrity of the "letter from the stars," they misrepresent its manner of meaning; and hence, beyond limiting human comprehension of it, they drastically misconceptualize the sidereal "text."

Since they are misinformative, their own word-concepts do not have the direct correspondence with "something else" that MAVO scientists take for granted as a property of language and thereupon transfer to the stellar communication. But inasmuch as they falsely promise it, they share with dreams the duplicity that *Mona Lisa* typifies. The name epitomizes the "dream" it designates. It applies primarily to that "dream"; and as a code-phrase for "monacholysis," its meaning is similarly self-contained. In its evocation of a world apart from the "dreaming cabinet," it is therefore speciously referential; and this makes *Mona Lisa* the paradigm of all word-concepts by which the mind imposes itself on the external world. Though seeming to mediate between the two, these really mirror the mind in which they originate; so that while they appear to open on the universe, they actually enclose the mind within itself. The mind thus becomes their prisoner, and also a prisoner of the world which it deals with through them as it does in dreams. Indeed, it transforms the outside world into the kind of dream that confounds Zipperupus and Ijon Tichy alike. An alien reality, entering into language in the way it enters into the dream-derivatives of language,[40] comes out as a dream-world. At the same time, its otherness, linguistically refashioned to fit anthropomorphic preconceptions of it, ceases to offer an escape from them, and instead delimits the bounds of human understanding.

Even so, responsibility for that entrapment rests with a certain view of language rather than with language per se. So long as the mind immediately refers individual words to a totally extralinguistic reality, it must project its categories of thought on a universe whose otherness it thus makes cognitively inaccessible. But the world which it thereby alienates has beforehand "injected its rules into human language" (*MV*, p. 25 [13]). Those "rules," to be sure, do not apply to language as a static set of discrete word-concepts, and hence do not guarantee that the latter correspond to anything outside the human mind. They do, however, govern language as a dynamic system; so that thanks to them, and also because human beings are inevitably the "inheritors of two evolutions, that of living matter and that of the material of informative language" (*MV*, p. 26 [13]), even the language of pure mathematics provides no hermetic refuge from the world (see *MV*, p. 24 [12]). Yet, paradoxically enough, this bondage holds a liberatory possibility. Through the very words which immure the mind in an infinitely regressive world of its own linguistic (re)construction when it takes them as "signs" of "something else" and instantly attaches to them some putative extralinguistic content, that mind may also transcend its (and their) limitations. But such freedom is available solely to the mind which, recognizing that words are self-referential, considers them first of all in their systemic relation to one another; for only if so regarded do they constitute language as an evolutionary system, and hence as a cybernetic model of an otherwise incomprehensible universe.

IX

More often then not Lem seems to be dealing directly with alien "natural" phenomena and the human difficulties of comprehending them. Nevertheless, he constructs his visions of the alien from language, and it is to language that they first of all problematically refer. As hermeneutic puzzles, they all possess in varying degrees the self-reflexivity most obviously exhibited in the parable of Zipperupus and Subtillion (and in "The Three Story-Telling Machines of King Genius" as a whole) and more narrowly instanced by the name *Mona Lisa* itself. A *Master's Voice*, a *Solaris*, or a *Futurological Congress*, of course, appears to have to do with human self-understanding as it bears on an understanding of the universe at large; and ultimately that is what they are about. But what they have to say respecting such matters they discover chiefly through a concern with how language makes their visions of an alien world possible. Like "the letter from the stars," their message pertains immediately to themselves and cannot be divorced from the self-referential structure of its transmission. Their meaningful content, in other words, is inseparable from their mode of linguistic derivation; and it is by reason of their self-generative principle that they finally stand as models of an extralinguistic universe.

In its hortative aspect, the significance of Lem's fictions follows from the self-transcendent power of language that they evince. "Striv[ing] to exploit every possible . . . combination inherent" in them, they present themselves as the linguistic equivalent of the universe over which Kelvin's "imperfect god" presides (see *Solaris*, pp. 204–6). That god, like Stapledon's Star Maker perceived temporally rather than from the standpoint of his eternal Being, is the apotheosis of perpetual self-creativity (and the self-doubt that goes with it), and thus is himself the projection, or theological concomitant, of a cosmos (and a consciousness) which, forever permuting itself, admits of no completion, no finality. Lem's texts are the linguistic analogue of such a cosmos. Indeed, by their self-referentiality, they not only reveal it; they configure, and constitute, it in terms of the endless self-evolution of language. Nor are they simply representational: as models *of* an alien universe, they are also—and above all—models *for* the cognitive freedom which accompanies the (linguistic) self-awareness they exact.

There is, however, another—satiric—side to Lem's normative enterprise.[41] Freeing the mind through language to a "cosmic" consciousness of its ever-evolving self necessarily entails freeing it from its bondage to word-concepts which perpetuate misconceptions of the self, the external world, and the relationship between them. Lem's fictions accordingly have, as they must, the kind of destructive impulse that Hogarth confesses to as the paramount motive of his own being (see *MV*, p. 29–30 [15–16]). Yet their linguistic possibility is nowhere more problematical than in this regard, as Lem makes clear in *"Rien du tout, ou la conséquence"* (*PV*, pp. 69–79).

The title belongs to an imaginary book by Soulange Marriot. That imaginary author, meaning to take the theory of the *antiroman* to its logical extreme, sets out "to write *nothing*" (*PV*, p. 71)—that is, to write a book which not only denies itself any reality, but does so without attaching metaphysical significance to that denial (see *PV*, p. 78). Her first chapter beings with "the nonarrival of . . . [a] train and the nonappearance of . . . Someone," and concludes with "[t]he contemplation of the nonbeloved heroine in nongravitational space"; "the next . . . discloses, straightaway, that this unbeloved is unbeloved for the simple reason that she *does not exist*" (*PV*, p. 76). This pattern of progressive repudiation in time extends to the narrational voice, which is finally consigned to nonexistence. "The novel does not end: it ceases," as its "language, having come to realize that it represents a form of incest—the incestuous union of nonbeing with being—suicidally disowns itself" (*PV*, p. 79).

Lem's account raises the suspicion that language itself foredooms *Rien du tout* to defeat. But regardless of whether this is so, there can be no doubt that Marriot's quixotic heroism is self-defeating. Her book must end in the suicide of language; for the reality which imprints itself on language cannot be annihilated altogether without also annihilating meaning.

This, Lem recognizes, is too high a price to pay for what in any event he calls the "arrant nonsense" of language's "absolute autonomy" (*PV*, p. 72). Nonetheless, the context in which Mme. Marriot's "novel" figures suggests that her intent is not totally opposed to the sort of negation that he himself aims at. *Rien du tout, ou la conséquence* can, after all, be found nowhere apart from the review of that name which is its metatext; and as such, it contributes to "*A Perfect Vacuum*—that is to say, a book [which is] 'about nothing' " by reason of the "nonexistence" of the books it is about (*PV*, pp. 6–7). On the other hand, those books have no less of a claim to existence than the "real" author whose "Introduction" "S. Lem" likewise displaces with a metatext, this one reminiscent of "Borges and I."[42] Furthermore, the same thing can be said of *A Perfect Vacuum* itself. It, too, exists in and through language and nowhere outside of language; and it is therefore the perfect vacuum which its opening commentary implies it is.

Yet a perfect vacuum, as realized in the volume so entitled, radically subverts the language on which it solely depends. It unites "nonbeing with being"; and in defying their linguistic distinction, it undermines the most fundamental of all "realities" which word-concepts inherently postulate. As metaphor, it thus identifies what

Lem is ultimately about. All of his fictions may be thought of as perfect vacuums—i.e., creatures of language directly corresponding to nothing in nature—and in that sense, their genre is incidental to their design. Purposing to disconnect words from the "reality" to which they speciously refer, he cannot deal in fictive worlds that mimetically reproduce (more or less) the constrictive universe which word-concepts, so to speak, conceive of.

His other worlds, then, must perforce be alien worlds; and this necessity, beyond explaining how it is that Lem generally "happens" to write science fiction,[43] also points to the reason for the puzzlement that they produce. By defining them either through their increasingly tenuous relationship to a "reality" which is itself a linguistic construct (as in *The Futurological Congress*) or in contradistinction to the linguistic categories that the human mind would impose upon them (as in *Solaris*), Lem does not intend to destroy language-as-meaning. He does, however, mean to destroy the prison of linguistic dichotomies. His "impossible" worlds are therefore baffling because—and to the extent that—he means them to be. His is a project for deconstructing language; his objective is to liberate human understanding as never-ending process; and his instruments are self-reflexive fictions—fictions, that is, which educe their alien worlds by referring language to itself and in thus "striv[ing] to exploit every possible . . . combination inherent" in it, exhibit it as a medium for perpetual discovery and self-discovery.

The Ideal Worlds of Science Fiction

George E. Slusser

> The painter's products stand before us as though they were alive: but if you question them, they maintain a most majestic silence. It is the same with written words: they seem to talk to you as though they were intelligent, but if you ask them anything about what they say, from a desire to be instructed, they go on telling you the same thing forever. And once a thing is put into writing, the composition, whatever it may be, drifts all over the place, getting into the hands not only of those who understand it, but equally to those who have no business with it; it doesn't know how to address the right people, and not address the wrong. And when it is ill-treated and unfairly abused it always needs its parent to come to its help, being unable to defend or help itself.—Plato, *Phaedrus,* 275d/e

If poetry can be said to aspire to the condition of music, then science fiction tends toward that of pure idea. That idea is, we are told, Science. But science fiction is two words, and it is strange if not paradoxical that, in this fiction, science, as idea almost synonymous with the original sense of that word, disembodied vision, should so strongly claim a precise locus, a literary form that is "ideal" in a very particular way. For the sense of this term, denoting as it does the absolute, unique and singular, is qualified in science fiction, the literature that, constantly reembodying the disembodied, claims as its ideal a condition of materiality equal to that of the material universe its science encounters. Indeed, within science fiction circles the word used to describe that condition is *hard.* And in fixing the center of those circles, readers and fans readily refer to the "hard core." As those who have been at gatherings with writers can attest, the science fiction world seems to form naturally around that small hard knot of authors who know science, who use their fictions to encase the workings, rigorous yet volatile, of this muse.

Extending this penchant for material qualifiers, these same readers also speak of "soft" science fiction. Seen from the hard core, this form is, as its name seems to imply, a debased version of the real, science muddled by sentimental "humanist" thinking. I wish to argue, however, that science fiction has at least two ideal worlds. Indeed, if we are to believe the proponents of the second form, the word *soft,* at least in its primary sense, is a misnomer. For these "soft" spokesmen, continually attacking their obdurate opponent, are every bit as aggressive, fanatics of mercy in battle with those of justice, Cordelia's soft music jarring with Lear's flinty wheel of fire. And like its hard counterpart, this softness perceives itself both as attacking and as attacked. Beset not by chimeras but this time by the clanking spawn of technology, this center proves every bit as fast, if not as "hard" in the material sense. Both extremes in fact see themselves, simultaneously, as shrine and fortress. And both, as vessels, would bear the same spark of science. Soft SF, in its claims for existence, is no less "scientific." What it does is seek to locate this idea, as unique center of its fictional world, in the human form rather than in some harder entity, in a warm brain rather than in cool intelligence, in the voice rather than in overwritten texts, in "characters" rather than concepts and backgrounds. Each of these forms, in making its absolute claims, seeks to exclude the other as condition for the existence of this idea of science. In that sense it is a struggle for the same unique center. And yet both these forms are strangely alike in their use of a same logical maneuver, an idealization that, declaring the opposite term illusion to its reality, would negate and annihilate it entirely.

Science fiction presents itself then as a genre in search of its center. What is unique, however, is that this center is not a metaphor, but, if we are to take these claims to hardness or softness seriously, an actual place with palpable qualities. In the beginning there was science, and that idea, fallen into its fictional incarnation, seems to need an operating locus that is both sufficient and efficient. The important word here is *need,* for it raises real questions. Why, for instance, is this genre, which many, in the wake of Gary Wolfe, see as committed to exploring the "growing edge" between the known and unknown, so obsessed with its core or center?[1] Even stranger, why should it seek to establish that center by means of a process like idealization? Why this prescientific reflex in a form that claims, along with the science that justifies its existence, to be self-corrective, receptive to continual change? Can we reconcile ideal worlds with its stated desire to give us new worlds for old? And one final question arises: if our two ideal worlds, so apparently opposed in their external textures, are in fact alike in their formative tactics and situation, what then is their opposite? What is this thing, something by definition unidealizable, that both hard and soft science fiction would close ranks against?

Seen in the general context of a "two cultures gap" these questions have implications that concern not only science fiction but the condition of all literature, as technology and written artifact, in this scientific age. To call science and the humanities, despite a sense of increasing, perhaps irreversible alienation between them, by the common term *cultures* is to hold out hope that they may some day reunite. Like the two parts of Aristophanes' hermaphrodite in the *Symposium,* they seem to have a common origin. Cut in half, their striving is ultimately to reform a whole. The gap between science and the humanities is often traced back to Descartes's famous division of mind and matter. On one hand Alfred North Whitehead views this division, because it bestows "independent substantial existence" on each term, as the crucial move that launched science's successful assault on material nature: "The whole Cartesian apparatus of Deism, substantial materialism, and imposed law, in conjunction with the reduction of physical relations to the notion of correlated motions with mere spatio-temporal character, constitutes the simplified notion of Nature with which Galileo, Descartes, and Newton finally launched modern science on its triumphant career."[2] On the other hand a thinker like Jacques Maritain condemns it as *"le principe et l'origine de la profonde inhumanité de notre science moderne."*[3] For Maritain, though, what still constitutes a man is not substance but spirit. And because these two opposites were once bound in a single frame, there resides in their encounter here a sense that they may again join to breach the gap, and that the result of this new joining may be a whole greater than the sum of its parts, some synthetic third term.

This wish may reveal the latent power of the progressivist belief today. But do hard and soft science fiction share that belief? In this same *Symposium* Socrates qualifies Aristophanes' creation myth of dividing and reforming substantial bodies with a further process of division, on a "higher" moral plane. Here, as wholes form and contend for the center, there must be another cleavage, where one whole is declared real because it is "good," the other "bad" because it is illusory. In the circularity of this argument, however, idealization easily becomes self-idealization. And hard and soft science fiction, as representatives of our "two cultures," are both self-idealizing forms in this same manner. As such their ancestor, in more modern thought, may be Pascal rather than Descartes. Pascal refers to Descartes as *"inutile et incertain."*[4] And if one looks at Pascal's notion of nature and of man's relation to it, which is as intricately complex as Descartes's is said to be simplified, one understands what he means. As a scientist, Pascal remained fascinated all his life with probabilities and uncertainties. In his *Pensées,* however, he sought to use uncertainty against itself in hopes of locating a certain and absolute way of dealing with the randomness of material nature.[5] Descartes's method is *"inutile,"* then, because it is not grounded in certainty, because his thinking opponent of nature is a mobile force (implied by the progressive form *res cogitans)* and not a center, not the fixed yet supple *roseau pensant* or thinking reed, progressive thought solidly rooted in organicity. Already here, as Pascal poses the problem, we must choose between methods that are wholes, entire "cultures." And he is moving, through the logic of idealization, to place his culture, absolutely, at the center of things. Pascal rejects the substantial center *("le moi,"* he states, the self in its objective form, *"est haïssable")* for a moral one. Against an infinitely extended universe Pascal's man as thinking reed sets himself absolutely apart by his capacity for moral thought.[6] At work in this passage is Pascal's famous doctrine of "orders," an idealizing maneuver that drives a wedge between contrary terms in order to silence and efface one of them. The logic here is all or nothing, the substitution of radical disproportion for promised comparisons, positive and negative superlatives for the geometry or relationships. Thus the reed is the *feeblest* thing in nature, and a vapor, the *tiniest* drop of water suffices to kill it. But at the same time that reed is of an infinitely different order, for it possesses a nobility that comes from thought, of which the universe has *none.*[7]

Pascal thus establishes his ideal world of thought, and by further fearful symmetry places it as unique center between two infinities of an infinitely different order.[8] What we have here, then, is no two cultures gap, but culture *and* the gap. Man's real adversary, for Pascal, was the horror of the void, the eternal silence of those infinite spaces that surround and isolate him on every side. In the same sense

Pascal's true antagonist was not Descartes but Montaigne, the skeptic who, in challenging the reliability of human perception and the power of reason to position itself through the formulation of reliable laws at the center of the natural universe, challenges the very idea of the center, the possibility of ideality itself. This skeptical current, running through Hume and Berkeley down to the modern metaphysics of science, not only alienates rational man from nature but seeks to dissolve this idea of a thinking self. Now no more than a "bundle" of perceptions, this "I" can no longer claim a constant and coherent self-identity. The notion of the gap, of those silences that are other and unrelatable by any logic, even the radical logic of the ideal, now invades the center itself. It is against this incursion that Pascal constructs his barriers, and it is because of this retrenchment, perhaps, that he continues to fascinate us today. But Pascal's core remains "soft," and had he written science fiction, it would have been soft science fiction. Indeed, thinking reeds still flourish at the center of this form, marked as it is by *silentium universi,* by its sense of an ever expanding, infinitely hostile cosmos and a continually contracting, but doggedly human, center, an idealization against despair that gives it existential overtones.

To this same situation our century has seen another response, a contender for this ideal center which names itself more efficient because it is simply "harder." As center of human operations, this new form modifies, in a particularly dynamic direction, the play of proportionality that kept Pascal's reed at the median. It does so by creating a curious rhythm of expansion and contraction, where the possibility of outward movement appears to abide, almost paradoxically, in man's constant ability to tighten and harden the core. According to J. D. Bernal, however, this paradox informs the very condition of modern rational man in nature. Like Pascal, Bernal is a scientist who offers a paradigm for literary response to this particular human condition. His 1929 book, *The World, the Flesh, and the Devil,* has in fact been most influential in shaping the hard core of science fiction. The subtitle of this book, "An Inquiry into the Future of the Three Enemies of the Rational Soul," sets forth all the parameters of his argument, and of hard SF. Here is the same "rational soul," or breath of scientific man, as in Pascal, set in the same adversary relationship to world and flesh. But now the direction of adversarity is the future, the promise of encounter both successive and progressive. With this declaration we seem to abandon the residual homocentricity of Pascal's paradigm, that proportionality between center and circumference which, in its balancing, still points to the medieval past. But notice Bernal's progression: world, flesh, devil. Forward movement here—the order in which we deal with these "enemies"—is simultaneously contraction, movement inward from world to body to mind as locus for the rational soul itself. It is implied, then, that the advancement of mankind (and this book is Bernal's profession of scientific faith) involves, at each step, the formation of harder and harder cores.

By *world* Bernal means both our own planet as it gradually becomes inadequate to sustain our technological and demographic evolution, and the material universe that, no matter how much we expand, remains on our periphery. Man meets this enemy, therefore, both by expanding and, simultaneously, by "terraforming" space, by creating concentric hard shells such as Dyson spheres and "ring-worlds" to encompass and protect that expansion. Wherever we go in space and time, wherever our evolution takes us, we form a hard core. But as we see with the next enemy, *flesh,* it is not only the more we expand the more we must harden, but that we harden in order to expand. The Cartesian duality of mind and body is made a literal condition here. Bernal believes the human mind an organ capable of great expansion, but limited by extensions that are not worthy of it. These extensions, the body's "soft" limbs and organs, must be rationalized and "hardened" by physiological engineering, or re-placed prosthetically by mechanical appendages, so that an even softer ectoplasmic brain can be given increasingly tougher and more functional casings. This is not reason dispossessed, expelled by dis-memberment from organic wholeness, but rather repossessed in evolutionary time from some original fall into imperfect flesh.

The third enemy, which Bernal calls the *devil,* is the most interesting and tenacious because it resides in the interstices, the unseen places of the rational soul itself. But these places are not, to Bernal, a priori unseeable. They are "soft" spots, named as the same inner desires and confusions that made a Pascal veer toward what here is called an irrational "humanist" reaction. This reaction, which constructs its protective wall around a center that remains soft, may be impossible to cope with in the present, but the future, Bernal predicts, can bring an answer. He sees, over the long range, the possibility of a technologically controlled evolution, psychology aid-ing the engineer, that will lead to a "dimorphism in humanity in which the conflict between the humanizers and the mechanizers will be solved not by the victory of one or the other, but by the splitting of the human race—the one section developing a fully balanced humanity, the other groping unsteadily beyond it."[9] But this "dimorphism" is clearly, in light of this devil at the core of humanity, an idealization of one term at the expense of the other. Seeing the humanizers as a separate form, the mechanizers purge them from the core; doing so, they advance. What they leave behind, the old green world of poetry and religion now "fully balanced," may seem ideal as well, but in reality it is a soft, empty illusion: "The world might, in fact, be transformed into a human zoo, a zoo so intelligently managed that its inhabitants are not aware that they are there merely for the purposes of observation and experiment."[10]

What is most significant, however, is that Bernal's vision of man's struggle with nature locates the third and final enemy at the core of the rational soul itself. Pascal, we have seen, traded the possibility of horror within for a horror without. His "devil" was not Montaigne and skepticism, but cosmic silence and menace, the ineffable things and events of a soulless external nature. By making this trade, Pascal lets the soul be surrounded and pressed inward and backward toward a primal center where the past guaranteed by Christianity overlaps with the promise of transcendence.[11] Bernal, though, is committed to a future. And by locating his devil in this same primal lair, then expelling it, he seeks to secure the center and propel things forward at the same time. In the forward sweep of time what is presently unknown can someday be known. This is so because it is named here, and clearly qualified, as something past and "soft," a persistent yet not eternal "humanist" indulgence in intuition. Bernal's mechanizers on the other hand are not afraid, they claim, to face these uncertainties of the unconscious as hard facts, to embrace a horror within so as to fix and control it, and in doing so to advance on the horror without and beyond. In relation to Pascal's soft core, then, Bernal has forced a shift in battle lines. The dimorphic wedge has brought softness, now seen as the enemy at the core, to redirect its efforts, to contend for the center by recasting its devil alien as hardness itself, to resurrect Faust the overreacher as the "mad scientist," false creator of that monstrous hardening which entombs the past, kills the organic and mystical roots of the rational soul. Thus, beneath what seems the central theme of science fiction—the struggle between man and universe, the known and the unknown—lies a hidden theme: the struggle between centers that hold and centers that do not. Writing about their alien encounters, then, our two ideal forms, hard and soft, are, on this deeper level of the text, in reality shaping and consolidating their respective centers. And as they do so the alien itself is redesignated. Indeed, for each of these centers the true alien has perhaps become, rather than some common external mystery, the all-too-persistent presence of its rival for the core.

But Pascal and Bernal are first and foremost scientists. They may offer what we can call soft and hard programs for the use of scientific reason, but they are not writing science fiction per se. To deal with hardness or softness in this strictly literary context, we must consider another element—writing itself, the medium that conveys and encases the rational soul so that it can operate in the literary universe. The ideal of science in terms of writing, at least since the 17th century, is transparency. From Bishop Thomas Sprat's admonition to scientists of the Royal Society in the 1660s to write with "mathematical plainness," to mathematician Paul Valéry's concern for making written prose a self-effacing medium for pure ideas, writing has been viewed by the speculator and experimenter as a necessary evil, an imperfect, hopefully someday dispensable, tool for reasoning.[12] But a form of writing that calls itself either hard or soft fiction, science or otherwise, would seem more apt to inscribe than describe, to resist rather than vanish, for hardness and softness are qualities, substantial textures in a medium that, insofar as it obeys the wishes of science, should strive to be textureless. For hard and soft science fiction, then, the actual writing done—inside the telling of all those tales of expanding knowledge and transcendence of matter—is to secure and fill out rival ideal centers, a writing against the other. And in seeking to give the core a written substance and opacity, what hard and soft SF are doing, in a sense, is designating the written text, in its total extension, an analogue for the material universe itself, a place not only where structures are created but where gaps and uncertainties occur. Here in this text-as-universe, what Stanislaw Lem calls "singularities," those unrelatable things and events of the physical world upon which all our theories go aground, are no longer simply unnameable but uninscribable as well.[13] Indeed, Lem is referring to cosmology here. And to scientists working in such a field, writing itself is seen as full of such singularities, signs and symbols that often seem completely unyielding to the operations of reason. But their vision, full of yearning for some original clarity of the idea, seems to mark writing, along with the phenomena it inscribes, with a stigma of the fall. If hard and soft SF then strive for ideal status, by their very designations they do so in a world of writing that has accepted its fallen nature, has made the necessary passage from the original insubstantial *logos* to a tangible science of traces capable of substantially fixing and holding in a universe of flux, of meeting singularities with singularity. Writing, in this postlapsarian world, is a *techno-logos,* an applied art where the re-uttering is also a re-ordering. And both hard and soft SF, as written forms, must be understood by the ways, the openly and consciously designated ways, they use this technology to shape their ideal worlds.

That this sense of writing as an extended world is increasingly urgent today is seen in the success of the works of Jacques Derrida. His vision of writing provides a necessary ground for discussing hard and soft science fiction precisely because it strives to be so resolutely post-technological, or should we say metatechnological, for the somewhat paradoxical consequence of his argument for universal writing is that it denies there was any fall into technology in the first place. Behind flesh and blood, he claims, "there has never been anything but writing."[14] In the beginning there was no ideal Word, but a system of language epitomized by writing, that is to say consisting of endless loops of "supplements" where no utterance exists in principio or per se but all bear traces or "grafts" of some prior or other utterance. There is no origin, then. But by the same token there can be no idealization, either. Indeed man, irrevocably embedded in a matrix of writing, a general text he did not write and which in a sense has written him, is denied the ideal. He may create hierarchies by positing dualities in order to favor one term over the other, such as speech over writing; but in the universe of writing these declared ideals—which must by definition be unique and absolute—are still subject to what Derrida calls *"différance,"* a process of endless differing and decentering which at the same time is a "deferral" of any claims to absoluteness. Finally, if there are no origins, and no ideal centers, there can be no singularities in Lem's sense, either. Derrida's "deconstructive" operations on individual texts indeed reveal knots of paradox, indeed revel in textual impasses and gaps. But here again, in this universe as endless chain of written traces and supplements, we never glimpse the unwriteable, the traceless presence that risks shattering the system of writing itself. Derrida's "aporias" flirt hazardously with the possibility of blankness, but they themselves can never be blank, never be pure state or quality. Indeed, what seems disorder is never really so, for it is something evoked only to be endlessly deferred. What emerges is, at best, something virtual—call it the horrific rather than horror.

Many today are uneasy, however, with such games of the horrifical. Sensing something grotesque in all this "grafting," they are tempted to summon a tangible figure, a Frankenstein monster, from these gaps. Such uneasiness, though, is usually only a provisional, monitory response, one that repels the looker into the abyss, drives him back to some ideal center. Commenting on the Derridian impasse, J. Hillis Miller, for example, finds such moments yielding "the deepest penetration into the *actual* nature of literary language, or of language as such."[15] At these places of potential disorder he is relocating visionary spots of time, seeing through these cruxes of randomness in the text into the life of things. He passes then through posttechnological holes in the writing process back to a pretechnological sense of language as *logos*, as original and ideal *presence*. This reaction is very much like that of soft science fiction vis-à-vis the technologies—that is, the themes and forms—that must shape its existence as science fictional writing. Rife with fascination for human extensions and futures, which are another form of supplement or deferral, these themes and structures themselves become, within the ideological field of soft SF, impasses that provoke a double response. Looking beyond them, as marks of a technological fall, we see a future of monstrous disorder. But at the same time they help us expel the horrific, place it "out there" as a tangible yet now inaccessible horror. Within the shield of this cleansed written text, we can relocate a center, the rational soul as *logos*.

Soft science fiction, therefore, can be called logocentric. One of the basic expressions of Western logocentrism is Plato's *Phaedrus,* with its distinction between "dead" and "living" discourse. And this dialogue is of interest to soft SF because its world has already fallen into technology. Plato's mouthpiece Socrates, in his invented legend of Theuth, gives us an Egyptian origin for writing, a technology that promises to make people "wiser and improve their memories." But the King of Egypt, in Socrates' parable, faults this invention within an invention as a mere recipe for "reminder" not "memory," for "telling" and not "teaching." Carrying this logic forward, Socrates names writing an illusion, falseness in relation to the true reality of dialectics. In this world, however, such idealization is already a defensive response. We are already under the impulsion of the rational soul in the *Phaedrus,* where Socrates' task is to define the "scientific" practice of language. But in warning this scientific practitioner about writing, Socrates describes something that could be a premonition of Frankenstein's monster: the dead simulacrum of a living force, something to which, because we seek to improve upon organic nature, we give the semblance of life, and which now threatens to escape from our control. Indeed, in this metaphor of "dead discourse" there is more than a hint of the horrific, where that which cannot speak on its own behalf shades toward becoming the unspeakable other, a singularity which, like some machine gone beserk, "goes on telling us the same thing forever." Plato, however, as he condemns writing, is using it, must use it as vehicle and time capsule to preserve the organic chain of voices within for future human memory. And he does so by incarnating, via Socrates' skilled metaphors, the absences and silences in his written text into a monstrous presence—the horrific into horror—which can then be bodily expelled from the core of the dialogue.

Plato's work, as logocentric ancestor to soft science fiction, helps us understand the latent paradox of that form as and in relation to writing. For while constantly warning against the hardness and deadness of this medium, in all aspects of which it sees traces of our technological fall from the original Word, soft SF, because it is writing, uses the same medium as necessary casing and protection for its center. We see a similar pattern in Pascal in fact. In one sense, his thinking reed is both successor and ancestor to that writing tool Plato's Egyptians invented. And it is under the sign and protection of the *Ecriture* or holy scripture that Pascal would construct his apology as casing for that stylus and stylistic point which is man, doing so in "thoughts" of lapidary prose, maxims as firmly engraved as the Twelve Tablets upon which his order of faith would found its alternate laws of operation to those of a blank and terrifying universe. Thus in Pascal's concentric vision, which remains that of soft SF, the center is the *logos* that must write. The circumference is the written text, an extended shell that thickens and hardens, but is always ready, at some epiphanic moment of inward vision, to melt away and reveal the soft core. Finally, beyond this shell lies horror. But because it has been written out its text as deadness, this horror is no longer simply silence, the wordless void. For in relation to that text, which now acts as its manageable surrogate, horror has become blankness, the unwriteable.

As writing, hard science fiction operates quite differently. We might begin to distinguish it from its soft precursor and antagonist by again citing Plato's distinction between memory and reminder. Writing in the former mode contracts upon a center. In the latter mode, however, the center extends along a continuum, analogous to that of space-time, but here rigorously controlled by these points of reminder. Because this second form offers a simulcrum of a visionary rather than rememorative order, we are tempted to evoke another distinction: that of Coleridge between fancy and imagination. This first, as form of writing, is characterized by "memory emancipated from the order of time and space; and blended with, and modified by that empirical phenomenon of the will, which we express by the word *choice*."[16] We should say rather by choice of words. For science fictional writing in this key, as controlled empirical structure aware it is working in its own present, combines the elements and themes of SF in order to encompass the ideal past of human memory and, in doing so, to free it from time/space as the order of chance and change. And by naming this order horror, the thing to be expelled, soft SF effectively thwarts whatever lure of the future its narrative materials may seem to promise.

In this sense hard SF is a literature of imagination because it inverts this formula: we have time and space emancipated from memory, and modified and shaped by the plastic power of the willed human intelligence. Hard SF is not writing around a center, but writing outward from a dynamic core that has been hardened and steeled by direct application of the will. It is dead discourse with a vengeance, narrative which, factoring its own cold equations, recognizes in its passion for sparse symmetrical forms, for directional charts and clean hard lines of action, the attraction of Derrida's endless possibilities of deferral, that emancipation from memory it renames progress, as well as Derrida's fascination with the textual game of the indeterminate, which it recasts in harder stuff as the alien *encounter*. Lem sees his cosmic singularities existing "in the continuum just as a stone exists here."[17] And hard SF, operating fully in that continuum, would render its alien singularities hard stones that can be met and hopefully built upon. Hard SF, then, encounters horror neither as silence nor as blankness but as tangible *presence*. At the same time it refuses the horrific, for it aims at every step to fill the gaps, to solidify all traces of human destiny across the text of cosmic expansion, to produce a man that is both self-made and self-written.[18] Hard SF writing is a declarative rather than a rememorative act, a figurative kicking of all the stones of universal singularity so as to affirm their thereness, and at the same time reaffirm the hard existence of a human intelligence that confronts its universe by means of hardened words.

In the emblematic sense, science fiction's relation to writing is perhaps best depicted, oddly enough, in that film of films: Kubrick's *2001: A Space Odyssey*. Indeed, the interpretational difficulties of this film may come from the fact that it presents both soft and hard iconographies, but does not choose between them. It is a "graphic" film in the original sense of the word, for mankind in it barely speaks, but is instead preoccupied with writing his evolutionary destiny across a blank cosmos. His progress in fact is marked by a series of deferred traces; a bone tossed in the air cuts to a spaceship, this in turn cuts to a white room at the end of the infinite. But what role, we ask, do these traces play? On one hand, we can see them as hard casings for an enduring soft center. For just as HAL is returned to his primal memories when Bowman, as representative of the race that transferred its functions to it so that machine can act as flesh's outer extension, enters and deprograms it, so man's own evolution at the same time nurtures the seed of devolution. When Bowman travels into the infinite, we witness that journey contracting to the soft center of his own eyeball. And Bowman's final adventure in the white room is likewise advancement-in-regression, where dying man and newborn child literally superimpose to form a new casing, this time softly amniotic in stark contrast to the hard shadowless room, around the knowing eye of the "star child," soft SF's emblem of the rational soul. This "soft" reading, however, ignores the presence and role of the famous slab, which in turn could epitomize the hard role of writing in science fiction. Throughout, this slab is a sort of *tabula rasa* over which a constantly yearning mankind passes his hands as if making traceless traces. As slate for our technological desires, it is a place where blank cosmic opacity has been quarried, cut, and polished with industrial precision: real manifestation of an ideal that would convert absence to tangible, useable presence.

The slab, then, represents the lure that brings man, throughout this film, to harden and solidify his evolutionary "statements." Writ against the cosmic void, forms such as the waltzing and coupling space stations, HAL, the Discovery, all are hardened versions of mankind, extended "reminders" of his presence. And the 18th century white room, enfolding the round red space pod that seems a steel surrogate for Bowman's eyeball, is Western man's most rational ideal further hardened, recast as stark walls, icy light, metallic echoes. But in this room the true hard core remains the black slab, still unwritten on, still luring mankind to new statements beyond these walls. If this film is seen to inscribe a return to biological consciousness, to racial memory, then the slab that traces this arc knows neither traces nor memory; it is a thing with no past, only a future. Clarke could not accept this unresolved tension in his novel, which coming after the film in a sense rewrites it. Significantly, he makes his slab transparent, a learning device whose stored images are mirrors of a softer human center. And in like manner the final room, in the novel, is an illusion, no hard artifact but the dissolvable projection of Bowman's brain.

2001 is ambiguous. But science fiction, as idealizing form, does not like ambiguity. Instead it strives to be singular, to establish a single center from which to operate against the singularities of nature. It demands, furthermore, that these external singularities be tangible. Metaphysics yields to physics and uncertainties become substantial presences, so that even Pascal's horrific silence, when manifest to the reed at the core, must appear as the drop of water that crushes. The way that singularity is dealt with in science fiction, however, depends on the kind of core. As we have seen, there are two in science fiction, cores that perceive each other, mutually, as opposite and other, so that seen from the hard center softness is an illusion, hardness from the soft core a bad copy, a skeleton to the living flesh. The remaining task of this essay then is twofold. First we will plot the narrative structures generated by these two cores, seeing them as related but *willfully* opposite responses to a basic narrative situation: the alien encounter. This element of willfulness, however, raises a second problem. Because both these cores are ideals, hence must be seen ultimately less as declarations than as categorical imperatives, centers established by fiat, the role of what Plato calls the "parent" in establishing and maintaining them is of prime importance. As opposed to the invisibility of the Derridean man in his text, or the godlike silence of Joyce's artist in his creation, the SF writer is eminently present in his creative universe. Indeed, those who are familiar with the vast secondary literature on SF—consisting of statements, interviews, and outright attacks on and defense of individual texts—know the inordinate desire of its writers to shepherd and guide their works toward one core or the other. As texts, science fiction generally is committed to the themes and forms of technology, and to its primary medium of writing. But the persistent presence of a "parent" indicates that these machines are not felt to be (unlike so many other modern systems) self-sustaining. A center must be located, it must be human, and it must be singular, for therein lies the strength to confront singularities both within and without. In a word, it must be ideal, and its "parents" must lead the text toward those mutually exclusive extremes of hard and soft discourse that Plato presented at the dawn of our technological age. Examination, then, of several hard/soft encounters at the core of SF by would-be "parents" will give us a clear strategic blueprint for its control.

But as was said of Arthur Clarke's Rama, and despite the neat binary logic of idealization, things always seem to come in threes. And in both cases above—that of defining hard and soft narrative situations, and that of establishing them as supertextual types of idealizing—a third presence is always felt: the horrific. This is the formal and metaphysical fascination not only with gaps in the text but with the center as indeterminacy, as a place where silence and blankness reign, where there can be no writing, no idealization, no defense possible. This horrific mode is constant companion to both hard and soft SF, and is therefore, beyond all ideals, perhaps their true opponent.

First, however, in order to determine how the hard or soft valence inflects a same narrative situation toward opposite ends of a formal spectrum, let's examine a variation on the alien encounter masterplot—the alien who fell to earth, who fell into the "text" of human culture. This is the situation of John W. Campbell's classic story, "Who Goes There?" (1938). It is also the situation of the two films based on this story, Howard Hawks's *The Thing from Another World* (1951), and John Carpenter's remake *The Thing* (1979). Here, though, all similarity stops. For if the story operates along hard parameters, its two avatars in film are, successively, classic statements in the soft and the horrific modes.

We begin with the Hawks film. In the course of Western thought, as we have seen, Pascal precedes Bernal, the soft response to scientific man's dilemma the hard. Here, however, things are inverted, and Campbell's tale has provoked a soft reaction. Significantly, this has occurred in the softer medium of film. For because we deal with images and not written words, the nameless "Thing" is less easily admitted as something singular. Indeed, the alien invader in the film is much too man-like, recognizably a man dressed as a walking vegetable. Bearing these traces of familiarity, he becomes an ambiguous presence. And it is as such that this film treats him, for the whole thrust of the action is in fact a reaction: the story of a creature who comes trailing clouds of humanity but who is progressively expelled, *rendered* alien as the invaded community reasserts its "living" structure at the center, finally negating the Thing as literal dead opposite.

There exists in the film, however, a third presence. From the outset the Thing is dumb, and as he is pushed out into the wastes becomes increasingly menacing in a silence that contrasts with the increasing garrulousness of the humans. But the scientist Carrington speaks for the Thing. But more than that Carrington, in his experiments on the creature, actually seeks to inscribe him into the text of rational inquiry. In this Hawksian world of casual and lively conversation, Carrington stands out by his "literary" manner of speaking. And quite literally his is a dead discourse. For not only does it bear little relationship to the concrete situation, but it addresses it wrongly, allowing the genetics of his text, in his laboratory conjugations, to proliferate uncontrollably, dangerously for the human community. What this film establishes (and celebrates), as its men and women unite spontaneously to expel both the ambiguous alien and its avatar, the discourse of the "mad" scientist, is Plato's organic chain of living speech, a world of dialogue in which even the journalist Scotty is deprived of his written story, and in the end delivers his message orally over the radio to the larger human circle listening beyond this center. Expelled to the periphery of this circle is Carrington. In the climactic scene, confronting the raging Thing in the corridor of the besieged camp headquarters, he advances to address the alien as if it had traces of reason, as if it could be integrated into that general scientific text he worships, only to be cast aside like some uncomprehended book. With this act of casting off, the Thing declares itself, finally, alien horror, that which is unassimilable and unique. At this point it can (and must) be annihilated, negated as this center closes around its ideal core—the *logos* as absolute and vigilant, watching the skies for more aliens.

Remakes are very Derridean things, because by openly functioning as supplement to a prior work they refute its claims to
uniqueness. Carpenter's 1979 remake of *The Thing* reinscribes that
film's soft center as if to reintroduce the horrific. By making his film
on one hand closer to the original written text, while on the other
playing this literalness off against verbatim quotes from the earlier
film, Carpenter creates a palimpsest on which he explores the ambiguities and puns of both sources. For instance, his Thing is no longer
the easily readible shape that James Arness in his carrot suit offered
us. By returning to the Campbell story for the body snatcher motif,
he is able to cast ominous doubt on even the most straightforward
cinematic presentation of the human form. All men then are potential aliens, absence-in-presence. And in another device taken from
Campbell, the "scientific" blood test devised to abolish this ambiguity by detecting the alien within, there is further deconstruction of
Hawks's ideal center. Surmising that, because this alien has such
advanced survival instincts, each of its cells must have independent
life, the hero McReady proposes to "read" blood samples from each
member of the infested community by thrusting a red hot needle in
them one by one. As he does so the soft ecosystem of the earlier film,
where individual elements like blood in our bodies do not have
identities of their own but derive their existence from the coordinated functioning of the whole organism, is rendered a web of gaps
and impasses. Subjected to the test of this remake, no single element
or group of elements in either preceding text can claim uniqueness,
for none is allowed to be self-contained, but when read properly is
seen to bear traces of the general text of survival, artistic as well as
biological. That text, however, is clearly horrific in nature. The
human body in Carpenter's film, on occasion, may be the place of a
grisly joke, a visual pun that illustrates the gulf separating the horrific
and horror. Such is the case when Dr. Copper, applying artificial
respiration to one of his "comrades" in hopes of reviving his human
spirit, sees the body he is pressing on suddenly gape to reveal a huge
mechanical jaw that then shears off his arms. Usually, however, the
human body only perpetuates ambiguity and impasse. In the final
scene of the film, for example, two men, having burned the camp in
hopes of destroying every last cell of the alien invader, meet in the
snow and prepare to die. Neither looks different from before, but we
know one or both of them must bear traces of the alien. These will
freeze, be thawed again, and go on in an endless text where, as gaps

are continuously created and written over, horror can only exist as virtuality.

Hawks's center has both men and women in it—or rather a single woman. She seems tough-minded and "liberated," but gives in to fetching coffee. And in the end, with a potential marriage to Captain Hendry in view, she promises to have a further softening impact on the core. Carpenter, following Campbell, gives us an all-male camp, and in an Antartic rather than timidly Alaskan location. But here all real resemblance between this film and the story ends. For Campbell's male core is not ambiguous, but openly and singularly hard. What is more, the alien that would invade it is really and uniquely something else. All the scientific analyses the men perform on it can find no traces of human biology. The only thing it shares with man in fact is its *hardness,* "a bred-in-the-bone instinct, a driving unquenchable fire that's *genuine.*"[19] Man then is not struggling with himself. Nor is he defending something. His fight with the alien focuses on a single shared quality which is essential to both—survival.

The alien, like man, wants the world all to itself. The world it wants, however, is, in Campbell's story, the particularly hard world of human technology. The core camp here is not, as in Hawks's film, a military outpost, a beleaguered Fort Alaska. It is a geographical expedition, man mapping the last uncharted waste, cold resolve against ice. Nor is there, as in Carpenter, any menace of disorganization from within. This system is a tightly written system, where each individual's resolve, his "stuff," is classified and hierarchized by the very name he bears. As text, it is something that cannot be written over, or even rewritten, but only effaced, cataclysmically replaced by the alien's adversarial alternate history. Unlike Carpenter's film, which hovers in a realm of virtuality, the story actualizes horror. And it sees it, significantly, as organic form gone wild—as a creature with three red eyes and "blue hair like crawling worms." The danger with this alien is that its rampant organicity threatens to inhabit hard human forms and "soften" them. We are looking, however, upon open horror here, and this, paradoxically, may be what is destined to save us. For this creature resembles a Medusa or a Gorgon, and to look on it, in the most fortunate sense, only hardens and steels the looker more. Emblematic of our encounter with this monster is this snaky tangle of hair set off against the *bronze* ax, a souvenir of its first contact with the excavation crew, that protrudes from its skull.

Among these hard men, some are harder than others, more predestined to look upon the Gorgon. In the same way, some scientific disciplines are by nature less permeable to alien incursions. It is no accident that the creature's main conduit into the human circle is via Blair the biologist. What is more, among those who meet the test, who survive as final hard core, are men like the physicist Norris: "Norris was all steel. His movements, his thoughts, his whole bearing had the quick, hard impulse of steel spring. His nerves were steel—hard, quick-acting—swift corroding'" (p. 55). Men's names clearly designate their hard or soft condition. Dr. Copper or the solid Van Wall we know will resist; but even before the test we suspect that those with ordinary "soft" names like Garry or Barclay will yield. Most formidable, however, proves the sentinel-like McReady: "McReady was a figure from some forgotten myth, a looming bronze statue that held life, and walked" (p. 49). If a myth, this bronze vision is surely the myth of technology itself, for the "life" this hard vessel contains is intelligence moving on the evolutionary vector of survival. Origin may be "forgotten," but its presence, in ideal form, is ready at any point in the future to step forth—a hard singularity engaging the singular alien menace. Well aware of his own ideality, McReady comes to life to articulate humanity's hard ideal core: "We'll fight. . . . We're real. You're imitations, false to the core of your every cell."

But the tactic of hard science fiction is not (as in Hawks's film) to reject and destroy the alien. Rejecting instead the "childish human weakness of hating the different," just as it rejects Derrida's game of "différance," hard SF seeks to enclose the alien in its steel trap. Note that the title of Campbell's story is not "what" goes there, but "who." The tacit goal here is to integrate the alien into our technology. Casting off the soft part of its existence, defeating its biological drives, man can keep the hard things—those machines and inventions that we can write into our text of evolutionary expansion, devices that can be motivated by the steel-cased intelligence that is its dynamic core. These men of steel close off the icy land in the eleventh hour and save their world: "No, by the grace of God . . . and the margin of half an hour, we keep our world, and the planets of the system too. Antigravity, you know, and atomic power. Because *They* came from another sun, a star beyond the stars. *They* came from a world with a bluer sun" (p. 104). This final sentence is not one of vigilance so much as jubilance. We have encompassed the alien, and we understand why. We name their technology. And by naming its makers as "they," not as "it," we in a sense subsume them, assume their hard extensions as our own, will use them in our race for these stars beyond the stars.

This process of idealization in science fiction surely reflects strong ideological differences in our culture as to the role of technology. What is unique here, however, is that these ideologies are not hidden or deviated, not concealed in texts, but aggressively drawn from them by "parents." There is perhaps no other genre today where writers take so much time "taking a stand," seeking to locate themselves at the core of SF so as to draw their works (and others if deemed fit) into a sphere of purity. As fitting to a form so committed to the idea of writing as technology, these apologies for SF address a higher, ideal bar of justice, where decrees take the form of Pascal's Twelve Tablets brought down from on high to specific works. We will briefly analyze three classic encounters between such legislating "parents," for in these we can plot the persistence of science fiction's idealizing, and of its dimorphism, the precipitation of soft and hard ideal worlds.

The first (and earliest) exchange—between Michel Butor and James Blish—reveals how accomodating SF is to "mainstream" incursions. For, coming to conquer SF's core, Butor can only divide it. In doing so he reiterates the now-familiar soft ideal. The second exchange, between Isaac Asimov and Jerry Pournelle, situates itself firmly at the hard core. We find, however, splitting even this core, that there can be no shadings, only mutual exclusions. For in order to assert his hard ideal, Pournelle it seems must force Asimov, once considered the father of hard SF, to "reveal," and defend, a soft stance. The third and final example, Ursula Le Guin's attack on Gregory Benford, reveals the power of idealization at the heart of today's science fiction. Le Guin and Benford are said to be the two most representative SF writers currently working in America. But put two such writers in the same space, and one it seems will invariably move to the furthest ideological corner. For Le Guin, that corner is the soft ideal in all its purity.

Michel Butor's pretentiously unassuming "Notes on Science Fiction" first appeared in English in the Fall 1967 issue of *Partisan Review*. In this article, however, the French "new novelist"—by then an established mainstream figure—is not simply commenting on the genre; he would usurp its very center. More curious than his aggressivity, perhaps, is his sense of this center is eminently "soft." Butor speaks from what clearly is a slender knowledge of specific SF texts. Yet the set of imperatives he utters could have been adhered to, if perhaps not stated, by a number of practicing SF writers at the time. The proper realm of SF, he proclaims, is not the future but the present. Speculative forays into time and space, he feels, the sort sanctioned by SF's "myth" of science and "inscribed" in its jargon, do not yield what they promise. For instead of actuality, such fictions give us only possibility, a place where, because everything is possible, nothing is. The pattern Butor describes here is quite familiar. The way of the future is the way to the void, passage through the horrific to horror. The only safeguard against this drift, in science fiction, is to secure the center, this time the classic soft core, a present firmly rooted in human tradition.

To Butor, SF's future is such a vague region because imagination there "no longer needs to make an effort of coordination." Indeed, it is this faculty of coordination, not speculation, that should characterize the genre. But, evoking Coleridge once again, we see he is choosing fancy instead of imagination, for he is asking SF to work within existing human systems, with their "fixities" as fictional counters, rather than through and beyond such systems. In fact he faults most of the SF he knows (precious little if we judge from his examples) for lacking "specificity," by which he means the shape bestowed on fictional actions and events by the human system of language, itself rooted in the equally human system of myth. Working within these systems, coordination works against the space/time continuum and its promise of change and newness, for its goal is to reconstruct a past rather than construct a future at the core of the fictional present.

Butor's core is the soft one of memory, a past that is immanent in, hence can be coordinated with, a human present assumed universal—a collective reality as opposed to those individual, and too individualistic, dreams he feels have spoiled science fiction. Citing Heraclitus that "those who are awakened are in the same world, but those who sleep are each in a separate world," Butor calls upon SF to become a collective enterprise. To do so, SF must eschew as so many empty nightmares the multiple cities of its uncoordinated future speculation. Instead it must create, collectively, a single city that "would become a common possession to the same degree as an ancient city that has vanished."[20] Through such collective creation both the postestablished and the preestablished, it is hoped, would collapse together to form a solid, and ubiquituous, core. Indeed, Butor calls upon SF to unify itself by limiting its field to just such a present, for to do so is to acquire "over the individual imagination a constraining power comparable to that of any classical mythology." The real danger, then, comes not from imagination alone, but from *individual* imagination—the single dreams. Proof that such are an invitation to chaos against which the center must resist is perhaps found in another work of "science fiction" by a non-science-fictional creator—Fellini's *Satyricon*. Fellini's stated purpose in this film, which abandons all pretense at historical reconstruction for a personal dream vision of mysterious actions and inscrutable faces, is to show that an ancient city like Rome is no more a "common possession" of humanity than a future city on Mars.[21] In that case however, if the past is as uncertain as the future, how can we privilege, as constraining and organizing force, memory over reminder, past over future?

Butor, therefore, it could be said, denies individuality to SF's core while at the same time imposing this denial by a fiat of individual will. And his remarks are perceived by James Blish, a long-time and scientifically literate practitioner of the genre, as just such a categorical statement, a total usurpation of the center of SF to which the sole response is an equally exclusive statement of an ideal. Blish's article "On Science Fiction Criticism," published not in *Partisan Review* (his note states that the piece, sent to that magazine, was returned six months later, with a note: "Sorry, a little too late . . . to use this now.") but in the "fanzine" *Riverside Quarterly,* matches absolutes with absolutes. Negatives abound: Butor has *never* read modern SF; he has *no* knowledge of science; the writers he cites are *not* SF writers because their work contains *no* trace of science whatsoever. Moreover, because Butor's audience is "literary" it is "*non*specialized." Stating that no other genre in history has been so consistently judged by its *worst* examples, Blish sees the self-fulfilling remarks of critics like Butor as acts of self-exclusion from the true center of SF—which he defines as the living author and his scientific interest in the future. On the contrary, any literary, nonscientific vision that looks to the past is not central but merely a fossilized cast-off. Indeed, the imagery Blish uses to depict his adversary is interesting. For what it bestows is not the flexible hardness of steel but the rigidity of fossils, of organic and historical residue. Butor's collective vision then is "antiquarian," and would turn SF and its future into dogma, something akin to "13th century canon law." His proposed single city is a "totalitarian" construct. All of these bring the weight of an unenlightened past to bear upon what he sees as SF's and mankind's, only hope: the free creative individual. If Blish's vision of this individual is hard, it is the right kind of hardness: the flexibility of the trained scientific intelligence operating in an open future. Where such a mind conceives a city, it must be an open city. In fact the SF that issues from this core of individual, rational, scientifically informed speculation will probably not build Butor's utopia at all. Its city may be less clean and well-lighted than our present cities. But it is only by opening our vision, and accepting what we see, that we can ever hope to act upon the future. We must, Blish proclaims, choose change itself, and with it even the possibility of abolishing this "folk custom of the huddling place" entirely.

Seen from Butor's center, Blish's argument will seem enclave rhetoric, and his insistence on the individual at the core a form of paranoia, the delusion that whole worlds can be centered on single beings. But Blish is equally reductive and declarative: there is only one center to SF and, as a place of rational extrapolation based on solid scientific knowledge rather than on vague myths or superstitions, it is hard. And writers like Isaac Asimov, by transposing the past "scientifically" into the future, have built whole edifices on this same hard core. Yet this same Asimov, usually considered a quintessential hard SF writer, has recently had his hardness challenged by another contender for this center, Jerry Pournelle. This is a struggle for the center, and what it reveals is a surprising softness in the hard ideal itself, the ease with which this core can split radically apart.

Holder of a Ph.D. in biochemistry, Asimov has stated with hard authority that SF *by its very nature* is the literature of a small core that values reason in a world that does not. And his famous definition of the genre, that SF is the branch of literature "concerned with the impact of scientific advance on human beings," conjures a vision of some hard juggernaut slamming into soft human beings. Pournelle, however, in a recent interview with Charles Platt in *Isaac Asimov's Science Fiction Magazine*, finds a soft spot in Asimov's rationality.[22] Referring to Asimov's statement that "violence is the last refuge of the incompetent" as an "asinine motto," Pournelle faults the good Doctor for minimizing the *effectiveness* of forces like violence in changing destiny. His incrimination may in fact point to an even deeper soft spot, a hidden humanism operating paradoxically at the heart of Asimov's seemingly rigorous and scientific view of the workings of the universe. Discussing Asimov's sense of freedom and necessity in his *Foundation Trilogy,* James Gunn uses a Christian analogy. "Psychohistory," Gunn tells us, "is no more restrictive of free will than the Judeo-Christian deity."[23] Such individual freedom, however, in Christianity, has meaning only in relation to a *telos* or determined pattern of events. Despite what Gunn says, this is freedom-in-determinism, and it seems to be the condition of Asimov's psychohistorical world as well. Indeed such freedom, to the degree that it hides from itself the fact that it is guided, must of necessity remain untested by notions like violence, hence in the eyes of a Pournelle offer a static view of mankind couched in pseudodynamic terms. And as "that branch of mathematics which deals with the reactions of human conglomerates to fixed emotional and social stimuli," psychohistory does seem to present a statistics of fixities, not variables, a determined envelope of cyclical occurrences that conceals and protects such unexamined "motions and impulses of humanity" as reason itself.

What Pournelle seems to protest, in Asimov, is this use of omnipotent law—the cyclical workings of his "all-human galaxy"—to sequester the operations of some representative "rational" few. Myth was the sanction for Butor's collective vision; social science is Asimov's. But the latter's view of human nature, in denying the individual will to violence, is just as "unrealistic" to Pournelle as Butor's vision seemed to Blish, again an illusion that hard reality will dispel. Open violence, however, is a force of uncertainty, something horrific. In *Foundation,* a work of much potential but little or no actual violence, Asimov controls the horrific by integrating it with psychohistory, but only at the cost of nesting a series of unexamined humanist fixities at the core of his fictional world. Pournelle, on the other hand, sees individuals and individuals alone controlling violence. Radically, he banishes all ideas of collective action to limbo. The spectrum he negates lies between Herbert Marcuse and John Norman—history on the Marxist flywheel, sex on the rape-rack—visions of the dullest determinism that must be effaced by a dynamic, liberated individualism, Heinlein's janissary fighting his way across the cosmos in order to keep the channels of energy open, loosing uncertainty so as to wrestle it into submission.

Pournelle's optimism of violence is an extreme ideal. Its extremeness in fact is seen in the author's swerve toward fantasy as its proper vehicle. To Pournelle fantasy is a hard form, ultimately harder perhaps than SF, because it is capable of "a fairly ruthless internal consistency." Indeed it is this internal hardness, rather than the rigors of Blish's scientific speculation, that may in the long run best reject that "tragic" view of fallen man that Pournelle sees invading, and deflating, the works of writers like Aldiss and Malzberg. To this view, as to Asimov's humanistic determinism, he opposes what he calls "redemption," the freedom of strong individuals to make a 100-billion-year-spree across the heavens. How can mankind be depressed, he asks, when the whole universe is there for the taking? Who knows what we can build? Maybe we are building God? This individual, like Heinlein's Lazarus Long, posits an ideal world where self is coterminous with universe, where man, seeking his origin and end in time and space, need only take up a mirror. The ultimate and most ruthlessly consistent fantasy that exists, then, is solipsism itself.

Ursula Le Guin is a writer of space epics who has consistently sought to keep mankind and his tragic existence alive at the core of a seemingly expanding universe. It is therefore not surprising that, increasingly, she opposes the hard vision of SF. She sees this hardness (Campbell bears her out) as male elitism, and its products, Pournelle's ruthless fantasies, as statements of masculine domination by violence and power. In an article called "American SF and the Other," Le Guin turns the tables, for in turn she holds up this "parochial" and "power-worshipping" SF as the true Alien, at odds with every possible form of community—sex, society, culture, race.[24] Emboldened perhaps by such professions of faith, she is recently seeking, through a series of pronouncements, to define an ideally soft and communal vision which she would place at the core of the genre. Le Guin is not seeking, as some feel, to withdraw from science fiction altogether. Her statements continue to be made in SF magazines. And they are about SF writers and the state of this particular art. To the contrary, she is placing herself closer and closer to the center. What is happening—and other commentators are helping her in this task—is the idealization of Ursula Le Guin herself.

A central event in this process is her contention with Gregory Benford. As a writer, Benford would appear to stand in ideal opposition to her sense of SF: he is male, a scientist (and a "hard" one at that), and seemingly a technophile. The bone of contention is Benford's own credo, "A String of Days," which appeared in the British journal *Foundation* as number 22 of their series "The Profession of Science Fiction."[25] In the subsequent issue of this journal Le Guin published a short satire on this piece, "A Day of Strings." But here, by plucking what she feels are a number of hard traits from Benford's text and holding them up to ridicule, she is defining her own stand, and offering herself as true center for the genre at the same time. Her strategy thus involves turning Benford's document into a hard SF manifesto. To understand this strategy, we must first see what his assumptions are.

First of all Benford seeks to give us, through the somewhat artificial simplicity of a day-to-day account, a view of the creative process purposely opposite from the reigning Romantic myth of the writer. What drives the creator here is not *angst* but a balanced metabolism. Creation is the result not of single-minded suffering or personal chaos, but of broad interests and vitality. Benford offers us a busy and varied, but always carefully controlled existence, in this case right down to the 3500-plus calories needed daily to sustain the machine. He rejects then the garret for the stockmarket and investment policies. Speaking of his writer's days as "some scraps of memory, a few bits of fiction, cancelled checks and tax returns," he trades hyperbole and high style for underromanticized banter and shoptalk. Drawn by his course of days away from the wellsprings of memory and myth, he presents himself as Blish's "specialist," seeking to control the multiple strands of his space-time continuum.

Of these strands there are two major ones, for Benford is, professionally, both a writer and a scientist. Like a modern Leonardo, Benford is offering his string of days as a model whereby the scientist-writer can control his particular field of activity, one which as scientist he sees steeped in movement, change, contingency— what he calls "life, whole." He offers examples that show writing, like science, to be a self-correcting process, one continuously open to the flow of new data and to changing perspectives. For instance he tells of calling the editor at Putnam (he is constantly travelling, constantly on the phone) to change one word in the galleys of his already many-times-revised novel *Jupiter Project* because "the latest notions about Ganymede," learned that very day from a scientific colleague, "make this necessary." Thus Benford proceeds scientifically as he creates fiction; and he writes it, predictably, about actually doing science. Another example hints at the way potential mystery might emerge from the seemingly undramatic day-to-day activities of the researcher—a major "plot" in Benford's fiction. He tells of coming across a Russian paper on Type III solar radio bursts. Through routine discussion with other scientists, and a fortuitous one with his brother who works for Defense, he begins to glimpse a possible connection between this paper and charged particle weapons research. Is this paper the tip of an iceberg, he asks? But if we are on the edge of "star wars" here, it is only the edge. To Benford, this literature of the investigating scientist never drifts into space opera or high espionage, but remains rooted, as something "falsely quiet," in the everyday job of work.

Benford is of course making a statement about SF's core here. But if that core is hard, there are nuances. He faults, for instance, both the readers and the critics of SF for not sensing the drama—the fiction—implicit in *real* scientific activity. He sees SF's current audience as split: on one hand, there are the adolescents seeking "wonder" fantasy; on the other, there are the "serious" establishment critics who (as he puts it) would rather "unearth Wells and embalm Le Guin." Both of these extremes are recognizably soft—the first soft-headed, the second an example of what Blish called "antiquarianism." Opposed to these, Benford clearly states, the real and viable core of SF is man doing science. This activity is, admittedly here, individualistic and competitive. Even so, what Benford describes is far from the militancy and violence of a Heinlein or a Pournelle. It is instead firmly based in the fabric of the author's daily life—in social events, in playing games with his children, in making sound investments. And Benford's definition of SF—his sort of hard SF—is both open-ended and muted in the same way. It is definition as a mode of operation, the writer trying to "enlist readers' responses to the devices of realism, in the cause of the fantastic."[26] The real here is science's daily encounters with the unknown, with those "singularities" Lem exposes. But by shifting the designation of this encounter from "horrific" to "fantastic," Benford offers us a situation of a slightly different order. His core is still positivistic. Yet because the use of the term "fantastic" suggests that the alien can be integrated into human systems in a more elegant and gracious manner that Campbell's tooth-and-claw struggle, there is greater space for routine human activity on the periphery of that core.

Le Guin parodies all this in her "Day of Strings." Her title, as mirror inversion of Benford's, is significant in revealing her own sense of the core. She rejects the open-ended string of days along with its sense of a need to master the continuum of time and space. Instead she proposes to draw all those strings, which she sees as fortuitous and irrelevant, toward one day as single center and central focal point. Her sense of the core, then, is of a centripetal force, not, as in Benford, of something expanding. She ridicules, for example, Benford's stopping the galleys at Putnam to change a word. Her idea of a creator, it seems, is that mythical shaper of wholes. The SF writer does not endlessly tinker with the external gadgetry of his fiction, using the latest discoveries in science and technology to erect some hard and impregnable, but ultimately hollow, structure. Instead all this external apparatus must be ready, at some moment of human revelation or epiphany, to collapse back effortlessly to its core. This is the case with Le Guin's physicist Shevek in *The Dispossessed,* whose discovery of a unified field theory is a moment of mystical vision, the moment when this entire Hainish universe in flux touches its solid core, the place back to which all mysteries and paradoxes now flow. Markham's "epiphany" in Benford's *Timescape* is quite different, merely the end of one time strand in a vast network of possible strands. Even so, if there is, in the loops and paradoxes of this "timescape," no simple riverrun of years, "there always remained the pulse of things coming, the sense that even now there was yet still time."[27] Still *time,* or *still* time? Benford or Le Guin? Hard or soft science fiction?

Recently Le Guin has been working to articulate her retreat to the soft core. By her own admission she has come, from her Hainish odysseys, back to earth. And it is to stay. In a recent interview for *Locus* (Vol. 17, no. 9, September 1984), she decries the Pournelle-Benford spirit as dominating our military-industrial times: "These are hard, gray times, and we need some reading that isn't all hard and gray and martial and threatening" (p. 56). A sample of such alternate reading might be her own recent work, "A Round, Buff, Speckled Poem." Here these same individualistic skygods—"steel eagles" laying "steel eggs" that hatch death—are set against the chthonian forces of the humble quail, the ever-abiding organic core of "nature" herself. To this new Le Guin it seems, if SF is to have a core, it must now be round and buff.

An article on Le Guin, which appeared in the January, 1984, issue of *Mother Jones,* is significantly entitled "In a World of Her Own." And what that world is is very interesting. For this article, working with a science fiction writer as world maker, is itself a world-building act of idealization, a transforming of the writer's own world into *the* world, the core to which all possible worlds in this genre must ultimately come. All flights of speculation are grounded in this place—Le Guin's Portland. We visit her simple house, its spare, clean children's rooms, its study opening out on well-rooted trees—the solid center from which, over the last twenty years, she has projected her SF worlds. This house in turn sits in the middle of an architypically "sensible" city. Portland has a low skyline and is full of substantial and "natural" things: good bookstores, whole food restaurants, and many parks visited by the beneficient spirits of ILWU martyrs and 1960s peace marchers. "It is a Le Guin city," the author tells us, "as if parts of it had been invented by her."[28] And it is also, like many of her fictional future cities, a Paul Goodman city, a place that is "messy, active, human-scale." Yet this is a "messiness" that offers little or no interface with the indeterminate, but rather disorder subjected to the same forces of inner coordination Butor prescribes for his single SF city. The city then can be the center to the degree that it can revert to the garden, to a place organized by "community," where "the human scale is always kept intact, and where all things are measured against it."

In the title finally of Le Guin's latest piece of fiction-in-progress, *Always Coming Home,* we have the ideal conjunction of centripetal motion and static absoluteness. The setting for this novel, she tells us, is both the distant future and the Napa Valley, her own family homestead, and a place of recurrent homecoming for some fifty summers. But this future Napa Valley is now isolated by earthquakes and continental shift. Conveniently, ugly modern cities like San Francisco (a metonym for Los Angeles, the future horroropolis we see in films like *Bladerunner*?) have slipped into the ocean, leaving old trapped rivers like the Humboldt free to flow. Le Guin, it seems, is using the possibility of future change here not to speculate but to calibrate—to return SF to those communally logocentric activities that should form its center. "I got less interested," she states, "in plot and wanted to see how these people lived, what they did, how they did it. They tell their own stories. They're highly literate, both oral and written literature."[29] The novel will present us with songs, recipes, artifacts. A web of "basic" social and cultural activities (they still make wine in this future Napa Valley for instance) is thus allowed to speak for itself, guided by an author who, like Plato with his dialogues, functions mainly as anthropological observer.

For Le Guin, then, the proper study of scientific mankind is not hard male aggressiveness but the female power to endure, the quail of her poem flying on short wings yet doing "long things," anchoring the organic chain. Against such, the hybris of the individual is ephemeral. Increasingly, however, to Le Guin, it has become dangerous as well. Compared with the soft idealizing of Pascal, or even of Hawks, where horror is finally pushed beyond the human perimeter or expelled from community, Le Guin's vision has become increasingly foreshortened. In her latest proclamations, horror is the very tangible force of war. Bringing it, the individual—Pournelle's hard apostle of violence—offers monstrous annihilation. The "steel eagle" then bears the apocalyptic mark of the beast, and the huddling place is no longer a folk custom but a folk necessity. Le Guin must retreat from space because it has become the place of death. If before (as in *The Thing from Another World*) the apparatus of SF—the narrative themes and figures of rationalist science—could be made, once their hardness is neutralized, to inscribe and even shield the soft core, now that same apparatus, ringing us in a "star wars" space, is blighted and menacing: "The little *Voyagers*? God, those were lovely. But what we are doing now I find in itself extremely depressing—the space shuttle. . . . It's all a bunch of crap flying around the world, just garbage in the sky."[30] Elsewhere she tells us: "I love the experiments, the little unmanned things." Again the ax of idealization falls, and a good "pure" science is separated from the impure crap. But this ideal form now is depicted as a helpless little child—a child whose clouds of glory have been all but consumed in the hard light of common day, whose only redemption lies in being recalled to the soft bosom of mother earth.

SF's map of the ideal stands at extremes today. On one hand there is Pournelle's hard megalomaniacal solipsism; on the other Le Guin's soft paranoia. And we can add to these radicalizations Stanislaw Lem's defection to the horrific. Already in 1977, in his review article on *Cosmology Now*, Lem denounces both the screens of blood and those of soft sentimentality that all SF throws over this "real" universe of cosmology. "It must be admitted," he proclaims, "that the universe presents the 'peak of indigestibility' for fiction writing in the whole field of our experience." In other words, SF can offer no center, soft or hard, against the singularities of nature. The true use of reason then—and "nothing today is so much held in contempt in SF as reason"—is to accept this truth, to stop writing useless barriers against the horrific silence. For Lem the defector all that remains is the horrific itself as ideal. And in the final flourish to this review, with its obvious bow to Plato, he confirms this: "SF fans should be discouraged from perusing *Cosmology Now,* unless they are willing to free their imagination from its imprisonment to discover in the brightness of real suns the true face of nature."[31]

One question remains—of crucial importance as Lem suggests for all of fiction and human experience alike: can we break the hegemony of idealization? In this essay I have sought to argue from all sides of SF's map of ideals, from all its cores. And we have seen that—no matter what its valence, hard or soft—as that core sets in its absoluteness it becomes something we are tempted, in the more pragmatic sense, to call "hard," inflexible. And we have seen, too, that the form with the hardest technological valence may, paradoxically, offer the most flexibility, the greatest potential for subverting the logic of the ideal. This is true precisely because this form, with its mobile center as constant *reminder* of mankind engaged in interplay with the singularities of nature, allows more room to act pragmatically. A passage from Benford's *In the Ocean of Night* is instructive here. The scientist-hero Nigel Walmsley has his world view challenged by a guru of the New Sons sect who, telling him that physical laws are but the bars of a cage, offers the following wisdom: "The central point is not to study the bars. It is to get out of the cage."[32] Such is the goal of most of the ideal centralities we have studied—to escape the cage. If Pournelle will do it by hard force, Le Guin seeks, by contracting within that cage, to pass through the needle's eye of epiphany. Benford's hero, however, offers another answer: "I think the act of reaching out is everything." Science may create bars; it may make nature, that cave of illusion, a cave of steel. Yet, even if mankind in science cannot break his chains, he at least has the power to turn, to continue to reach out. To show "science as a human enterprise" is Benford's key phrase to describe his fiction. And that fiction promises to reorganize past and future, memory and reminder, soft and hard, in relation to this progressive present time of doing and showing. Indeed, if a new ideal emerges from Benford's fiction, I can think of no better description than a line from Peter Tosh's song "Mystic Man": something that accomodates that "man of the past, living in the present, but walking in the future."

Notes
Biographical Notes
Index

Notes

The Unconscious City

1. Henri Pirenne, *Economic and Social History of Medieval Europe* (1933; rpt. New York: Harcourt, Brace & World, 1962), pp. 52–53.
2. Raymond Williams, *The Country and the City* (New York: Oxford Univ. Press, 1973), p. 272.
3. Brian Aldiss, ed., *Science Fiction Art: The Fantasies of SF* (New York: Crown Publishers, 1975), p. 89.
4. Jean Raynaud, "*La Ville dans la science fiction américaine contemporaine,*" *Revue Française d'Etudes Américaines,* no. 11, April, 1981, p. 67. This and subsequent translations are mine.
5. Merrell A. Knighten, "The Caves of Steel" in Frank N. Magill, ed., *Survey of Science Fiction Literature* (Englewood Cliffs: Salem Press, 1979), p. 320.
6. Peter Nicholls, "Hardcore SF" in Peter Nicholls, ed., *Science Fiction Encyclopedia* (Garden City, NY: Doubleday, 1979), p. 273.
7. Brian Ash, *The Visual Encyclopedia of Science Fiction* (New York: Harmony Books, 1977), p. 167.
8. Ihab Hassan, "Cities of Mind, Urban Words: The Dematerialization of Metropolis in Contemporary American Fiction" in Michael C. Jaye and Ann Chalmers Watts, eds., *Literature & the Urban Experience* (New Brunswick: Rutgers Univ. Press, 1981), pp. 107, 109.
9. Brian Stableford, "Cities" in Peter Nicholls, ed., *The Science Fiction Encyclopedia* (Garden City, NY: Doubleday, 1979), p. 120.
10. Ibid., p. 120.
11. Raynaud, p. 68.
12. Ibid., p. 68.
13. Ibid., p. 69.
14. Ibid., p. 69.
15. Gary K. Wolfe, *The Known And The Unknown: The Iconography of Science Fiction* (Kent, OH: Kent State Univ. Press, 1979), p. 88.
16. Ibid., pp. 88–92.
17. Gaston Bachelard, *The Poetics of Space,* Maria Jolas, trans. (1958; rpt. Boston: Beacon Press, 1969), p. 72.

18. Gaston Bachelard, *The Psychoanalysis of Fire*, Alan C. M. Ross, trans. (1938; rpt. Boston: Beacon Press, 1968), p. 19.

19. Sharon Spencer, *Space, Time and the Structure in the Modern Novel* (Chicago: Swallow Press, 1971), p. 14.

20. Darko Suvin, *Metamorphoses of Science Fiction* (New Haven: Yale Univ. Press, 1979), p. 64.

21. Ibid., p. 65.

22. John Wyndham, *Re-Birth* (1955; rpt. New York: Ballantine Books, 1978), p. 1.

23. Ibid., p. 172.

24. Ibid., pp. 173–74.

25. Ibid., p. 180.

26. Ibid., p. 185.

27. Isaac Asimov, *The Caves of Steel* (1954; rpt. Greenwich, CT: Fawcett Publications, 1972), p. 88.

28. Arthur C. Clarke, *The City and the Stars* (1953; rpt. New York: Harcourt, Brace & World, 1969), p. 3.

29. Ibid., p. 7.

30. Max Lüthi, *Once Upon a Time: On the Nature of Fairy Tales*, Lee Chadeayne and Paul Gottwald, trans. (1962; rpt. New York: Frederick Ungar, 1970), p. 111.

31. Clarke, *The City and the Stars*, pp. 16–17.

32. Ibid., p. 17.

33. Ibid., p. 213.

34. Julian S. Krupa, back cover illustration for *Amazing Stories*, August, 1939, rpt. in Aldiss, *Science Fiction Art*, p. 89.

35. Lewis Mumford, *The City in History* (New York: Harcourt Brace Jovanovich, 1961, pp. 12–13.

36. Leo Morey, cover illustration for *Amazing Stories*, July, 1932, rpt. in Aldiss, *Science Fiction Art*, p. 92.

37. Abraham Merritt, *The Metal Monster* (1920; rpt. Westport, CT: Hyperion Press, 1974).

38. Hugo Gernsback, *Ralph 124C 41+* (1911; rpt. New York: Frederick Fell, 1950), p. 40.

39. Ibid., p. 82.

40. Tim Brooks and Earle Marsh, *The Complete Directory to Prime Time Network TV Shows 1946–Present (Revised Edition)* (New York: Ballantine Books, 1981), p. 341.

41. Eugene Zamiatin, *We*, Gregory Zilboorg, trans. (1924; rpt. New York: E.P. Dutton, 1959), p. 22.

42. Cyrano de Bergerac, *Other Worlds*, Geoffrey Strachan, trans. (1657; rpt. London: New English Library, 1976), p. 68.

43. François Rabelais, *Gargantua* in *The Portable Rabelais*, Samuel Putnam, trans. (1532; rpt. New York: Viking Press, 1946), p. 200.

44. Zamiatin, *We,* p. 171.

45. Ibid., p. 77.

46. John Pfeiffer, "Metropolis" in Magill, *Survey of Science Fiction Literature,* p. 1384.

47. Thea von Harbou, *Metropolis* (1926; rpt. New York: Ace Books, 1963), pp. 109–10.

48. Ibid., p. 54.

49. W.H. Auden, "In Memory of Sigmund Freud" in *The Collected Poetry of W.H. Auden* (New York: Random House, 1945), p. 167.

50. Samuel R. Delany, *Dhalgren* (1974; rpt. New York: Bantam Books, 1982), p. 278.

51. J.C. Cooper, *An Illustrated Encyclopedia of Traditional Symbols* (London: Thames and Hudson, 1978), p. 194.

52. C.G. Jung. *Symbols of Transformation* (1956), cited in J.E. Cirlot, *A Dictionary of Symbols,* Jack Sage, trans. (New York: Philosophical Library, 1962), p. 47.

53. C.G. Jung, *Psychology of the Unconscious,* Beatrice M. Hinkle, trans. (1912; rpt. New York: Dodd, Mead and Company, 1949), pp. 234–35.

54. Sigmund Freud in John Bartlett, *Familiar Quotations,* 15th ed. (Boston: Little, Brown and Company, 1980), p. 679.

55. James Blish, *Cities in Flight* (1957, *They Shall Have Stars*; 1962, *A Life for the Stars*; 1955, *Earthman Come Home*; 1958, *The Triumph of Time*; rpt. in one vol. New York: Avon Books, 1970), p. 231.

56. Ibid., p. 362.

57. Joanna Russ, quoted in Paul A. Carter, *The Creation of Tomorrow* (New York: Columbia Univ. Press, 1977), p. 173.

58. Cf. Wolfe, *The Known and the Unknown.*

59. Cf. Mark Rose, *Alien Encounters* (Cambridge, MA: Harvard Univ. Press, 1981).

60. David Ketterer, *New Worlds for Old* (New York: Doubleday, 1974), p. 102.

61. St. Augustine, Preface to *City of God* (415).

62. John Robert Colombo, "Babylon" in *The Great Cities of Antiquity* (Toronto: Hounslow Press, 1979), p. 10.

63. N.G.L. Hammond and H.H. Scullard, eds., *The Oxford Classical Dictionary*, 2nd ed. (Oxford: Claredon Press, 1970), s.v. "Helen."

64. Christopher Marlowe, *The Tragical History of Dr. Faustus* (1601) sc. 13, 11, 112–13.

65. John Dos Passos, *Manhatten Transfer* (1925; rpt. Boston: Houghton Mifflin, 1953) pp. 116–17.

66. J.D. Bernal, *The World, the Flesh & the Devil* (1929; rpt. Bloomington: Indiana Univ. Press, 1969), pp. 18, 19, 24.

67. William Morris, ed., *The American Heritage Dictionary of the English Language* (Boston: Houghton Mifflin, 1976), s.v. "metropolis." I am

grateful to Professor Sandra Gilbert for bringing this etymology to my attention.

68. Ibid., s.v. "kei-¹."

69. Italo Calvino, *Invisible Cities,* William Weaver, trans. (1972; rpt. New York: Harcourt Brace Jovanovich, 1974), p. 44.

Hard-Core Science Fiction and the Illusion of Science

1. Quoted in *H.G. Wells: The Critical Heritage,* ed. Patrick Parrinder (London: Routledge & Kegan Paul, 1972), pp. 101–2.

2. For a recent sophisticated discussion of the issue of realism and SF, see chapter four of Christine Brooke-Rose, *A Rhetoric of the Unreal: Studies in Narrative and Structure, Especially of the Fantastic* (Cambridge: Cambridge Univ. Press, 1981).

3. Robert Heinlein, "Science Fiction: Its Nature, Faults, and Virtues," in *The Science Fiction Novel: Imagination and Social Criticism* (Chicago: Advent, 1959), pp. 29–30.

4. Cf. Fredric Jameson, *The Political Unconscious: Narrative as a Socially Symbolic Act* (Ithaca, NY: Cornell Univ. Press, 1981), p. 232.

5. See Pierre Macherey, *A Theory of Literary Production,* trans. Geoffrey Wall (London: Routledge & Kegan Paul, 1978), p. 169.

6. Despite a certain overlap, I want to distingish the idea of hard-core SF I am describing from that "engineering mentality" attacked a decade ago by Richard Lupoff for its "dedication to control, to predictability, to the finite, closed-end solution." "Science Fiction Hawks and Doves: Whose Future will You Buy?" *Ramparts* (Feb. 1972), p. 27. The qualities Lupoff attacks do not seem to me evil in themselves; to a rather large extent the future good of humanity depends on them. My own complaint is to a misapplication of these otherwise praiseworthy aspirations.

7. "Teaching Science Fiction: Unique Challenges," transcribed and edited by John Woodcock, *S-FS* 19, 251.

8. The story has been anthologized more than a dozen times. The edition I am using is that found in *The Science Fiction Hall of Fame,* Vol. 1A, ed. Robert Silverberg (New York: Avon, 1970), pp. 543–69.

9. The story has not received much detailed attention, but it is often mentioned in discussions of hard-core SF, and usually when it is mentioned it is treated as a paradigm of the hard core. Typical is James Gunn who calls it "The touchstone story for hard-core science fiction." *The Road to Science Fiction #3: From Heinlein to Here,* ed. James Gunn (New York: New American Library, 1979), p. 244.

10. "Teaching Science Fiction," 250.

11. See Jameson, *The Political Unconscious,* pp. 267–68.

12. See, for example, Gaines in Heinlein's "The Roads Must Roll." "On the surface, Gaines' exceptionally intelligent mind was clicking along with the facile ease of an electromechanical integrator—arranging data at hand, making tentative decisions, postponing judgments without prejudice until necessary data were available, exploring alternatives. Underneath, in a compartment insulated by stern self-discipline from the acting theater of his mind, emotions were a torturing storm of self-reproach. He was heartsick at the suffering he had seen." *The Science Fiction Hall of Fame, Vol. 1A,* pp. 91–92.

13. The concept of the author must be understood in a particular way in this story. In Godwin's original version of "The Cold Equations" Marilyn was saved. It was John W. Campbell, his editor, who insisted that her death was the "right" ending. (I am indebted to James Gunn for this valuable piece of SF lore). If this anecdote is true, here we have two authors who are to some extent in conflict within the same story. Though it is convenient to continue to use the term "author" to speak of the intention we postulate behind the story, we need to keep in mind that in this case the term does not refer to an actual person. It may be more useful to conceive of the "author" of "The Cold Equations" as the ideological context in which Godwin and Campbell find themselves and which unites them even in their difference.

14. *PMLA* (1971), 17.

15. *Criticism and Ideology: A Study in Marxist Literary Theory* (London: Verso Editions, 1976), p. 89.

What Makes Hard Science Fiction "Hard?"

1. "Ainsi la matière nous révèle nos forces. Elle suggère une mise en catégories dynamiques de nos forces. Elle donne non seulement une substance durable à notre volonté, mais encore des schèmes temporels bien définis à notre patience. Aussitôt, la matière reçoit de nos rêves tout un avenir de travail; nous voulons la vaincre en travaillant. Nous jouissons par avance de l'efficacité de notre volonté. Qu'on ne s'etonne donc pas que rêver d'images matérielles—oui, simplement les rêver— c'est aussitôt *tonifier* la volonté. Impossible d'être distrait, absent, indifférent, quand on rêve d'une matière resistante nettement désignée. On ne saurait imaginer gratuitement une résistance. Les matières diverses, déployées entre les poles dialectiques extrêmes du *dur* et du *mou* designent de très nombreux types d'adversités. Réciproquement, toutes les adversités qu'on croit profondément humaines, avec leurs violences cyniques ou sournoises, avec leur éclat ou leur hypocrisie, viennent, dans des actions contre des matières inanimées particulières, trouver leur réalisme. Mieux que n'importe quel complément, le com-

plément de matière spécifie l'hostilité." Gaston Bachelard, *La Terre et les rêveries de la volonté* (Paris: José Corti, 1948). Unless otherwise indicated, translations are my own.

2. William James, *Pragmatism*, (1907), cited in F.O. Matthiessen, *The James Family Including Selections from the Writings of Henry James, Senior, William, Henry, & Alice James* (New York: Knopf), pp. 238–39.

3. John W. Campbell, "The Invaders," (1935) in *The Best of John W. Campbell*, ed. Lester del Rey (Garden City: Nelson Doubleday, 1976), p. 64.

4. Ibid., p. 61.

5. Ibid., p. 66.

6. Ibid., p. 68.

7. Campbell, "Rebellion" (1935) in *Best of John W. Campbell*, p. 94.

8. "Das Objekt wird dem Ich, wie wir gehört haben, zuerst von den Selbsterhalungstrieben aus der Außenwelt gebracht, und es ist nicht abzuweisen, dab auch der ursprüngliche Sinn des Hassens die Relation gegen die fremde und reizzuführende Außenwelt bedeutet. . . . Das Äußere, das Objekt, das Gehabte wären zu allem Anfang identisch." Sigmund Freud, "Triebe und Triebschicksale," (1915) in *Psychologie des Unbewußten*, Vol. III of *Sigmund Freud Studienausgabe*, ed. Alexander Mitscherlich, Angela Richards, and James Strachey (Frankfurt on the Main: S. Fischer, 1975), pp. 98–99.

9. "Besonders vom Wibtrieb gewinnt man häufig den Eindruck, als ob er im Mechanismus der Zwangsneurose den Sadismus geradezu ersetzen könnte. Er ist ja im Grunde ein sublimierter, in Intellektuelle gehobener Sprößling des Bemächtigungstriebes." Sigmund Freud, "Die Disposition zur Zwangsneurose," (1913) in *Zwang, Paranoia und Perversion*, Vol. VII of *Studienausgabe* (1973), p. 116.

10. H.G. Wells, *The War of the Worlds*, (1898) in *The Complete Science Fiction Treasury of H.G. Wells* (1934; rpt. New York: Avenel Books, 1978), p. 265.

11. Ibid., p. 387.

12. Ibid., p. 371.

13. Ibid., p. 349.

14. Robert Scholes and Eric S. Rabkin, *Science Fiction: History. Science. Vision.* (New York: Galaxy–Oxford Univ. Press, 1977), p. 54.

15. Roland Bainton, "Sebastian Castellio, Champion of Religious Toleration" in *Studies on the Reformation* (1963; rpt. Boston: Beacon Press, 1966), p. 145.

16. John Calvin, *The Institutes of the Christian Religion* (1559), ed. John T. McNeill, trans. Ford Lewis Battles (Philadelphia: Westminster Press, 1960), I, 72.

17. "Die Götter können die Furcht nicht vom Menschen nehmen, deren

versteinerte Laute sie als ihre Namen tragen. Der Furcht wähnt er ledig zu sein, wenn es nichts Unbekanntes mehr gibt. Das bestimmt die Bahn der Entmythologisierung. . . . Aufklärung ist die radikal gewordene, mythische Angst." Max Horkheimer and Theodor Adorno, *Dialektik der Aufklärung, Philosophische Fragmente* (1947; 1969; rpt. Frankfurt on the Main: Fischer Taschenbuch, 1971), p. 18.

18. "Jeder Versuch, den Naturzwang zu brechen, indem Natur gebrochen wird, gerät nur um so tiefer in den Naturzwang hinein. . . . Die Abstraktion, das Werkzeug der Aufklärung, verhält sich zu ihren Objekten wie das Schicksal, dessen Begriff sie ausmerzt: als Liquidation." Horkheimer and Adorno, p. 15.

19. Samuel R. Delany, "Shadows" (1974–75) in *The Jewel-Hinged Jaw: Notes of the Language of Science Fiction* (New York: Windhover-Berkley, 1977), p. 80.

20. Robert Heinlein, *Starship Troopers* (1959; rpt. New York: Berkley, 1968), p. 95.

21. Ibid.

22. Ibid., p. 96. Emphasis in original.

23. "Diese Wendung ist schon die zum falschen Bewußtsein; hätte der Löwe eines, so wäre seine Wut auf die Antilope, die er fressen will, Ideologie." Theodor Adorno, *Negative Dialektik* (1966; rpt. Frankfurt on the Main: Suhrkamp, 1970), p. 340.

Is There a Technological Fix for the Human Condition?

1. See David Samuelson, *Visions of Tomorrow* (New York; Arno Press, 1975), Ch. 2, pp. 45–84.

2. Martin Bridgstock, *SFS* 10, 1983, pp. 52–56.

3. Liam Hudson, *Contrary Imaginations* (London; Harmondsworth, 1972), p. 55.

4. Brian M. Stableford, *Foundation 15*, 1979, pp. 28–41.

5. *Contrary Imaginations*, p. 55.

6. Gregory Benford, in *Bridges to Science Fiction* (Carbondale: Southern Illinois Univ. Press, 1981), pp. 53–63.

7. Thomas Disch, *Science Fiction at Large*, edited by Peter Nicholls, (London; Victor Gollancz, 1976), pp. 139–55.

8. Gregory Benford, *The Patchin Review* 3, 1982, pp. 5–9.

9. S. Finch-Rayner, *Journal of Popular Culture*, Vol. 18 (Spring 1985), 727–34.

10. Gerard Klein, *SFS* 4, 1977, pp. 3–13.

11. Richard D. Erlich, *Foundation 27*, 1983, pp. 64–71.

12. Jerry Pournelle, *Destinies*, Vol. 2 No. 2, (New York; Ace, 1980).

13. *Visions of Tomorrow*, pp. 56–57.

14. Gregory Benford, "Why is There so Little Science in Literature?" in
    Nebula Award Stories 16, ed. by Jerry Pournelle, (New York: Holt
    Reinhart Winston, 1982).

Thomas Burnet's *Sacred Theory of the Earth* and the Aesthetics of Extrapolation

1. The first edition, containing only the first two parts is: Thomas Burnet,
   Telluris Theoria Sacra (London, 1681). This appeared in English as *The
   Sacred Theory of the Earth: Containing an Account of the Original of the
   Earth and of All the General Changes Which It Hath Already Undergone
   or Is to Undergo, till the Consummation of All Things* (London, 1684).
   The final two parts were added to the Latin edition of 1689 and included
   in the English translation of 1690 and in subsequent English editions.
   For a study of Burnet's influence on English aesthetics, especially
   attitudes toward mountains and poetic descriptions of them, see Mar-
   jorie Hope Nicolson, *Mountain Gloom and Mountain Glory: The Development of the Aesthetics of the Infinite* (Ithaca: Cornell Univ. Press,
   1959). For the political context of Burnet's ideas see M.C. Jacob and
   W.A. Lockwood, "Political Millenarianism and Burnet's *Sacred
   Theory*," *Science Studies*, 2 (1972), 265–79; and Margaret C. Jacob, *The
   Newtonians and the English Revolution 1689–1720* (Hassocks, Eng.:
   Harvester Press; Cornell Univ. Press, 1976).
2. Frank E. Manuel, *The Religion of Isaac Newton* (Oxford: Clarendon
   Press, 1974), p. 39.
3. Stephen Toulmin and June Goodfield, *The Discovery of Time* (1965; rpt.
   Chicago and London: Univ. of Chicago Press, 1982), p. 93.
4. For the exchange between Newton and Burnet see *Correspondence of
   Isaac Newton,* II: 1676–1687, ed. H. W. Turnbull (Cambridge: Pub. for
   the Royal Society at the University Press, 1960), pp. 319, 321–35. In
   Newton's view the biblical account of creation is neither fiction nor an
   objective scientific description but rather a kind of phenomenological
   extrapolation backwards in time to narrate events during planetary
   formation as they would have appeared to an observer on earth without
   any knowledge of science: "As to Moses I do not think his description of
   ye creation either Philosophical or feigned, but that he described realities in a language artificially adapted to ye sense of ye vulgar. Thus
   where he speaks of two great lights I suppose he means their apparent,
   not real greatness. . . . To describe them distinctly as they were in them
   selves would have . . . become a Philosopher more than a Prophet. He
   mentions them therefore only so far as ye vulgar had a notion of them,
   that is as they were phaenomena in our firmament, & describes their
   making only so far & at such a time as they were made such
   phaenomena. . . . For Moses accommodating his words to ye gross

conceptions of ye vulgar, describes things much after ye manner as one of ye vulgar would have been inclined to do had he lived & seen ye whole series of wt [sic] Moses describes" (pp. 331, 333). Genesis is here taken by Newton as using scientifically correct extrapolations to present a version of the distant past that is not fantasy (not "feigned") but factual. It is "not an Ideal or poetical but a true description" Newton insists elsewhere in the same letter to Burnet (p. 333). But in this view Genesis is factual in an incomplete way and resorts to a non-scientific (not "Philosophical") vocabulary that allows but does not compel informed readers to recover the scientific basis of its account. Anyone thus trying like Newton and Burnet to reconstruct the facts of planetary formation alluded to in Genesis would face a problem curiously like that of some reader of a scientifically accurate narration which presents events as they might have been perceived by an *imaginary* protagonist ("had he lived & seen ye whole series") who saw things that really happened although from a limited perspective in space and without the scientific knowledge to understand them.

5. For the text of Newton's manuscript "Treatise on Revelation" see Manuel, *The Religion of Isaac Newton*, pp. 107–25; see too ch. IV, "Prophecy and History," pp. 83–104. A related discussion of these issues is provided in Frank E. Manuel, *A Portrait of Isaac Newton* (Cambridge, Mass.: Harvard Univ. Press, 1968), pp. 361–80..

6. Arlen J. Hansen, "The Meeting of Parallel Lines: Science, Fiction, and Science Fiction," in *Bridges to Fantasy*, ed. George E. Slusser, Eric S. Rabkin, and Robert Scholes (Carbondale: Southern Illinois Univ. Press, 1982), pp. 51–58.

7. David Ketterer, *New Worlds For Old: The Apocalyptic Imagination, Science Fiction And American Literature* (Bloomington & London: Indiana Univ. Press, 1974), pp. 13, 91.

8. Thomas Burnet, *The Sacred Theory of the Earth*, 6th ed., 2 vols. (London, 1726), I, xx. All subsequent references are to this edition. Following each citation volume and page numbers are given in parenthetical notation.

9. Joseph Keill, *An Examination of Dr. Burnet's Theory of the Earth*, 2nd ed. (London, 1734), pp. 22, 139. The first edition of Keill's *Examination* appeared in 1698.

10. H. Bruce Franklin, *Future Perfect: American Science Fiction of the Nineteenth Century*, rev. ed. (London: Oxford Univ. Press, 1978), pp. 101–2.

11. For discussion of other borderline relationships between fiction and fact in literature see Leo Braudy, *Narrative Form in History and Fiction: Hume, Fielding and Gibbon* (Princeton: Princeton Univ. Press, 1970; Patricia M. Spacks, *Imagining A Self: Autobiography and Novel in Eighteenth-Century England* (Cambridge, Mass.: Harvard Univ. Press,

1976); Hayden White, *Tropics of Discourse: Essays in Cultural Criticism* (Baltimore: John Hopkins Univ. Press, 1978); Lennard J. Davis, *Factual Fictions: The Origins of the English Novel* (New York: Columbia Univ. Press, 1983); and William R. Siebenschuh, *Fictional Techniques and Factual Works* (Athens: Univ. of Georgia Press, 1983). For an explanation of how scientific theories may be incorporated into literary fantasy while retaining something of their status as assertions about the real world, although on a different basis, see Robert M. Philmus, *Into the Unknown: The Evolution of Science Fiction from Francis Godwin to H. G. Wells* (Berkeley and Los Angeles: Univ. of California Press, 1970), pp. 108–26.

12. Burnet stresses, too, the utility of those hypotheses which in the normal course of science must be displaced by more accurate conjectures: "He that in an obscure Argument proposeth an *Hypothesis* that reacheth from End to End, tho' it be not exact in every Particular; 'tis not without a good Effect; for it gives Aim to others to take their Measures better, and opens their invention in a matter which otherwise, it may be, would have been impenetrable to them" (I, 130) Cf. Newton's more evasive assertion added to the "General Scholium" of the second edition of the *Principia* in 1713: "Hypotheses con fingo."—"I frame no hypotheses." For comments on the relationship to Newton's actual methods of this notoriously perplexing assertion, see N. R. Hanson, "Hypotheses Fingo," in *The Methodological Heritage of Newton*, ed. Robert E. Butts and John W. Davis (Oxford: Basil Blackwell, 1970), pp. 14–33.

13. For the 17th- and 18-century contexts of "admiration" as an aesthetic category, see Samuel H. Monk, *The Sublime: A Study of Critical Theories in XVIIIth Century England* (New York: Modern Language Association, 1935); H. T. Swedenberg, Jr., *The Theory of the Epic in England, 1660–1800* (Berkeley: Univ. of California Press, 1944); and J. V. Cunningham, *Woe or Wonder: The Emotional Effect of Shakespearean Tragedy* (Denver: Univ. of Denver Press, 1951).

14. Burnet resorts to a dismissive variation of the knot-metaphor when he rejects one astrological theory of stellar motion—the circle of retrogradation—as "a Bundle of Fictions tied up in a pretty Knot." He calls it this because he finds it a theory "merely imaginary" which "hath no Foundation in the true Nature or Motion of the coelestial Bodies" (II, 41). Here Burnet is not discussing "a *kind* of Fiction," as he calls scientific hypotheses to underscore their resemblance to the storyteller's art from which they nevertheless differ in point of application to the real world. Instead Burnet is dismissing ideas that are from a scientific viewpoint entirely fictions because they are based upon erroneous premises and therefore inevitably *wrong:* such theories, unlike those with true or at least possibly true explanatory force are at best merely decorative and thus no more than a "pretty Knot" which

may ornament a package without serving any other purpose. In Burnet's use of the metaphor elsewhere scientists, unlike astrologers and other pseudoscientists, tie knots that invite (informative) untying, not just appreciation of how pretty they look, and thus have a function although untying them also has its pleasures.

15. For Burnet's rejection of astrology see *"The Sacred Theory of the Earth,* II, 37–40, esp. p. 40: "I do not see how we are any more concern'd in the Postures of the Planets, than in the Postures of the Clouds; and you may as well build an Art of Prediction and Divination, upon the one, as the other." For a survey of shifting attitudes toward astrology, as well as an account of its persistence, see Bernard Capp, *English Almanacs 1500–1800: Astrology & the Popular Press* (Ithaca: Cornell Univ. Press, 1979).

16. Burnet follows what he calls "the receiv'd Rule of Interpreters" that "the literal Sense . . . is never to be quitted or forsaken, without Necessity" (II, 218). Accordingly he rejects the view "that *darkening of the Sun, shaking of the Earth*, and such like Phrases of Scripture . . . are to be understood only in a moral Sense" (II, 131). Eclipses, earthquakes, and the like apparently predicted in the Bible thus always invite Burnet to attempt scientific explanation even when the phenomena might not be anticipated on the basis of science alone.

17. For classic essays by R. F. Jones on "Science and English Prose Style in the Third Quarter of the Seventeenth Century" and "Science and Language in England of the Mid-Seventeenth Century" see *Seventeenth-Century Prose: Modern Essays in Criticism*, ed. Stanley E. Fish (New York: Oxford Univ. Press, 1971), pp. 53–111. Jones's essays are also conveniently available along with other related material in Richard Foster Jones, *The Seventeenth Century: Studies in the History of English Thought and Literature* (Stanford: Stanford Univ. Press, 1951).

18. Taking science fiction as a mode of what David Ketterer calls the apocalyptic imagination opens a useful window to the past without, however, precluding other ways of defining science fiction and accounting for different aspects of its development. I have stressed Ketterer's definition in this essay in order to suggest the relevance of Burnet. For the history of science fiction taken as a form of the gothic tale and rooted accordingly in another part of the 18th century, see Brian W. Aldiss, *Billion Year Spree: The True History of Science Fiction* (New York: Doubleday, 1973). For the connections of science fiction with varieties of mythology see: Robert M. Philmus, *Into the Unknown: The Evolution of Science Fiction from Francis Godwin to H. G. Wells* (Berkeley and Los Angeles: Univ. of California Press, 1970); and Casey Fredericks, *The Future of Eternity: Mythologies of Science Fiction and Fantasy* (Bloomington: Indiana Univ. Press, 1982). For the history of science fiction since *Frankenstein* in relation to the rise of modern

science, see Robert Scholes and Eric S. Rabkin, *Science Fiction: History, Science, Vision* (New York: Oxford Univ. Press, 1977). For a useful survey of the problems that bedevil any attempt at definition, as well as a brilliant solution of many of them via the idea of science fiction as cognitive estrangement—with, accordingly, yet another 18th-century text, *Gulliver's Travels*, identified as the model for all science fiction—see Darko Suvin, *Metamorphoses of Science Fiction: On the Poetics and History of a Literary Genre* (New Haven and London: Yale Univ. Press, 1979). For a consideration of the liberating possibility that the whole generic system which created science fiction as a distinct form may be in the process of breaking up into more fluid relationships that call for casting our historical nets even more widely, see Mark Rose, *Alien Encounters: Anatomy of Science Fiction* (Cambridge, Mass.: Harvard Univ. Press, 1981).

The Language of the Future in Victorian Science Fiction

1. *Works of William Morris*, ed. May Morris (London: Longmans, 1910–1915), XVI, xxviii.
2. *News from Nowhere* (London: Routledge and Kegan Paul, 1970), ch. 1. Further references are given in the text by chapter.
3. Robert Currie, "Had Morris Gone Soft in the Head?" *Essays in Criticism*, 29 (1979), 341–56.
4.. For discussions of the complex relation of *News* to the Victorian realist novel see Patrick Brantlinger, " 'News from Nowhere': Morris's Socialist Anti-Novel," *Victorian Studies* 19 (1975), 35–49; Patrick Parrinder, *"News from Nowhere, The Time Machine* and the Break-Up of Classical Realism," *Science Fiction Studies*, 3 (1976), 265–74; Bernard Sharratt, *"News from Nowhere*: Detail and Desire," in *Reading the Victorian Novel: Detail into Form*, ed. Ian Gregor (New York: Barnes and Noble, 1980), pp. 288–305.
5. See the discussion of the use of metaphor and metonymy in defining the genre of science fiction in Mark Rose, *Alien Encounter: Anatomy of Science Fiction* (Cambridge, MA: Harvard Univ. Press, 1981), 14–23.
6. *Looking Backward: 2000–1887* (New York: Signet, 1960), p. 80. ch. 10.
7. "Looking Backward," *The Commonweal*, June 22, 1889. Reprinted in *Science-Fiction Studies*, 3 (1976), 287–89.
8. Ian Watt, *The Rise of the Novel* (Berkeley: Univ. of California Press, 1967).
9. *The Political Unconscious* (Ithaca: Cornell Univ. Press, 1981), p. 104.
10. *Academy* (May 23, 1891), 483–84. Reprinted in *William Morris: The Critical Heritage*, ed. Peter Faulkner (London: Routledge & Kegan Paul, 1973), p. 340.
11. *The Left Hand of Darkness* (New York: Ace Books, 1976).

Science and Scientism in C. S. Lewis's
That Hideous Strength

1. James Gunn, ed., *The Road to Science Fiction: From Gilgamesh to Wells* (New York: New American Library, 1977), p. 3; Robert Scholes and Eric S. Rabkin, *Science Fiction: History, Science, Vision* (New York: Oxford Univ. Press, 1977), 42–51; Robert A. Heinlein, "Science Fiction: Its Nature, Faults, and Virtues," in *Turning Points: Essays on the Art of Science Fiction*, ed. Damon Knight (New York: Harper & Row, 1977), p. 7; the question of genre in the trilogy is alluded to briefly in Patrick G. Hogan, Jr., "The Philosophical Limitations of Science Fiction," in *Many Futures, Many Worlds,* ed. Thomas D. Clareson (Kent State Univ. Press, 1977), p. 270.
2. Scholes and Rabkin refer to Lewis as having "pitted magic against science," (p. 50).
3. Donald M. Hassler's discussion of "newness" in hard science fiction, for example, includes the statement that "'science fiction can only be credible as a genre if within the story there appears only a 'single allowable deviation from known phenomena.' " *Comic Tones in Science Fiction: The Art of Compromise with Nature* (Westport, CT: Greenwood Press 1982), p. 76. Hassler in turn cites Eric S. Rabkin, "Genre Criticism: Science Fiction and the Fantastic," in *Science Fiction, A Collection of Essays*, ed. Mark Rose (New York: Prentice Hall; 1976), p. 96.
4. "On Science Fiction," in *Of Other Worlds: Essays and Stories*, ed. Walter Hooper (New York: Harcourt Brace Jovanovich, 1966), p. 69.
5. *That Hideous Strength* (New York: Macmillan, 1979), p. 70. All subsequent references are to this text (second hardcover edition).
6. *Out of the Silent Planet* (New York: Macmillan, n.d.), p. 139. All subsequent references are to the hardcover edition.
7. Note here Scholes's and Rabkin's discussion of the trilogy and Merlin's role in it.
8. (Athens, Ohio: Ohio State Univ. Press, 1981), pp. 105–23.
9. "On Science Fiction," in *Of Other Worlds.* ed. Walter Hooper (New York: Harcourt Brace Jovanovich, 1966), p. 63.

"You Can Write Science Fiction if You Want To"

1. Poul Anderson, "The Queen of Air and Darkness," *Magazine of Fantasy & Science Fiction,* 40 (April 1971), 5–6. Anderson's comment on the story was made at an author's panel (moderated by the writer of this paper) at Desert Con III, Tucson, Arizona, February 25, 1975.
2. Carol Renard, in "Letters," *Isaac Asimov's Science Fiction Magazine,* 6 (December 1982), 185, also citing a letter by C. M. Fitchett in *Analog,* May 1982.

3. Dean R. Lambe, in "Brass Tacks," *Analog Science Fiction/Science Fact,* 102 (December 1982), 170.

4. Leigh Brackett, "The Science-Fiction Field," *Writer's Digest,* 24 (July 1944), 22.

5. Ross Rocklynne, "Science-Fiction Simplified," *Writer's Digest,* 21 (October 1941), 25.

6. Brackett, "The Science-Fiction Field," pp. 21, 22, 23. Compare the judgment of "Thornton Ayre" (John Russell Fearn), in a similar article "The Fantasy Field," *Writer's Digest,* 23 (August 1943), 36: "It cannot be too strongly stressed that you must be sure of your scientific facts . . . No science fiction editor will allow glaring faults of science to slide past him."

7. Rocklynne, "Science-Fiction Simplified," p. 26. An update on Pluto, popularly written by a professional astronomer, is Derral Mulholland, "Ice Planet," *Science 82,* 3 (Dec. 1982), 64–68. Incidentally, there is a good Pluto story to be written from the information in this article—as any alert pulp writer in the Golden Age would have seen instantly.

8. Alfred Bester, "The Broken Axiom," *Thrilling Wonder Stories,* 13 (April 1939), 64–65.

9. Groff Conklin, "On Science Fiction by Scientists," editorial introduction to *Great Science Fiction by Scientists* (New York: Collier Books, 1962), p. 9.

10. "Eando" (Otto) Binder [Gordon A. Giles, pseud.], "Via Asteroid," *Thrilling Wonder Stories,* 11 (February 1938), 29, 30.

11. Alfred Bester, "Guinea Pig, Ph.D.," *Startling Stories,* 3 (March 1940), 116.

12. Manly Wade Wellman, "Hok Draws the Bow," *Amazing Stories,* 14 (May 1940), 96.

13. Even given the assumptions of that era, it was possible to treat *Homo neanderthalensis* with more compassion. Compare Lester del Rey's touching short story "The Day Is Done," *Astounding Science-Fiction,* 23 (May 1939), 39–50.

14. Robert Bloch, Guest of Honor address to the 9th annual convention of the Tucson Science Fiction and Fantasy Association (TusCon IX), November 14, 1982.

15. Isaac Asimov, "Now You See It—," *Astounding Science-Fiction,* 40 (January 1948), 21, 25. "Electronic computers," the Good Doctor has since acknowledged, were "not invented until I was half through the series." Asimov, "Viewpoint: The Story Behind the Foundation," *Isaac Asimov's Science-Fiction Magazine,* 6 (December 1982), 41. Earlier in the series Asimov had tried to play ahead of the state of the scientific arts by having the Foundation's nuclear power plants powered by something more advanced than uranium fission; "I didn't have the wit (at 21) to think of controlled hydrogen fusion, so I threw in

praseodymium as the most complicated elementary name and hoped that would be a code-word for 'better than fission." Isaac Asimov to the present writer, December 7, 1982. Between the magazine and the book versions of the story Asimov thought better of that choice—perhaps because praseodymium in the natural state is 100 percent atomically stable, in addition to being fiendishly difficult to separate chemically (at least, by techniques known in 1942!)—and substituted plutonium. Compare Isaac Asimov, "Foundation," *Astounding Science-Fiction* 29 (May 1942), 43, and Asimov, *Foundation* (New York: Gnome Press, 1951), p. 60.

16. Andrew Feenberg, "An End to History: Science Fiction of the Nuclear Age," *John Hopkins Magazine,* 28 (March 1977), 13–14. A recent, knowing fictional account of serious scientists subverted by—and eventually outwitting—just such an academic entrepreneur is Charles Sheffield, "Rogueworld," *Magazine of Fantasy and Science Fiction,* 64 (1983), esp. p. 15.

17. Scaled down to a slightly less implausible 875 in the book version of the story. Smith made many such small alterations between the magazine and book versions of his space operas, sometimes to resolve discrepancies that happened in developing a long and complicated plot, but sometimes also to supply technical words which at the time of the first serial publication had not yet existed; e.g., "radar," in the *Skylarks*.

18. E. E. Smith, "Gray Lensman," Part II, *Astounding Science-Fiction,* 24 (November 1939), 30, 39–40.

19. Theodore Sturgeon, "Microcosmic God," *Astounding Science-Fiction,* 27 (April 1941), 46.

20. Raymond F. Jones, "The Great Gray Plague," *Analog Science Fact/ Science Fiction,* 67 (February 1962), 17–18, 63. Some *Analog* readers have never reconciled themselves to Mr. Kidder's demise. Editor Stanley Schmidt received a complaint in 1983 from a reader who thought he had detected a "steady drift to the scientific right" since John Campbell's death in 1971, claiming "it has been years since scientific orthodoxy has been questioned here"—a claim which Schmidt vigorously disputed. Stanley Schmidt, "Those Nasty Ol' Censors," editorial in *Analog,* 103 (January 1983), 7.

21. Norbert Wiener, *I Am a Mathematician* (Garden City: Doubleday, 1956), p. 270. Fairness requires us to note that Wiener inconsistently had written a quite creditable science fiction short story of his own, which the *Tech Engineering News* published in 1952 (under the pseudonym "W. Norbert"). It appears (under the author's own name) in Groff Conklin, *op. cit.*, pp. 299–313, and once it gets going it is good, Golden Age-style science fiction pulp.

22. Ray H. Ramsay, in "The Vizigraph," *Planet Stories,* 4 (November 1950), 106; Bruce Hapke, in *Planet Stories,* pp. 107–8.

23. Ivan Efremov, *Fantastika, 1962* (Moscow, 1962), p. 472, and interview in *Texnika molodeži*, No. 1 (Moscow, 1971), p. 19; both as translated and quoted in G. V. Grebens, *Ivan Efremov's Theory of Soviet Science Fiction* (New York: Vantage Press, 1978), p. 11.

24. Isaac Asimov in "Galaxy Stars," *Galaxy Science Fiction*, 32 (May 1972), 176.

25. Algis Budrys, "Books," *Magazine of Fantasy & Science Fiction*, 64 (January 1983), 23. I am aware that this statement occurs in the context of a blast against a previous collection of Eaton Conference papers; however, one takes wisdom wherever one can find it. The point Budrys makes here is perfectly valid, namely, that the forcing of "speculative fiction . . . into pseudogeneric containers labeled 'science fiction and newstand fantasy,'" in the course of that mass saturation, demands the vigilant attention of "scholarship . . . informed by the ideal that clear communication of clear thought is the most noble human enterprise." Budrys is not the only SF writer who is worried about the prospect of the final corruption of the genre by the corporate conglomeratization of Publishers' Row; George R. R. Martin delivered some characteristically pungent remarks on the same theme during a panel at Westercon 35 (Phoenix, Arizona, July 4, 1982).

26. L. S. Blanchard, "Mirror of the Soul," ibid., pp. 28–60; Robert L. Forward, "Rocheworld," *Analog*, 102 (December 1982, 12–63) 103 (January, 1983, 106–58; February, 110–56). The editorial headnote (or "blurb," as the pulp era would have called it) with the Blanchard story noted that this was a first sale. Striking initial appearances by new writers, of which there have been several instances of late, are a sign of the continuing good health of magazine SF.

Noise, Information, and Statistics in Stanislaw Lem's *The Investigation*

1. Stanislaw Lem, *The Investigation* (New York: Avon, 1976), p. 1. All subsequent references to this novel will appear within parentheses in the text and will be to this edition. The text of my essay is identical to the text of the paper I read at the fifth Eaton Conference. Approximately a year and a half after that conference, John S. Nania's intelligent essay on Lem's detective novels appeared ("Exploding Genres: Stanislaw Lem's Science Fiction Detective Novels," *Extrapolation*, 25 [1984], 266–79). Although our essays deal with some of the same passages in Lem's *Investigation* and are in general mutually supportive, their emphases differ radically. Nania, for example, devotes only a single sentence to the Sherlock Holmes connection and at no place in his essay touches upon my own fundamental topic—information theory. In addi-

tion, after I presented my paper at the fifth Eaton Conference, an English translation of Lem's *His Master's Voice* became available (New York: Harcourt Brace Jovanovich, 1983). This novel frequently and overtly refers to numerous aspects of information theory, especially that of noise. Although I am pleased that its contents lend weight to the arguments in this essay, I am disappointed that it appeared too late for me to refer to it repeatedly.

2. A. Conan Doyle, *The Sign of the Four* (New York: Ballantine, 1979), p. 9. All subsequent references to this novel will appear within parentheses in the text and will be to this edition.

3. Cf. a passage in the last chapter of *A Study in Scarlet*; Holmes is speaking: "Most people, if you describe a train of events to them, will tell you what the result would be. They can put those events together in their minds, and argue from them that something will come to pass. There are few people, however, who, if you told them a result, would be able to evolve from their own inner consciousness what the steps were which led up to that result." Summing up the events relevant to the case at hand, Holmes says: "You see, the whole thing is a chain of logical sequences without a break or flaw" (A. Conan Doyle, *A Study in Scarlet,* in *The Complete Sherlock Holmes,* Vol. I [Garden City, NY: Doubleday, n.d.], pp. 83–84, 85).

4. "The Adventure of the Speckled Band," in *The Complete Sherlock Holmes,* Vol. I, 257.

5. *The Complete Sherlock Holmes,* p. 20.

6. At one point in the story in another connection, Gregory says of Sciss: "Maybe Sciss is insane . . . maybe he has a split personality or a divided ego" (p. 128).

7. In this regard, it is worth noting that, as in the Sherlock Holmes stories in general, Scotland Yard in *The Investigation* employs a detective named "Gregson," as well as one named "Gregory." See pp. 119, 132–33.

8. See, for example, Jeremy Campbell, *Grammatical Man: Information, Entropy, Language, and Life* (New York: Simon and Schuster, 1982), pp. 15–49, especially.

9. P. 11. Hereafter cited within parentheses in the text.

The Cybernetic Paradigms of Stanislaw Lem

1. Wiener, *The Human Use of Human Beings* (New York: Avon, 1967), p. 130. All subsequent references to Wiener are to this text.

2. The parallels with Rabelais—and with Joyce (Lem parodies *Finnegans Wake* in "Gigamesh": see *PV,* pp. 28–40)—are particularly evident throughout much of *The Cyberiad* and in *The Futurological Congress.*

3. In an unpublished essay entitled "On Translating the Grammatical Wit of

Stanislaw Lem into English," Michael Kandel, who is easily the most conscientious and the best of Lem's English translators, discusses the peculiarities of Lem's use of Polish. He points out that Lem's texts abound in word-play. With its basis in Polish grammar, this mostly takes the form of neologisms which are portmanteau words. *Grobot,* for example, a robot grave-digger, comes from a conflation of *grób* (= grave) and *robot*; while *trupeć* combines *trup* (= corpse) with *rupieć* (= junk), and hence signifies the remains of a discarded robot. Such "[g]rammatical play," Kandel observes, "is not an empty game. . . . For Lem language reflects and also shapes the pattern of man's mind and civilization"—a matter which I address in the last three sections of the present essay.

4. Lem, in a brief essay on Borges, declares his admiration for "this great master of the logically immaculate paradox" and confesses that "I have been trying for years to enter ['by quite another road'] the territory in which the Argentinian's best work was created." However, Lem also avers that the "cultural-mythical sources" of Borges's "imagination" are "dying off as far as their power to explain a [changing] world . . . is concerned." "He has explicated to us [*sic*] paradises and hells that remain forever closed to man." Lem concludes: "we are building newer, richer, and more terrible paradises and hells; but in his books Borges knows nothing about them." See Lem's "Unitas Oppositorum: The Prose of Jorge Luis Borges," trans. Franz Rottensteiner, *SF Commentary* [Melbourne], No. 20 (Apr. 1971), pp. 33–38.

5. See also Lem's "On the Structural Analysis of Science Fiction," trans. Franz Rottensteiner and Bruce Gillespie, *Science-Fiction Studies* [hereafter *SFS*], 1 (1973), 26–33; and his "The Time-Travel Story and Related Matters of SF Structuring," trans. Thomas H. Hoisington and Darko Suvin, *SFS,* 1 (1974), 143–54.

6. Cyrano, *Other Worlds* [*L'Autre monde*], trans. Geoffrey Strachan (London: Oxford Univ. Press, 1965), pp. 178–80, 181.

7. Ibid., pp. 156–65 and *The Invincible,* pp. 214ff. The latter, and other works by Lem which I refer to, are cited according to the following editions (listed alphabetically by title):

The Chain of Chance, trans. Louis Iribarne. New York and London: Harcourt Brace Jovanovich, 1978, 179 pp.

The Cyberiad, trans. Michael Kandel. New York: Avon, 1974, 236 pp.

The Futurological Congress, trans. Michael Kandel. New York: Avon, 1974, 142 pp. [**FC**]

The Investigation, trans. Adele Milch. New York: Avon, 1974, 189 pp.

The Invincible, trans. [from a German trans.] Wendayne Ackerman. New York: Ace, 1973, 223 pp.

Master's Voice. [**MV**] See *La voix du maître.*

Memoirs Found in a Bathtub, trans. Michael Kandel and Christine
Rose. New York: Avon, 1973, 192 pp. [**Memoirs**]
Mortal Engines, trans. Michael Kandel. New York: Seabury Press,
1977, 239 pp.
A Perfect Vacuum, trans. Michel Kandel. New York and London:
Harcourt, Brace Jovanovich, 1979. 229 pp. [**PV**]
Solaris, trans. [from a French transl.] Joanna Kilmartin and Steve Cox.
New York: Berkley, 1970, 223 pp.
The Star Diaries, trans. Michael Kandel. New York: Avon, 1977, 321
pp.
La voix du maître, trans. Anna Posner. Paris: Denoël, 1976, 254 pp.
[**MV**]
Abbreviations bracketed in boldface on the above list are those used to
identify a title in the body of my essay.

8. See J. S. Spink, *French Free-Thought from Gassendi to Voltaire*, (Lon-
don: Athlone Press, 1960), pp. 63, 89–90, and Thomas S. Kuhn, *The
Copernican Revolution* . . . (Cambridge, MA, and London: Harvard
Univ. Press, 1957), p. 240.

9. For a further discussion of Cyrano in this regard, see my *Into the Unknown: The Evolution of Science Fiction from Francis Godwin to H. G.
Wells* (Berkeley and Los Angeles: Univ. of California Press, 1970),
pp. 136–40.

10. Lem's debt to Turing, and more especially to Wiener, is something he
himself acknowledges in the footnotes to his *Summa Technologiae*.
Kandel has also remarked upon it in "Stanislaw Lem on Men and
Robots," *Extrapolation*, 14, no. 1 (Dec. 1972), 14–15 et seq., as has
Dagmar Barnouw in "Science Fiction as a Model for Probabilistic
Worlds: Stanislaw Lem's Fantastic Empiricism," *SFS*, 6 (1979), 156.

11. Leslie Fiedler, in the course of reviewing half a dozen of Lem's books,
uses a similar term: "[Lem] . . . favors the anti-mystery story, which,
though structured like a tale of detection, ends without a revelation"
("Travelers in Space and Time," *Quest*, 1 [May–June 1977], 81).

12. Compare Lem's parable, "How Trurl and Klapaucius Created a Demon
. . . to Defeat the Pirate Pugg," in *The Cyberiad*, pp. 119–34.

13. Kandel quotes this passage (his translation) in "Stanislaw Lem . . . ,"
p. 20, from which I have borrowed it.

14. The argument in Dostoyevsky I am alluding to occurs in *Notes from
Underground*, trans. Constance Garnett (New York: Dell, 1960),
pp. 46–47.

15. "The Experiment," trans. Michael Kandel, *The New Yorker*, July 24,
1978, p. 32. The first of my quotations from this text may be found in
"Non Serviam," *PV*, p. 180; but the second, which is equally crucial for
understanding what Lem is about, somehow got left out of that repara-
graphed version.

16. In a review of Joseph Weizenbaum's *Computer Power and Human Reason* (1976), Lem concedes that "no computer will ever become a duplicate of a human being." But he also points out that "it has proved impossible to decide once and for all whether a computer, an information-processing machine, can be educated toward creative intelligence." "I know well since I took part in [it]" the "tempestuous discussion between supporters and opponents of artificial intelligence" that raged "in the USSR 20 years ago"; and "[t]o put it succinctly, we know as little about the future course of computer evolution now as we did then": "On Science, Pseudo-Science, and Some Science Fiction," trans. Franz Rottensteiner, *SFS*, 7 (1980), 331–32.

17. Kilmartin and Cox, following the example of the French, also render "Snaut" as "Snow." It is unfortunate that in this and other respects *Solaris*, which is in many ways Lem's greatest work to date, should have been so badly served by its English translation.

18. My choice of the word *dispossessed* is calculated to evoke the book of Ursula Le Guin's which bears that title; for by the end of her fiction, Shevek has succeeded in exorcizing the past just as (by my reading) Kelvin has. (Whether Le Guin had read *Solaris* before writing *The Dispossessed* [1974] I do not know.)

19. *Solaris* is not alone is possessing this ability. The Black Cloud transforms itself into Rohan's image in *The Invincible*, p. 215.

20. Compare Mark Rose's discussion of Solaris as "a figure precisely located on the border between inanimate nature and animate creature," in *Alien Encounters: Anatomy of Science Fiction* (Cambridge, MA: Harvard Univ. Press, 1981), p. 82 et seq.

21. Chance-versus-purposiveness is one of a number of antinomies that Lem aims at discrediting. For its bearing on the creative process, see Lem's "Metafantasia: The Possibilities of Science Fiction," trans. Etelka de Laczay and Istvan Csicsery-Ronay, *SFS*, 8 (1981), 58ff; also Rose, *Alien Encounters*, pp. 157ff. For the speciousness of the opposition as it is applied to biological evolution, compare H. G. Wells's argument in the essay "Bye-Products in Evolution" (1895): that if Nature, selecting *chance* variations for their biological utility, "may . . . have truly engendered all the nobler [and nonutilitarian] attributes of the human soul," that apparent *design* is owing to the principle, "You cannot make a hay-cart that will refuse to carry roses" (*H. G. Wells: Early Writings in Science and Science Fiction*, ed. R. M. Philmus and David Y. Hughes [Berkeley, Los Angeles, and London: Univ. of California Press, 1975], p. 205).

22. Apart from numerous allusions in *Master's Voice* (on which, see below), Lem also broaches the idea of an intentional universe in the concluding chapter of his *Fantastyka i Futurologia*. For a translation of the relevant passage, see "Metafantasia," pp. 55–57.

23. Cf. *PV*, pp. 223–24: "theoretically, if the energy that Earth's science invests in elementary-particle research were to be multiplied 10^{19} times, that research as a *discovering* of the state of things would turn into a *changing* of that state! Instead of examining the laws of Nature we would be imperceptibly altering them" (emphasis in the original).

24. "Metafantasia," p. 60.

25. See ibid., p. 57: given the "thesis: the universe created by God" and "its antithesis: the universe as non-intentional object," "their synthesis," emerging from "the empirical interrelation of th[ose] two . . . models," "does away with transcendence and replaces it wi[th] intergalactically plural Reason."

Lem's "synthesis" is very close to the one Anthony Wilden hints at when he argues that "the non-mechanistic cybernetic perspective," as it contradicts "the Newtonian-Cartesian *epistemology* of science," approaches the prescientific cosmology of the Middle Ages in that it *seems* "teleological and anthropomorphic": "Changing Frames of Order: Cybernetics and the Machina Mundi," in *The Myths of Information: Technology and Postindustrial Culture*, ed. Kathleen Woodward (Madison, WI: Coda Press, 1980), pp. 219ff.

26. A like analogy, minus any explicit commentary on its significance, appears in *The Investigation*, pp. 41–42.

27. *His Master's Voice* (New York: Harcourt Brace Jovanovich, 1983, 199 pp.) follows the example of later editions of *Glos Pana* in leaving out the Author's Foreword I refer to. Nor does it otherwise count as one of Michael Kandel's best efforts at rendering Lem into English. By adding a personal pronoun to the title, Kandel obliges himself to speak of the "HMV Project," whereas the terms *Master's Voice* and *Mavo* appear in the Polish text; and his translations of certain passages which I consider crucial are often obscure, if not inaccurate.

La voix du maître, however, is equally unreliable—for which reason I have, with the generous assistance of Elizabeth Kwasniewski, verified my translations from the French against the original Polish and modified them accordingly. To facilitate comparison, I include in brackets the corresponding page number(s) of *His Master's Voice*.

28. The discovery that the point of detonation of any real quantity of the "stellar" substance is indeterminate, that a large-scale explosive effect cannot be localized, finally makes the use of "Lord of the Flies" in global warfare impracticable (see *MV*, p. 214 [166]).

29. Thus one of the latecomers to the MAVO project opines that "the signal provides guidance, not information, and is addressed to the cosmos, not to any creatures in particular": *MV*, p. 239 [187]).

30. Kandel, in "Stanislaw Lem . . . ," p. 20, quotes from the *Summa Technologiae* Lem's dictum, "I believe in no final solutions"; and Barnouw, op. cit., pp. 160–61, singles out the "non-assertive properties of SF" as

what chiefly attracts Lem to that generic model (but see also my
subsequent discussion).

31. *An Apologie,* in *The Essayes of Michael Lord of Montaigne,* trans. John
Florio (1603; rpt. London: Routledge, n.d.), p. 226.

32. See, for example, "The Twenty-First Voyage" from *The Star Diaries,*
pp. 203ff., as well as *"Non Serviam,"* in *PV,* pp. 187–96.

33. On this theme in Swift and his successors, see the chapter on "The
Measure of Man" in my *Into the Unknown,* ed. cit., esp. pp. 56–65.

34. See note 5. Franz Rottensteiner has communicated to me what I take to
be the complementary point that "The Seventh Voyage" "is not an
empty game but a literary one" whose "reference is to science fiction:
Lem complicates the time-loops and duplications of Tichy to the
utmost, and his hero behaves so much more stumblingly than the usual
hero of time-travel stories that [his appears as] a deliberate send-[up] of
such stories."

35. It is telling in this regard that a portrait of Queen Victoria dominates the
room which is the opening scene of *The Investigation,* (p. 7).

36. Fredric Jameson argues that "what is indeed authentic about [science
fiction] . . . is not at all its capacity to keep the future alive, even in
imagination. On the contrary, its deepest vocation is over and over
again to demonstrate and to dramatize our incapacity . . . [for] imagin-
[ing] the future, to body forth . . . the atrophy in our time of what
[Herbert] Marcuse has called the *utopian imagination,* the imagination
of otherness and radical difference." This would account for the
tenuousness of the future which *The Futurological Congress* at once
envisions and repudiates—i.e., a future which is "fictifact." Indeed, as
"an *auto-referential* discourse, whose content is a perpetual interroga-
tion of its own conditions of possibility," *The Futurological Congress*
illustrates the following remark of Jameson's better than the example
he is actually referring to does (viz., Le Guin's *The Lathe of Heaven*):
"in the very process of exploring the contradictions of . . . [the] production [of a Utopian future], the narrative gets written, and 'Utopia' is
'produced' in the very movement by which we are shown that an
'achieved' Utopia—a full representation—is a contradiction in terms."
See Jameson, "Progress Versus Utopia; or, Can We Imagine the Future?," *SFS,* 9 (1982), 153, 156, and 157, respectively.

37. The connection between the sidereal "message" and a genetic code is
something Hogarth intimates when he reports that after studying "a
quantity of works devoted to the decipherment of the genetic code of
man and animals," it occurred to him that the "counterpart [*pendant*] of
the [stellar] phenomenon . . . was the double identity of every organism, which is at once itself and the carrier of information effectually
addressed to the future" (*MV,* p. 160 [123]). An exchange in *Memoirs*
implies a similar analogy. Prandtl's assertion that "absolutely every-

thing ['is code']. Yourself included," prompts K. to muse aloud: "Perhaps, . . . if you are thinking about genetics, heredity, those programs of ourselves we carry around in every cell." Significantly, this thought follows soon after a passage anticipatory of *Master's Voice*: "The eye," Prandtl tells K., "converts a light wave into a neural code, which the brain must decipher. And the light wave, from where does it come? A lamp? A star? That information lies in its structure; it can be read" (see *Memoirs*, pp. 64–65).

38. Hogarth adumbrates the analogy in *MV*, p. 167 [128–29]: "Each sentence of a book signifies something, even if detached from its context; but within it, its signification unites with that of other phrases preceding and following it. From this interpenetration, from this accumulation and concentrated addition there emerges, frozen in time, the thought which is the [literary] work. In the stellar code, it was not a matter of the signification of elements, of 'pseudo-phrases,' so much as of their destination. . . . The synthesis of Frog's Eggs had been obtained after wrenching from the code elements to which atomic and stereochemical 'significations' were attributed."

39. I have taken the term *analytico-referential* from Timothy Reiss's *The Discourse of Modernism* (Ithaca, NY: Cornell University Press, 1982). There Reiss mainly considers fiction of the 17th and early 18th centuries, the period in which the notion that language corresponds to and discloses "the order of things" becomes predominant. Compare Michel Foucault's *Les mots et les choses* (Paris: Gallimard, 1966) for a like approach to neoclassical discursive texts.

40. The idea that dreams are derivatives of language—that they are essentially "idiolectic," so to speak—is implicit throughout Freud's *Die Traumdeutung*, as Jacques Lacan has in effect demonstrated. See the latter's "Fonction et champ de la parole et du langage en psychanalyse," esp. sect. 2 ("Symbole et langage comme structure et limite du champ psychanalytique"), in *Ecrits* (Paris: Editions du Seuil, 1966), pp. 266ff.

41. Lem has an abiding concern with the question of what (and how) ethical norms can be (re)validated and preserved in a world where "technologies, hammer[ing] away at the foundation of institutional values," have caused "the whole edifice of autonomous value" to crumble. For his most explicit statement on this subject, see his "Culture and Futurology," trans. anon., *Polish Perspectives* [Warsaw], 16, no. 1 (Jan. 1973), 30–38, from p. 33 of which I have taken the phrases quoted.

42. See Borges, *Labyrinths*, trans. James E. Irby et al. (New York: New Directions, 1964), pp. 246–47, and also note 4.

43. Lem in a recent interview responded to the inquiry, "Do you consider yourself strictly an SF writer?," by saying: "As a matter of fact, I do not consider myself an SF writer. The question of genres is simply unimpor-

tant for me, and very often I turn to different modes of writing. . . . One could simply say that I attempt certain mental experiments and try to create certain situational models. I would also add that the conventions of normal, realistic literature, or whatever you call it, are insufficient for me." See Raymond Federman, "An Interview with Stanislaw Lem," *SFS*, 10 (1983), 3.

From those words, it should be evident that the genre of Lem's fictions is consequent upon the models he deliberately experiments with. Mark Rose, op. cit., pp. 82–95, makes this point in regard to *Solaris*, and he touches on it again in his even more penetrating analysis of "The Mask" (pp. 157–65).

The Ideal Worlds of Science Fiction

1. Gary K. Wolfe, *The Known and the Unknown: The Iconography of Science Fiction* (Kent, OH: Kent State Univ. Press, 1979), pp. 13–16.
2. Alfred North Whitehead, *Adventures of Ideas* (New York: New American Library, 1955), p. 118.
3. Jacques Maritain, "Descartes et l'incarnation de l'Ange," in *Trois Reformateurs* (Paris: Plon, 1925), pp. 92–93.
4. Blaise Pascal, *Pensées et Opuscules*, ed. Léon Brunschvicq (Paris: Hachette, 1923), p. 361 (Pensée #78).
5. See, for example, *Pensées*, #234 (p. 442): "Or, quand on travaille pour demain, et pour l'incertain, on agit avec raison."
6. *Pensées*, #347 (p. 488): "Travaillons donc à *bien* penser: voilà le principe de la morale."
7. *Pensées*, #347 (p. 488): "Mais, quand l'univers l'écraserait, l'homme serait encore plus noble que ce qui le tue, parce qu'il sait qu'il meurt, et l'avantage que l'univers a sur lui; l'univers n'en sait rien." In this logic of radical disproportion, "plus noble" is a false comparison. For, as we learn, thought alone bestows nobility, and the universe has none.
8. Pascal has numerous meditations on man's relation to the two infinities: the infinitely large and the infinitely small. In proportion to these two extremes of radically different order, man is held at the midpoint (see *Pensées* #419, p. 516: "S'il se vante, je l'abaisse; s'il s'abaisse, je le vante").
9. J. D. Bernal, *The World, the Flesh and the Devil: An Inquiry into the Future of the Three Enemies of the Rational Soul* (London: Jonathan Cape, 1968), p. 56.
10. Bernal, p. 23.
11. See *Pensées* #552 (p. 573) on the centripetal fate of Christ the redeemer on earth: "C'est le dernier mystère de la Passion et de la Rédemption. Jesus-Christ n'a point eu où se reposer sur terre qu'au sepulcre."

12. Seeking to distinguish "pure poetry" from impure prose, Valéry says the following: "Tandis que le fond unique est exigible de la prose, c'est ici la forme unique qui ordonne et survit. C'est le son, c'est le rythme, ce sont les rapprochements physiques des mots, leurs effets d'induction ou leurs influences mutuelles qui dominent, au dépens de leur propriété de se consommer en un sens défini et certain." From "Commentaire de *Charmes,*" cited in André Lagarde and Laurent Michard, *Le vingtième siècle* (Paris: Bordas, 1964), p. 304.

13. Stanislaw Lem, "Cosmology and Science Fiction," *Science Fiction Studies,* 4 (1977), 110.

14. Jacques Derrida, *De la grammatologie* (Paris: Editions de Minuit, 1967), p. 228.

15. J. Hillis Miller, "Steven's Rock and Criticism as Cure," *Georgia Review,* 30 (1976), p. 335.

16. Samuel Taylor Coleridge, *Biographia Literaria* (New York: Dutton, 1967), p. 167.

17. "Cosmology and Science Fiction," 110.

18. The hero of Heinlein's newest novel, *JOB: A Comedy of Justice,* is just such a self-written man. Suffering the same indignities as the classical Job, this figure, we learn, has been writing his memoirs along the way. By doing so, he has literally rewritten the world, softening the kicks and pricks by hardening all the illusory beings and places he encounters into a private vision of the end, a text of edenic harmony.

19. John W. Campbell (as Don A. Stuart), "Who Goes There?" in *The Science Fiction Hall of Fame,* vol. IIA, ed. Ben Bova (New York: Avon Books, 1974), p. 97. Future references in the text are to this edition.

20. Michel Butor, "Notes on Science Fiction," tr. Richard Howard, *Partisan Review,* 34, no. 4 (Fall 1967), 602.

21. See Dario Zanelli, "From the Planet Rome," in *Fellini's Satyricon* (New York: Ballantine Books, 1970), p. 8: "It's a film about Martians, a science-fiction film. It should be as fascinating to its spectators as the first Japanese films were to us: films which left you with a continuous feeling of uncertainty."

22. "Profile: Jerry Pournelle," in *Isaac Asimov's Science Fiction Magazine,* 6, no. 13 (December 1982), 20–39. Asimov's response to Pournelle's comments about his "asinine motto" is found in the same issue, his editorial "Violence and Incompetence," pp. 5–9.

23. James Gunn, *Isaac Asimov: The Foundations of Science Fiction* (New York: Oxford University Press, 1982), p. 43.

24. Ursula Le Guin, "American SF and the Other," in *The Language of the Night: Essays on Fantasy and Science Fiction* (New York: Putnam's Sons, 1979), pp. 97–101.

25. Gregory Benford, "A String of Days," in *Foundation,* 21 (February

1981), 5–17. Le Guin's reply, "A Day of Strings," appeared in *Foundation,* 22 (June 1981), 89–90.

26. "A String of Days," 17: "It is an unusual act, doing science and writing about it in fiction at the same time. Lately I've been trying to enlist the reader's responses to the devices of realism, in the cause of the fantastic. An odd enterprise."

27. Gregory Benford, *Timescape* (New York: Simon and Schuster, 1980), p. 412.

28. Nora Gallagher, "Ursula Le Guin: In a World of Her Own," in *Mother Jones,* January 1984, 23–27, 51–53. The poem, "A Round, Buff, Speckled Poem," was Le Guin's entry in *The Faces of Science Fiction* (New York: Bluejay Books, 1984).

29. "Ursula K. Le Guin—Down to Earth," in *Locus: The Newspaper of the Science Fiction Field,* Issue #284, vol. 17, no. 9 (September 1984), 1, 56.

30. "In a World of Her Own," 53.

31. "Cosmology and Science Fiction," 110.

32. Gregory Benford, *In the Ocean of Night* (New York: The Dial Press/ James Wade, 1977) pp. 115–16.

Biographical Notes

PAUL ALKON is Leo S. Bing Professor of English at the University of Southern California. He is at work on a book on fiction of the future in 18th–19th century literature.

GREGORY BENFORD is Professor of Physics at the University of California at Irvine. His most recent book is *Artifact: A Scientific Romance.*

DAVID BRIN teaches astrophysics at San Diego State University and is the author of *Sundiver.* He won a Hugo Award for best novel in 1984. He won a Hugo Award in 1984 for Best Novel (*Startide Rising*).

PAUL A. CARTER is Professor of History at the University of Arizona and author of the classic study *The Creation of Tomorrow.*

DAVID CLAYTON teaches English at the University of California at Santa Cruz and writes on romantic literature.

MICHAEL COLLINGS teaches English at Pepperdine University in Malibu and has written on C. S. Lewis and Piers Anthony.

DR. ROBERT L. FORWARD is Senior Scientist at the Hughes Research Laboratories and author of the hard science fiction classic *Dragon's Egg.*

GEORGE R. GUFFEY is Professor of English at UCLA and is noted for his work on the use of computers in the humanities.

JAMES GUNN is Professor of English at the University of Kansas and a well-known science fiction writer.

JOHN HUNTINGTON is Professor of English at the University of Illinois at Chicago.

FRANK MCCONNELL is Professor of English at the University of California at Santa Barbara and the author of *Storytelling and Mythmaking.*

ROBERT M. PHILMUS is Professor of English at Concordia University in Montreal and editor of *Science Fiction Studies.*

ERIC S. RABKIN is Professor of English and Chairman of the Linguistics Department at the University of Michigan.

GEORGE E. SLUSSER is Curator of the Eaton Collection and Adjunct Professor at the University of California at Riverside. He is at work on a book on science fiction.

HERBERT L. SUSSMAN is Professor of English at Northeastern University and author of *Victorians and the Machine.*

PATRICIA WARRICK is Professor of English at the University of Wisconsin-Center and an authority on cybernetics.

Index